THE HOME PET VET GUIDE

DOGS

Other Books by Martin I. Green

THE HOME PET VET GUIDE FOR CATS

**A SIGH OF RELIEF:
THE FIRST-AID HANDBOOK FOR CHILDHOOD EMERGENCIES**

THE HOME PET VET GUIDE

DOGS

Created and Produced by Martin I. Green

BALLANTINE BOOKS • NEW YORK

Published in the United States by Ballantine Books, a division of Random House, Inc., New York,
and simultaneously in Canada by Random House of Canada, Limited, Toronto.

This edition published by arrangement with Martin I. Green and Berkshire Studio.

Manufactured in the United States of America
First Edition: APRIL 1980
789

CREDITS

Created, Designed & Produced by	MARTIN I. GREEN
Edited by	ROSS FIRESTONE
Research Director	PAUL A. CIRINCIONE
Illustrated by	BOBBI BONGARD
Associate Designer	BOBBI BONGARD
Consulting Veterinarian	DR. HARVEY RHEIN
Editorial Assistant	BERNICE CIRINCIONE
Proofreader	CIA ELKIN
Mechanical Art by	FRANK OSSMANN

Thanks to Leonard Rubin for his invaluable advice and input, and to
Ben Schawinsky and Herbert Sipp for their help and assistance. Thanks, too,
to Michael Albano, Seymour Z. Baum, Martha Donovan, Gail Firestone,
Leslie Kamerling, Jeff Young and Typographic Concepts.

I am indebted to Nancy Neiman for her ongoing faith and support,
and to Nancy Coffey and Bill Shinker for their enthusiastic participation in
making this book happen.

A very special thanks to Ann Sipp, without whom it would not have been possible.

Finally, to Mary Sipp Green, for her encouragement, understanding and love.
MIG

BERKSHIRE STUDIO
PRODUCTION
West Stockbridge, Massachusetts 01266

ACKNOWLEDGMENTS

We wish to thank the following veterinarians for providing us with information and for reviewing and commenting on the manuscript during its various phases:

William J. Kay, D.V.M.
Chief of Staff
The Animal Medical Center
Speyer Hospital and Caspary Research Institute
New York, New York

Chris Lawson, D.V.M.
The Animal Medical Center
Speyer Hospital and Caspary Research Institute
New York, New York

Andrew Breslin, D.V.M.
Lenox, Massachusetts

For information provided, we would also like to thank:

Patrick Concannon, Ph.D.
New York State College of Veterinary Medicine
Cornell University
Ithaca, New York

Donald Lein, D.V.M., Ph.D.
New York State College of Veterinary Medicine
Cornell University
Ithaca, New York

Thanks, too, to the following for making their facilities available to us and for their research on our behalf:

Bianca Beary
President
Washington Humane Society
Director of Humane Education, A.S.P.C.A.
Washington, D.C.

Joan Weich
Coordinator of Communications
National Headquarters
American Society for the Prevention of Cruelty to Animals
New York, New York

Marie Fabrizi
Assistant Librarian
The American Kennel Club
New York, New York

Ada Ferrer
Assistant Librarian
The American Kennel Club
New York, New York

FOR
MY SON JARED,
MY NIECE BONNEE
AND
ALL DOG LOVERS EVERYWHERE

CONTENTS

INTRODUCTION

BY HARVEY RHEIN, D.V.M.

Former President of the Long Island Veterinary Medical Association
Dix Hills Animal Hospital
Huntington, New York

Over the past few decades veterinary medicine has made enormous strides forward. Veterinarians working in private practices, veterinary schools and animal medical centers have developed any number of new and more effective procedures for diagnosing and treating the conditions that beset our pets. Many of the recent advancements in human medicine have also been successfully applied to pet care. As a result, veterinary medicine has now reached a level of sophistication where virtually any type of treatment including brain and cardiac surgery—even the use of pacemakers—is available if required.

Yet for all these advances, many health problems that might have been easily eliminated or prevented continue to persist.

The health of a dog requires the cooperative efforts of both the owner and the veterinarian. And on a day by day basis it is the owner, not the veterinarian, who has to provide the essentials necessary to maintain the dog's good health. The owner must make sure the dog has a nutritious diet, sufficient exercise, adequate grooming and clean, safe living quarters. He must also adhere to the veterinarian's recommendations about inoculations, periodic physical examinations and other routine care. By meeting these responsibilities, the owner should be able to spare his dog many of the painful and debilitating disorders that might otherwise afflict it.

To be sure, even the best preventive care cannot guarantee that the dog won't suffer some illness or injury at some point in its life. When this happens, prompt, effective treatment is often vitally important to minimize the effects and assure a rapid, uncomplicated recovery. Here again, owners play a crucial role, for it falls to them to perceive the symptoms, then either provide the necessary care at home or consult the veterinarian if that is what's required.

Major, even life-threatening problems often arise when owners delay seeking veterinary help because they are not sure something is really wrong or hope that the situation will somehow take care of itself if given enough time. Frequently, a single telephone call could have made the difference. Dog owners should never feel reticent about calling a veterinarian to discuss the symptoms they have observed in their pets. Veterinarians are busy people, but they much prefer to be distracted by a false alarm than have an illness worsen because the treatment was unnecessarily delayed. By listening to you describe your pet's symptoms and questioning you about them, the veterinarian will probably be able to determine whether you ought to bring the animal in for an examination. He may even be able to guide you to the right treatment without actually having to see the dog. In a very real sense, the owner serves as the dog's voice to the veterinarian. But there is no way for him to bring his training and skills into play if this voice remains silent.

Over the course of my many years as a practicing veterinarian I have come up against such silent voices over and over again, and I think I know why. It certainly isn't because owners don't care about the well-being of their pets. Obviously they do, just as they care about the well-being of all the other members of their households. Rather, it seems to me that the problem is rooted in the fact that so little proper information in a truly useable form has been available to the owners when it was needed.

Through a lack of information I have seen any number of health problems created or compounded by errors in the way dogs were housebroken or trained. Any number of times I have seen diseases and other serious conditions allowed to develop because well-intentioned but uninformed owners neglected to give their dogs the normal care and maintenance they require. Inadequate diet, pest control, sanitation and immunization may easily lead to illnesses that can seriously impair the dog's health. Perhaps the most dramatic and heart-wrenching example of what can happen from lack of information is when a dog has an accident or other emergency and professional veterinary care isn't immediately available. I have seen countless cases where the owner's best intentions failed to help a pet or even worsened its condition because he didn't know what to do or how to do it.

Up until now, there has been no single comprehensive, concise source of accurate information telling the pet owner what he or she needs to know in easily understandable, nontechnical terms. This book should make up for that deficiency.

The early chapters detail how to prevent health problems from arising in the first place. You will find discussions of such vitally important subjects as nutrition, grooming, housing and sanitation as well as housebreaking and training.

The sections that follow tell you how to cope with the illnesses and emergencies that are most likely to beset your dog. For each illness you will find the major symptoms, the special precautions to be taken and instructions about what has to be done to bring your pet back to health. For each emergency you will find the symptoms that will help you identify what is wrong and step-by-step first-aid procedures to be followed until veterinary aid can be obtained. These procedures are printed in easy to read large type and supported by clarifying illustrations.

To make the information about illnesses and emergencies as accessible as possible, a unique Symptom Recognition Index has also been included. When you notice a particular symptom in your dog, you need only consult this Index to discover what may have caused it. By comparing the symptom you observe in your pet with those described for each of the listed disorders, you should be able to identify the problem, get some sense of its seriousness and find out what to do about it. For emergencies, there is also a special indexing system on the back cover to give you immediate access to the appropriate first aid.

I suggest you begin acquainting yourself with the Symptom Recognition Index as soon as possible and read through the sections on illnesses and emergencies so you will have some familiarity with the recommended procedures before you ever need to use them. You should also keep this book in an accessible place known to everyone in your family.

In my opinion, having this book nearby should do a great deal to put concerned pet owners at ease and make them confident about their ability to deal with almost any health problem that may arise.

PART ONE

A DOG IN THE FAMILY

OF DOGS AND MEN

The relationship between humans and dogs goes back many thousands of years, though no one knows for certain exactly when or where it first started. Cave drawings, fossil remains and other archaeological evidence strongly suggest that the practice of keeping dogs in the household was already well established in prehistoric times. One can only guess why this relationship might have begun. Perhaps it was a matter of mutual benefit: man fed the dog, and the dog stayed nearby to warn of approaching enemies and predators. Or perhaps a family of humans found and raised the young of some early canine and discovered them to be useful, intelligent, loyal companions. Whatever the origin, it is generally agreed that the dog was probably the first animal to be domesticated and incorporated into the daily life of the human family. It is also likely that the dog's popularity spread as its versatility and usefulness became more fully recognized and appreciated.

Our ancestors' great skill was finding ways to use the dog's keen senses and instincts to make their own lives easier and more secure. Dogs were used to hunt game, herd livestock and protect people and property. They have accompanied men into battle, rescued them from avalanches and other dangers, tracked down their fugitives, found their lost children, pulled their sleds, warmed their bodies against the cold and, perhaps most important of all, kept them company.

Dogs with the best appearance and temperament were selected over other varieties, and in this way varied breeds possessing unique qualities became established in widespread parts of the world. Continued selective breeding of the best animals produced litters that had still better, more uniform qualities than their predecessors. Sometimes two different varieties were allowed to breed in the hope that the resulting litter would possess the best characteristics of each of its parents. Some of these breeds spread from place to place as their owners explored new territories, fought wars and colonized and traded in foreign countries. Others were closely and jealously guarded by their masters and never seen outside their native regions. Rare and exotic dogs were among the most precious gifts exchanged by monarchs. In some parts of the world, they were even exalted as deities.

In our own time, the dog has fit comfortably into every setting where human beings are to be found. It is at home in high-rise apartments and accommodates itself admirably to traveling by car and jet plane. And as it continues to serve many of its traditional functions, it constantly adds on new ones. Dogs are now taught to lead the blind and aid the deaf. They have learned how to uncover contraband and explosives. They are even being used to help withdrawn, emotionally disturbed children and adults break out of their isolation and form relationships with other living things. Their adaptability to new circumstances and demands seems almost infinite.

To a great extent, the success of the relationship between human and dog is attributable to this ability to adapt to man's ever changing life-style and needs, to accept and share willingly the circumstances of our lives, whatever they may be. No other animal has ever been so fully incorporated into our lives because none can participate in so many of our varied activities. The very fact that this relationship has endured so long says a great deal about its strength.

THE DECISION TO GET A DOG

It has not been one relationship, of course, but millions of separate and distinct ones all differing from one another, each taking its particular form from the multiple interplay of individual dog, person, need and circumstance.

Still, several common reasons are usually involved, either singly or in combination, in the decision to get a dog:

• The single most popular reason is for the companionship it provides. A good dog that is given proper treatment, handling and training is a happy animal that brings energy, activity and good cheer into a home. And the dog is not content simply to be **in** the home. It wants to be **part** of the home, a member of the family. It is always ready to accompany you wherever you go, wants to be included in everything you do and is never more forlorn than when it feels itself left out. Dogs can adjust to any household, whatever its activity level. They make excellent pets both for people who live alone and for families of adults. And, of course, their energy, exuberance and readiness for fun and play make them particularly good companions for children.

• Another, increasingly common, reason for getting a dog is for the security it provides. Its bark serves to alert you that someone is at your door (or window), and the fear of discovery and attack is usually enough to drive away all but the most determined prowlers. Outside the home, you are much less likely to be accosted if your dog is with you. In recent years, guard and attack dogs have become highly popular. These are usually medium-sized or larger dogs that have been trained to protect people or property on command. When trained and handled properly, they are always under their owners' control and are completely safe. However, the quality of the training is crucially important. Dogs that are poorly trained or improperly handled can be extremely dangerous even to their masters and the other members of their family.

• Dogs are still widely used for sport and work, though less than they once were. For most people, hunting has changed from an unavoidable necessity of everyday life to an occasional recreational pastime. Some dogs continue to herd sheep and perform the other traditional duties of the work-dog, but social changes have also altered their roles substantially. Most sport and work-dogs are now used for guard and other defensive purposes.

• Some people decide to get purebreds so they can breed them. This is a more costly and demanding undertaking than a novice might suppose. Most inexperienced owners who breed their pets actually lose money. It doesn't usually become profitable until done on a larger, more efficient basis.

• Few owners decide to get pets specifically so they can enter them in dog shows, but many people ultimately do find this an interesting and challenging hobby. Preparing the dog to compete is not a simple matter. It requires months of training and grooming. But if the dog does well in the competition it is awarded points that are applied toward championship status. Along with the satisfaction that comes with raising a champion, the dog's value for breeding purposes is also increased significantly. This is why professional breeders are especially interested in having their dogs do well in shows.

There are all sorts of reasons for adding a dog to the family, but these benefits do not come without cost, effort and increased responsibility. You would do well to keep this fact in mind before making a final decision to bring a dog into your home. Every year a significant percentage of new pets are sold, given away, abandoned and even destroyed by families that have changed their minds for one reason or another. Some of these reasons have to do with the dog itself. It may grow too large for the available space or turn out to be vicious without provocation or refuse to be housebroken. Other reasons have more to do with the owner's inability or disinclination to provide the care, training and attention the dog requires. Sometimes problems develop that could not have been anticipated. You might not know someone in your family is allergic to dog hair. But, unfortunately, the problems are all too often entirely predictable.

Prospective owners must carefully and honestly consider whether they and the other members of their household are truly prepared for the extra work and effort that necessarily come with a dog. It must be fed once or twice a day, walked several times, housebroken, groomed, trained to be obedient, kept in good health —the list of responsibilities goes on and on. And they continue seven days a week, 52 weeks a year. Remember also that the dog cannot be left alone for any extended period, certainly not for more than one day at a time.

If you are considering getting a dog for your children to "teach them responsibility" or because they desperately want one, you should make sure they are old enough to treat it properly. If your youngsters aren't yet sufficiently mature to understand that a dog has feelings like all other living beings and may not tolerate being chased, shouted at, teased or hurt, it would be better to postpone the gift until they are older.

The point is, if there are good reasons to suspect that a dog would not fit into your home right now, do not get one. Wait until the time is more opportune. Then, if and when you do decide to add a dog to your family, the experience is much more likely to be pleasurable for all the parties involved in the relationship —you, your family and the dog itself.

SELECTING THE RIGHT DOG

Once you have decided to get a dog you are still left with the question of what sort of dog to get. Will it be a puppy or a fully grown animal? A male or a female? Long-haired or short? Purebred or mixed breed? If a purebred, which one? There are dozens to choose from. If you are considering a mixed breed, the decision isn't any easier. They come in a virtually unlimited number of combinations. Unless you already have your heart set on a particular animal, the whole matter can be terribly confusing.

It will help clarify your thinking if you first ask yourself what purpose you want the dog to serve. Do you want a family pet? A watchdog? A hunter? A show dog? A certain kind of dog may be well suited to some of these purposes but not to others. It will also help to keep in mind practical considerations shaped by the specific circumstances of your life. If you live in an apartment, remember that a large dog takes up more space and requires more exercise than a small dog. If you're concerned about hairs all over your newly upholstered furniture, remember that long-haired dogs do shed more than shorthairs. Obviously, it makes sense to fit the givens that come with certain dogs with the givens of your own situation.

Although there are often significant differences between dogs of the same breed and even between members of the same litter, experience suggests that there are some reliable generalizations that may help guide you toward the best dog for your purposes. Retrievers, for example, are known to be excellent around children. Hunting dogs are also gentle with youngsters but are so active they may be difficult to control within the limited confines of a small home. In general, male dogs tend to be more aggressive than females. Spayed females usually have the fewest health problems and often make ideal companions for young children. On the other hand, a small dog probably isn't the best choice for a family with youngsters under the age of eight or so because the kids are likely to be at it constantly and it may strike back to protect itself. Because your dog will be an integral part of your family, you must have a realistic sense of the pros and cons of each option before coming to a final decision.

PUREBRED OR MIXED BREED?

Whether you select a purebred or mixed breed will be influenced by your personal preference, budget and the future plans you have for the dog. Purebreds have some value for breeding purposes. Mixed breeds do not. Purebreds can participate in dog shows sanctioned by the American Kennel Club. Mixed breeds cannot. Neither choice, however, assures you of a healthier, smarter or more lovable pet.

As the name suggests, a purebred is a dog whose predecessors for many generations have all come from the same breed. Although there are millions of them in this country, they represent only a small minority of all dogs.

Purebreds are initially more costly than mixed breeds but do not usually cost more to feed and maintain. The higher initial cost is due in part to stud fees, veterinary care before and after whelping and the other expenses the breeder incurs to produce a salable puppy. As might be expected, puppies from championship bloodlines or from rare and unusual breeds are the most expensive of all purebreds.

Perhaps the main advantage of purebreds is that so much is known about them. Owners, breeders, veterinarians and others with a special interest in a breed have observed and written about all the specific characteristics that have been passed down through the generations, and this information is widely available to anyone who cares to seek it out. If you are considering a particular breed, you can easily find out about such things as the expected thickness and color of the hair, the dog's size and structure, its special skills and problems and even its temperament and personality. With some of the older breeds, such observations may have been accrued over the course of hundreds or even thousands of years. The availability of such detailed information has also made it possible for these dogs to be improved through systematic selective breeding that emphasizes their best qualities and reduces or eliminates their hereditary faults. The end result is to give the prospective buyer the best possible basis for making an informed decision by doing away with much of the guesswork involved in predicting the qualities a puppy will have when it matures. The section on **THE BREEDS OF DOGS** gives you a good distillation of what you may expect to find in the most popular breeds available in this country.

Keep in mind, however, that the fact that a dog is a purebred does not necessarily assure you of quality. Before making a purchase, you must always evaluate the particular dog you are considering as well as the reputation of the breeder. Poor quality purebreds often result from indiscriminate or irresponsible breeding practices, such as mating two dogs from the same litter. Typically, such practices follow close behind a sudden increased demand for a particular breed because of the interest generated by a movie, book or news story. Efforts to produce more dogs quickly to satisfy this demand may result in litters with poor characteristics or hereditary defects.

If you are thinking about buying a purebred, make a point of becoming somewhat familiar with the "standards" or ideal characteristics of that breed. One of the main factors determining the price you will have to pay is the extent to which a given dog fits these standards. You might find it both enjoyable and informative to learn about the breed at first hand by attending a dog show. You will be able to watch how each breed is judged, talk to some of the owners and breeders in your area and discover the qualities that may lead you to or away from a particular breed. Keep in mind, though, that owners and others with a special commitment to one kind of purebred may not offer very much information about its limitations or shortcomings.

The overwhelming majority of dogs are mixed breeds. This means that their characteristics are more a product of genetic luck than of carefully planned selective breeding. It is, therefore, much more difficult to predict what the appearance and temperament of a mixed breed puppy will be when it matures. Even puppies from the same litter may vary widely from each other and from their parents. Each puppy is a truly unique individual, different from all others in the world.

There are exceptions, but mixing of the breeds usually produces sturdy, intelligent offspring that possess the best qualities of their predecessors. They are also much less likely to embody hereditary defects than purebreds are.

PUPPY OR MATURE DOG?

Should you be thinking about a puppy, remember that it will require more time, care and patience than a mature dog. It will have to be fed more frequently, housebroken and carefully taught the rules of its new home. Moreover, a puppy does not have the resistance and strength of an older dog, so an illness may have much more serious consequences.

The extra effort is certainly not without its compensations. A puppy is one of the most adorable babies in the animal world and provides endless pleasure and enjoyment to everyone around it. Most puppies learn quickly and adjust easily to other pets and all the other aspects of a new home. Understandably, if you raise a puppy to maturity, it will be closer to you and the other members of your family than a newly arrived mature dog could ever be.

The age at which the puppy is adopted is crucially important. Newborn pups are wonderfully appealing, but they shouldn't be separated from the mother too early, certainly not before they have completed nursing and no longer require her milk. The ideal age for adoption ranges from about six or eight weeks to around four months. If the puppy is taken from its mother and littermates too early and kept only in the company of humans, it will form strong attachments with people but have very poor relationships with dogs. Such animals routinely get into fights with other dogs. On the other hand, puppies older than four months may have already begun to pick up bad habits from littermates and adult dogs which may be too late to change. If the puppy has been pretty much isolated from human contact for these first four months, it will probably not make a suitable pet. For some reason, such dogs fail to form the strong attachment to human beings that is one of the species' principal characteristics and virtues. These animals tend to run away over and over again and seldom return home by choice.

For some people, fully grown dogs offer certain important advantages. They are stronger, better able to take care of themselves and much less susceptible to illness. Since they are likely to have been already immunized and neutered, they also save their new owners the cost of these early medical expenses. Mature dogs only need to be fed once or twice a day and usually need less sustained attention than puppies.

Nor do they need to be housebroken. When a fully grown dog is brought into a new home and subjected to a new routine, it may make an occasional mistake, but this period of uncertainty usually passes quickly. Although it does take more time for a mature dog to adjust to new surroundings, especially if there are other pets in the house, by and large it is probably a better choice if you don't have the time, energy or inclination to deal with the not inconsiderable needs of a pup.

The single most important personal quality in a dog is probably its personality. Since you have not trained the mature dog from the outset and are getting the product of someone else's efforts, you must be sure it has the qualities of temperament you want or at least does not have the qualities that you don't want. It is usually far easier to judge a fully grown dog's disposition than a puppy's, and you can be reasonably sure that its personality will remain pretty much the same after you take it home with you. Adult personality is exceedingly difficult to predict in a puppy even when the parents are known, especially if it is a mixed breed. Only time will tell how it will turn out.

Still, it takes a fair amount of observation and judgment to determine what a mature dog is really like. What its present owners tell you has only limited value. For one thing, their judgment of the dog's disposition may simply be wrong. They may believe, for example, that because the dog has never bitten anyone it never will, when the fact is any dog will bite if sufficiently provoked or placed under high enough stress. For another thing, the present owners' evaluation is necessarily based upon their experience with the animal in their own environment, and your household may be very different. If the dog has only known a tranquil existence among considerate adults, it may exhibit a radically different personality when taken to a home full of noisy, rambunctious children. Changes from one sort of household to another may bring out problems that never existed before (as well as put an end to problems that previously seemed insoluble). Particularly if your home differs from the sort of place it grew up in, you ought to spend considerable time observing how the dog reacts to various situations before you decide to adopt it.

MALE OR FEMALE?

Both male and female dogs make excellent pets, and either one is a good choice. In the most general sense, females are likely to be more cautious, gentle and quiet. Spayed females are commonly held to be the most pleasant dogs with the nicest dispositions and fewest undesirable traits. Males tend to be somewhat larger than females as well as tougher and more aggressive, characteristics that are entirely desirable if what you want is a watchdog. They are also much more likely to get into fights with other dogs, particularly other males.

Older dogs tend to develop physical problems that are characteristic of their gender. As they age, some females develop urinary conditions that cause them to lose control of their urine. They are also prone to uterine infections and ovarian, uterine and breast cancer. Older males commonly have inflammations, abscesses, infections and tumors in their prostate glands and tumors around the anus. Some of these problems can be alleviated with prescription drugs. Others may require surgery, sustained treatment or ongoing care at home. The point is that neither males nor females are necessarily healthier or less subject to illnesses.

Obviously, a female is preferable if you look forward to having puppies around your home.

LONG-HAIRED OR SHORT?

If you are considering a long-haired dog, be aware that those beautiful, showy coats do shed and do require substantial care and grooming. To maintain the dog's appearance and keep its hair from becoming knotted and matted, you will have to brush and comb it at least once a day. Matting is a serious problem and can only be prevented by continuous attention. Regular brushing is also necessary to cut down on the amount of loose hair the dog swallows when it grooms itself, as well as to hold down the amount deposited on floors, furniture and clothing. Keep in mind that some long-haired breeds shed more than others and that large long-haired dogs tend to leave more loose hairs around than small ones do.

Should you decide on a long-haired pet, you will also routinely have to clean the area under the tail to prevent the formation of packs of matted hair. Unless cleaned away promptly, they can obstruct the dog's normal bowel functions and lead to painful irritation, inflammation and infection. Particularly when the dog gets older, flies may be attracted to this area in hot weather and seriously threaten the animal's health by depositing maggots in its flesh.

Short-haired dogs also require regular grooming, of course, but not nearly as much.

WHERE TO GET YOUR DOG

There are so many mixed breed puppies and dogs looking for homes that you should have no trouble finding one that suits you perfectly if you are willing to look around a bit.

Mention to your friends and neighbors that you want a dog, and it probably won't be long before someone with a new litter offers you one.

You can also check your neighborhood bulletin boards and the classified section of your local newspaper. They are usually filled with ads offering to give away puppies at no cost to good homes.

Your local Society for the Prevention of Cruelty to Animals (SPCA) and Humane Society Shelter probably have large numbers of mixed breeds available for immediate adoption. Should you select one of these animals, you are likely to be saving it from an early, if painless, death. With luck, you may even find some purebreds waiting for homes. It may not matter to you, but be aware that the ancestry of such dogs is uncertain and therefore they have no value for breeding or show purposes.

Pet shops are another good traditional source for dogs. Many offer both mixed breeds and purebreds, though they tend to sell only the breeds in greatest demand. If you have a more unusual sort of dog in mind, the store may not be able to get it for you right away.

Purebreds can also be obtained from amateur and commercial breeders. Keep in mind that the quality and cost of purebreds vary widely and do not necessarily have a direct relationship to each other. Some breeders are seriously dedicated to offering only fine examples of a breed that are free from hereditary defects and temperamentally well-suited to modern family life. Others are more concerned with selling quantity than quality. Be particularly wary if the breed you are considering has become highly popular within the last year or two.

If it is at all possible, check the reputation of a pet shop or breeder with owners who have gotten their pets there. What they tell you should give you a pretty good idea of what to expect. In the final analysis, of course, the responsibility for selecting the pet falls to you and the other members of your family.

CHECKING THE DOG OUT

The dog you choose is going to be yours for some years to come, so take the time to look at a number of pets before making your final decision. If it turns out that the first dog you saw is ultimately the one you like best, you can always go back for it. It is usually better to take the chance it might be gone than to select impulsively the first nice animal you see. Even if you have had no previous experience judging dogs, the process of looking around and comparing will help sharpen your judgment.

When you have narrowed your choice down to a particular dog, spend a few minutes observing its appearance and behavior to make sure it is in good health. Of all the factors to keep in mind when coming to your final selection, this is the single most important.

• A healthy dog is active, alert, curious, responsive and able to move about freely without hesitation. It should not seem unusually shy, frightened or dejected.

• The body should be muscular and firm without a potbelly or wobbly back legs.

• When you run your hands over the dog's chest, you should be able to feel the ribs but not be able to stick your fingers between them.

• The animal ought to be relatively clean. A healthy dog is able to care for itself; a sick dog is not.

• The fur should be smooth, thick and glossy, with no bare or bald spots.

• Check the skin underneath. It should be clean and have a healthy pink color, without lumps, redness, scales, dryness or evidence of fleas.

• Make sure there are no symptoms of respiratory illness such as sneezing, coughing, wheezing, discharges from the eyes or nose, or debris around the lips or mouth.

• Signs of diarrhea around the dog's tail may also indicate illness. The anus should not look swollen or protrude.

• Examine the inside of the dog's ears to make sure they are clean and free of foreign matter.

• Check the inside of the mouth. The teeth should be white; the gums pink, firm and without sores or angry red areas.

• If you are looking at a puppy, check the conditions in and around the litter as well as the appearance of its littermates. They should tell you something about how well it has been cared for. As a general rule, the less contact a puppy has had with other dogs and cats, the better its chances of being free of infectious diseases and parasites. Find out from the seller whether it has been wormed and inoculated or if this will be your responsibility.

Final confirmation that the dog is healthy should come from a veterinarian. Plan to have it examined within three or four days after you bring it home. Make sure it can be returned to the seller within some reasonable period, say ten days to two weeks, if the vet finds it in poor health or unacceptable for any other reason. Most responsible pet dealers are willing to agree to this sort of conditional sale. The incubation period for many infectious diseases is between a week and ten days, and the symptoms may not become apparent before then.

Almost equally as important as the dog's health is its disposition. This should always be evaluated in terms of the purpose you want it to serve. Obviously, it makes more sense to pick a dog that is predisposed to being a family pet, watchdog, or whatever, than one that will require you to change its basic disposition through later training.

It is extremely difficult to make accurate predictions about a dog's personality if you haven't been able to observe it over a long period of time in a wide variety of circumstances. Even then, owners who have had their pets for years are often startled by the personality changes that can be produced by particularly stressful situations. The changes that take place in a puppy as it matures can be especially dramatic. Still, by placing the dog you are considering in a mildly stressful situation and carefully watching how it reacts, you will have a fairly sound basis for deciding whether or not it is temperamentally suited to your needs.

With the seller's permission, take the dog out of the sight of its kennel or littermates. Place it down on the floor, walk a few steps away, then drop down, offer the dog your hand and call to it. Notice the way it responds. Also observe its reactions when you try to pet, handle and restrain it. Does it welcome your hand? Does it struggle? Does it run away from you? How does it react when you walk away as if you were leaving?

In responding to these situations, the dog will show characteristics either of dominance, submissiveness or independence. To be sure, these characteristics can be manifested in many different ways. The following descriptions are simplified, but they should convey a general sense of the three basic personality types and may save you a good bit of regret and frustration in the years to come.

• **The Dominant Dog: Approaches readily. Growls and protects itself with its paws or teeth if you pet it too hard, handle it a bit roughly or try to restrain it.** If the animal reacts this way, it will probably do better as a guard or watchdog than as a companion for young children or elderly adults.

• **The Submissive Dog: Approaches cautiously, per-**

haps with its ears back or tail down. **May lick your hand when you pet it. Struggles only briefly, if at all, against being handled or restrained.** Usually the best choice for a family with young children.

• **The Independent Dog:** Does not seem at all anxious to get involved with you and would prefer to be left alone to go its own way. **When handled and restrained, may react either dominantly or submissively.** Independent dogs often require considerable training. Characteristically, they tend to be habitual runaways.

THE FIRST DAYS AT HOME

You should begin to make preparations for your new pet even before you bring it home:

• Unless you have chosen a mature, well-trained animal that can be trusted anywhere in the house, it will be necessary to set aside an area where the new arrival can be confined safely and comfortably. A small warm room with few furnishings and an easily cleaned tile floor would be just about ideal.

• Do everything you can to make the room as safe as possible for the dog. For example, electrical wires that might be chewed should be removed or placed out of reach. The same should be done with toxic chemicals, glassware and small objects that could be swallowed. Remember that a dog is a curious animal and may stand on its hind legs or even climb up on furniture to reach something it finds particularly interesting.

• Since the object is to confine your pet, not isolate it, put an expandable gate across the doorway of the area and leave the door open so the dog can see the members of the family if not join them.

• If the dog isn't yet housebroken, cover the entire floor with several thicknesses of newspaper.

• Place the dog's bed in the room. Also put in a few toys—a rubber ball, a large rawhide or fiber bone, etc.

The dog's arrival at your home is an understandably exciting event, especially if you have children. Still, you must make every effort to keep things as subdued as possible. Keep in mind that your new pet is in the midst of an unusually stressful period of change. It has just been separated from its previous owner or mother and littermates, and every aspect of its usual routine has been disturbed. What happens over the next few weeks will influence how it feels in its new home for years to come.

The dog will need at least a few days to explore its new surroundings and gradually adjust to them. Until it understands that you mean it no harm and will provide food, water, shelter and companionship, it is bound to feel a fair amount of uncertainty. If you have another dog or a cat, it might be wise to keep it elsewhere in the house until the new arrival has had a chance to begin its adjustment. After a few days, the two animals can be allowed to meet under your supervision.

During this period, patience and gentle handling are among the most important things you can provide. Make sure that everyone, especially the children, understands that loud noises, heavy hands and sudden movements can frighten the dog and prolong the adjustment

period. Children under about six years old should be closely supervised when they are around the pet. Particularly if it is a young puppy, they may unintentionally injure it. You may notice that while the dog is still gaining confidence and adjusting to its new surroundings, it may not bark or be at all playful. This sort of mild withdrawal is fairly common and no cause for concern unless accompanied by other symptoms of illness. As the adjustment period proceeds, the dog will perk up and become its normal noisy, playful self.

The first day is usually the most difficult. Place the dog in the area you have prepared for it, and give it a bowl of water and a small amount of bland food such as cooked hamburger or semi-moist dog food. Don't be surprised if it isn't immediately hungry. Particularly if you have a puppy, it would be best to find out what your pet had been fed by its previous owner and continue this diet until it adjusts to its new surroundings. If its usual diet is abruptly changed to something radically different, it may stop eating altogether. This can lead to **HYPOGLYCEMIA,** a potentially life-threatening illness; see page 120. Once your dog begins to adjust, its diet can be gradually changed without any ill effects.

You can begin the process of housebreaking the dog immediately by taking it out for a walk after it eats and whenever it appears about to relieve itself. Just before you retire for the night, take it out again for the last time.

If you are very fortunate, the dog will be so tired out by all the excitement of the first day that it will fall into a sound sleep and not awaken until the next morning. A more realistic expectation is that it will probably cry, whine and carry on for most, maybe all, of the night.

The options about how to cope with this situation range from ignoring the dog completely to bringing it into the bedroom with you so it won't have to spend the night alone. If you have a puppy, you may be able to make it feel secure enough to sleep by simulating a littermate out of a hot water bottle filled with warm water and wrapped in a towel. This has the best chance of working if you place the towel in with the litter of puppies to get their scent on it before you bring your new pet home. A loudly ticking alarm clock or a radio tuned in to an all-night talk show might also do the job. Every situation is different and requires a somewhat different approach, so experiment a bit to find the method that works best for you. And though it may be difficult, try to keep your patience and hold on to your temper. Within a few nights, the dog will settle down and everyone will be able to sleep peacefully once again.

Even if care of the dog will ultimately be your child's responsibility, these early weeks are too important to getting the dog off to a good start to be left exclusively to a child. The youngster may be able to feed, groom and walk the animal perfectly well, but children usually do not understand all the complexities of housebreaking and basic obedience training. Dogs also tend to be less cooperative and obedient with youngsters because of the children's smaller size and subordinate position in the household. Your child can certainly help, but it is far better for everyone, including your pet, if the dog is supervised and trained by an adult. Housebreaking and obedience training should be started immediately to ensure the fastest possible development of good behavior patterns. The training will only be harder to accomplish if it is deferred for these crucial first weeks and the dog begins to settle into habits you find unacceptable.

SELECTING A VETERINARIAN

At about the same time you decide to get a dog, begin looking for the veterinarian who will provide the health services it will periodically require throughout its life. These services range from routine examination and preventive care to treatment of acute illnesses and life-threatening emergencies. The three main factors to consider in making your choice are professional competence, the facilities and equipment available for diagnosis and treatment and the attitudes and personality of the veterinarian as they may affect your relationship.

The practice of veterinary medicine is restricted to men and women who have been graduated from an accredited school of veterinary medicine and met the state licensing requirements. Beyond that, competence can vary widely, just as it does in all the other healing arts.

Unless you are already familiar with a veterinarian from an earlier pet, begin by asking dog owners you know for the names of veterinarians they would recommend. Try to determine the kind of care their dogs required and what their experience has been. Predictably, most owners will have only good things to say about their vets, so it might be valuable to ask if they have switched veterinarians recently and, if so, why. Keep questioning friends and relatives until you have a list of three or four veterinarians who have been enthusiastically recommended by their clients. As an alternative, you can consult your telephone directory or the veterinary medical association in your area for the names of local practitioners.

Beginning at the top of your list, call the veterinarian's office and request information about the fee structure and the facilities and services available. They can vary widely from one vet to the next. You should be able to get this information about such basic matters as routine examinations, inoculations and neutering.

Armed with as much preliminary information as you

can gather, call the veterinarian back and introduce yourself to him. Indicate that you are about to buy a dog and are telephoning at the recommendation of one of his clients. Tell him you would like to meet him personally and tour his facilities if that's at all possible. Veterinarians have busy schedules, but they will usually oblige this sort of request.

When you meet the vet face to face you will begin to form some preliminary impressions about what a professional relationship with him might be like. What you are seeking is an individual who inspires confidence in his skills, seems to have sincere concern and compassion for his patients and shows sensitivity to your feelings as a pet owner.

As you look around the facilities, notice whether the examination and treatment areas seem clean and well-equipped. Do the patients look well cared for and reasonably content? Are healthy animals kept separated from sick ones? If boarding is available, are the housing and exercise facilities adequate? You might also tell the vet about the type of dog you are considering and ask him for his opinion about your choice.

In all likelihood, this brief meeting is the only direct basis you will have for deciding whether or not you want your dog treated by this person. Have confidence in your feelings and judgment. They are probably correct. If for any reason you come away with a negative impression, move on to the next veterinarian on your list.

THE FIRST TRIP TO THE VETERINARIAN

If your new dog seems healthy, it is usually best to wait three or four days before taking it to its first visit to the veterinarian. Your observations about how it behaves at home before then can provide the vet with a good bit of important information. Does it have a good appetite? Do its bowels and bladder seem to function normally? Does it walk, run, play and appear to be enjoying itself? Have you noticed any symptoms of illness?

Take along a specimen of the dog's stool in a closed container. The veterinarian will perform a routine analysis and, if necessary, treat the animal for internal parasites. Also bring a record of any vaccinations the dog may have already had.

A puppy should see the vet when it is about six or eight weeks old. If this is the first visit, the veterinarian will take the dog's health history and give it a general examination. He will also give it the first in a series of immunizations that will protect it from several serious illnesses. Unvaccinated puppies are particularly susceptible to illnesses and are poorly prepared to survive them. The incubation period for certain types of sickness is ten days or longer, so the symptoms may not appear until after the vet has examined the puppy and found it in good health. Should this happen, inform the veterinarian immediately, as well as the dog's previous owner.

REGISTERING A PUREBRED

The American Kennel Club (AKC) was formed about 100 years ago to promote the protection and advancement of purebred dogs in the United States. Since that time the organization has maintained a systematic registry that now includes more than 20 million names.

Every puppy bred from two registered dogs is itself eligible for registration. Usually the breeder registers the birth of a purebred litter with the AKC and gives one of the forms he receives to the buyer of each puppy. The new owner then completes the form, submits it to the AKC with the appropriate fee, then is sent a certificate of registration.

Occasionally, the breeder may not have applied for or received the AKC registration forms by the time the new owner takes the puppy home. In that case, he must provide a signed statement or bill of sale stating the breeder's name, the puppy's date of birth, breed, color and sex and the registered names and numbers of both parents. Without this information, it may not be possible to register the puppy with the AKC. It is your responsibility as the buyer to secure the information before you accept the dog. Do not complete your purchase if the breeder is unable or unwilling to give it to you.

ENVIRONMENT

THE OUTDOOR DOG

If you live in the country or suburbs and have a yard or other open space, you may want your dog to spend much of its time outside the house. Dogs like the outdoors. They enjoy the opportunity it gives them for exercise, exploration and adventure. To determine how much time your pet ought to spend there, you will have to take into account the climate and the dog's particular physical characteristics.

Some breeds such as Shepherds, Malamutes and Huskies actually prefer living outside, particularly in winter. Others were never intended by nature to endure cold weather or have lost some of nature's protection from the elements through generations of selective breeding and domestication. Such animals are much more comfortable sharing man's increasingly indoor style of life. Most dogs, though, are quite content to spend some or even all of the daylight hours outside the house if they can come inside for companionship in the evening and aren't forced to endure the discomforts of snow or rain. Dividing their time up in this way between inside and outside seems to strike a happy balance and works well in respect to the dog's dual role as family pet and watchdog.

There are, however, a number of precautions to take before letting a new dog outside the house by itself:

• Because of their susceptibility to illness, puppies should be at least three months old before they are permitted outside.

• To give a new dog time to adjust, outdoor periods should be short at first, then gradually lengthened over the next week or two. Particularly in a young dog, sudden exposure to extremes of temperature can result in serious illness.

• Don't let your dog go out alone until you have taught it its name and to come when you call. A dog will learn its name easily if you repeat it often as you groom, feed and pet it. It can also be quickly trained to come to you at the sound of a whistle.

• Your pet should have received its first series of vaccinations before coming into contact with other dogs outside the home.

• Dogs have a way of straying, so make sure your pet has a tag on its collar giving your name and telephone number in case it gets lost or becomes injured far from home. If your community requires dogs to be licensed, the tag should also include its license number.

• To prevent unwanted litters, you might also consider having your dog altered before permitting it to roam.

Especially if you let your dog go out unsupervised, you should make adequate provisions for its safety, health and comfort. One very important thing you can do is restrict it to a particular area rather than turn it loose to roam at will. Keeping the dog on your own property is not only a matter of law in many communities but obvious good sense. It will keep your pet from becoming a real or imagined nuisance to the neighbors, limit the mischief it can become involved in and, most importantly, protect it from automobiles, the single greatest threat to its life.

Many dog owners keep their pets in an enclosed yard area. This is handy but far from ideal. For one thing it may wreak havoc on your flower beds and vegetable gardens. For another, you may suspect your dog is part groundhog if it takes a fancy to digging up holes in your lawn. You will also have to clean up the dog's droppings regularly to maintain a reasonable standard of sanitation and hygiene, and this can be something of a challenge in a yard with grass, bushes and sheltered areas. The clean up effort will never be as complete or effective as it should be, and internal parasites that may be present in the dog's stool will find themselves quite safe and comfortable while they wait to reinfest your pet or some new host. The matter of cleanliness is even more important if children and other members of the family use the yard for recreation.

A much better solution, especially if the dog is to live outdoors, is to set aside an area exclusively for your pet's use and enclose it with a high wooden or chain link fence. Keeping the dog out of reach will prevent it from fighting with other animals in the neighborhood and make it more difficult for it to catch and eat small game, which often carry parasites and infectious diseases. You will also save yourself a lot of nuisance and potential legal headaches.

Here are some points to keep in mind about the dog's space:

• The enclosure should be large enough to allow it

23

to run around and play without being cramped.

• The ground should be cleared down to the soil, then covered with sand or small pebbles so it will be easy to clean and hose down.

• If possible, choose an area that is partially shaded throughout the day and near a convenient source of water.

• The surrounding fence ought to be high enough to discourage the dog from jumping over it. To be sure, few enclosures are truly escape-proof. Dogs have the ability to scale or burrow under seemingly impossible barriers. But, fortunately, they are usually content to make only a few half-hearted attempts at escape before they settle down and accept confinement.

If it isn't feasible to build a fenced-in enclosure, you may have no choice but to tie the dog while it is outdoors. This will successfully restrict its movements, but it also creates the potential for other problems you will have to take care to prevent.

• Choose a strong but lightweight metal chain for tethering the dog. It may chew through a fiber rope either in play or in an effort to escape.

• Secure the chain to a post or other firmly fixed object so it won't pull free when the dog strains against it.

• Many dogs pull constantly against their ties, and the resulting friction can wear away fur and irritate the neck, causing acute discomfort and serious infection.

To keep the dog from hurting itself, choose the correct sort of collar and make sure it fits properly. Long-haired dogs should be given round collars. Round or flat collars are appropriate for shorthairs. The collar should fit snugly enough so it can't slip over the dog's head but loose enough to move freely around its neck. Never tie your pet to a chain with a training collar that tightens as the dog pulls against it.

• The area within reach of a tied dog should be cleared of obstacles so the animal won't become snagged, wrapped or tangled in the chain. If you tie it near a fence or porch, make sure the chain is long enough to reach the ground no matter where the dog goes. It is not unusual for dogs, particularly puppies, to hang themselves when they jump over a fence or fall through the protective railings on a porch because their chains were too short to reach the ground.

• Even when the enclosure is cleared of obstacles, chances are the dog will sooner or later tangle its feet in the chain if it is fairly long. Usually no great harm results, although occasionally a dog will catch a toenail and may tear it off when it tries to pull itself free. Many owners deal with the problem by using a relatively short length of chain connected to a metal ring that moves freely along a thin metal cable suspended between two fixed points. This allows the dog the freedom to move along the entire length of the cable but does away with a trailing chain that can be caught underfoot. If you install this sort of device, make sure the chain connecting the dog to the ring is long enough to let it lie down and move somewhat away from the cable. Also make a point of stringing the cable seven or more feet above the ground so no people will be injured by walking into it.

• Exercise the dog regularly to keep it in good physical condition. As paradoxical as it may seem, dogs kept tethered outdoors often do not get as much exercise as they need.

• Also give it the human companionship and attention it requires. A tethered dog can become aggressive if constantly ignored, particularly if people are always walking past it or its view of nearby activities is blocked by obstacles. Regular visits and play periods will satisfy its social needs and keep it a trustworthy member of your family.

• If the dog stays outside every day for any appreciable amount of time, you should provide it with a comfortable, well-insulated, weatherproof shelter. The characteristics of a well-designed doghouse are discussed on page 26.

• Also keep close watch on the dog to make sure it stays in good health. Because outdoor dogs are not as much under their owners' eyes as indoor dogs, health problems are less likely to be noticed until they have become quite serious.

THE INDOOR DOG

Most dogs adapt quite well to an indoor life and are happy to be in more or less continuous contact with people. There are, however, a number of things you can do to ensure the animal's well-being:

• Dogs confined to a relatively limited space, such as a small apartment, are likely to gain weight and lose their physical tone unless they are exercised regularly. In addition to taking your pet on its regular walks, you should also set aside at least ten or fifteen minutes a day for vigorous exercise, preferably outdoors. Continuous confinement without regular exercise is unhealthy because neither the appetite nor the circulatory system is properly stimulated. Pets kept in this condition are likely to become obese and old before their time.

• A house dog should have some special area set aside where it can go when you don't want it elsewhere in the house. Select a spot that is comfortably warm and easy to keep clean. Clear it of rugs and other furnishings that may become spoiled if the dog has an accident or becomes ill. Furnish it with the dog's bed and a few toys so it can be comfortable and content.

• If you house the dog in a basement or garage, cover its space with a mat, blanket or section of old carpet to protect it from the concrete floor. Dogs that spend extended periods in direct contact with concrete tend to develop arthritis at a relatively early age. It is not unusual for dogs to seek out the coolness of concrete in warm weather, but this should be discouraged in older and arthritic animals.

• Make sure the dog gets enough human contact to keep it friendly and socialized. Dogs kept isolated for long periods may develop behavior problems and grow less reliable as house pets, particularly with the children in the family.

• Most dogs have a natural urge to chew on things. To save the legs of your dining room chairs and other valued possessions, provide your dog with a large sturdy bone, hard ball or some other suitable toy it can gnaw on and play with.

DOGGY BONE

LIVING QUARTERS

A dog can find a comfortable place to sleep almost anywhere, but it should be given its own sleeping quarters.

If your dog sleeps indoors, it will probably feel most safe and secure sleeping in the area you have chosen as its special place. Select a warm, quiet spot for its bed, well away from heavy household noise and activity. A great variety of dog beds are available at pet shops, or you can make one yourself. A heavy three-sided cardboard box or carton will do nicely as long as it is large enough to keep the dog from feeling cramped. Line the bottom with a pillow or soft pad protected with several layers of washable covers. To minimize cold drafts and dampness, elevate the bed several inches above the floor.

If your dog sleeps outdoors at night, it will need a sturdy, well-insulated, draft-free shelter to protect it from wind, cold and rain. You can purchase a doghouse or construct one yourself. Plans for various types of dog shelters can be found in the public library or in the numberous magazines published for the weekend handyman.

Here are some important points to keep in mind when buying or building the dog's shelter:

• It should be made entirely of waterproof materials suitable for outdoor use.

• All paints must be lead-free and nontoxic.

• The doghouse will be easier to keep clean if the roof is removable or hinged to permit full access to the interior.

• There should be an awning-like overhang over the entrance so the dog will always have a shaded, relatively cool area during warm, sunny days.

• There also ought to be a small entry area that separates and protects the main interior space from the outside weather.

• To block out wind and rain, the entrance and the opening between the entry area and main space ought to be curtained with canvas or some other heavy cloth. The curtains should be slightly wider than the entranceways and hung so the air can circulate freely and the dog doesn't have any difficulty getting in and out.

• All exposed wooden edges should be covered with smooth metal so the dog can't chew at them.

• The entire structure ought to be elevated four or five inches above the ground.

The doghouse should be placed somewhere within the same fenced-in area you have chosen for the dog

to play in, in a spot sheltered from cold winds. If possible, face the doorway away from the north wind. Since the ideal location may be different in summer than winter, it ought to be possible to move the structure as the seasons change.

Pad the floor of the shelter with a blanket, rug or other soft material so the dog will be able to sleep in comfort. Remember to wash the bedding regularly.

Decide where you want the dog to eat and drink, and make sure this spot is always accessible to the animal. If you feed the dog outdoors, make certain the area is protected from sun and rain as well as from ants and other pests that might be attracted to the food.

Food and water should be placed near each other. The water bowl ought to be heavy and stable enough to keep the dog from tipping it over. Inexpensive bowls with weighted bottoms are available in almost any pet shop. For the dog's food, use a shallow dish or pan rather than a bowl so your pet won't have to use its paws to get the food out of the bottom. It will make clean up easier indoors if you put several thicknesses of newspaper under the containers. Make a point of changing the paper frequently.

SANITATION AND HYGIENE

The dog's feces must also be removed regularly, preferably every day, and buried, burned or flushed down the toilet. This will minimize the hazard of internal parasites that have not yet been detected. The eggs of many of the parasites that infect dogs are passed on in the animal's feces and will contaminate everything they touch, reinfesting the dog and building up an enormous parasite load that can seriously impair its health. Even dogs that have been successfully treated for parasites can be reinfested by contaminated ground. Whipworms and some other parasites can live outside a host for long periods of time, especially in warm weather. Once the ground has become contaminated, the only way the parasites can be killed is by plowing the surface under. The possibility of reinfestation through contaminated ground is one important reason why you should have a veterinarian analyze your dog's stool at least once a year.

Some parasites can be passed to humans, so it is especially important to clean up after your dog if it defecates anywhere near where children play. In warmer parts of the country roundworms are a particular risk to youngsters who walk around barefooted and play in moist soil that may be contaminated.

An increasing number of communities are adopting laws that require dog owners to clean up after their pets. As inconvenient as it might be, this is not an unreasonable requirement. Feces in the street can be a serious public health problem as well as an unsightly nuisance. A plastic bag and small shovel or one of the new clean up devices sold for this purpose makes the task simple.

Be sure to take note of any changes in your dog's toilet habits such as straining, constipation or diarrhea. They can be symptoms of a wide variety of illnesses. If they don't clear up immediately, check the relevant entries in the illness section of this book and, if necessary, consult your veterinarian.

NUTRITION

For good health and appearance, vitality and long life, your dog requires a diet that provides the proper amounts of protein, fat, vitamins, minerals and other nutrients. At each major stage of your pet's life its nutritional needs change to reflect the changing needs of its body. A puppy requires a diet suited to rapid growth, the development of strong teeth and bones and well-functioning internal organs and metabolism. An adult dog needs a diet that provides energy and good nutrition to fuel a healthy body at its peak. Even an older dog that has begun to slow down with advancing age will enjoy vigorous good health longer if its special dietary requirements are met.

Although commercial dog foods have gained enormous popularity, homemade dog foods are still a popular alternative. Dog food you prepare yourself is just as satisfactory as long as it meets the dog's full nutritional requirements. These needs are broader than the animal's designation as a carnivore (meat eater) might suggest. It also needs greens and grains in its diet. If you are going to prepare the food yourself, you will have to make a point of providing them.

• Add bran or cooked cereal to the dog's meat several times a week.

• Every meal ought to contain some high protein food such as cooked fish, meat or fowl combined with cooked vegetables.

• Raw egg yolks are also an excellent source of protein and can be included in the diet two or three times a week.

• Vegetables should be ground and thoroughly mixed into the meal so the dog can't remove or ignore them.

• Occasionally include high fat foods such as whole or dry milk, meat fat, cheese and cream. These foods are also an excellent source of additional protein.

• For a healthy, lustrous coat, add a teaspoon of unsaturated cooking or salad oil to the dog's meal two or three times a week.

For reasons of health or safety, certain foods should be avoided entirely and others given only occasionally or in small quantities:

• Large amounts of raw egg whites and organs such as liver, kidney and heart can upset the dog's vitamin balance and lead to serious physical problems.

• Raw meat may contain parasites and should be cooked thoroughly before being served to the dog. (Pork and pork products should be avoided altogether.)

• Starch must also be well cooked.

• Fish and chicken bones are dangerous because they may splinter into sharp pieces and stick in the dog's throat, catch between its teeth or become lodged in its rectum. Large beef bones are safer, but it would be better to get your dog a rawhide or fiber bone that won't splinter.

Rather than prepare the dog's food themselves, many owners find it more convenient to feed it commercial dog food. These foods are perfectly fine as long as they are produced by a reputable company that stays abreast of current nutritional information and research. Most supermarkets and grocery stores offer a great variety of such foods for sale:

• Maintenance foods that provide a fully balanced diet for the adult dog. They are available in many different flavors, and come both in cans, where the food is already moistened with water, and the more economical dry form to which water can be added. Dry foods have become increasingly popular because they are resistant to spoiling and can be left in the dog's dish.

• Special formula foods. Some are specifically designed for puppies that have just been weaned or for older dogs that have begun to slow down. Others are for dogs that have suffered heart disease, stress or some other illness that requires a special diet. Your veterinarian will tell you when any of these special formulas are appropriate.

• Specialty foods in small cans that are intended to supplement or add variety to the dog's staple diet. These serve as a flavorful change, but since they do not provide a fully balanced diet by themselves, they should not be used as a replacement for maintenance foods.

To give your dog a variety of tastes and textures you might try out various combinations of flavors, moist and dry maintenance foods and specialty brands. Once you have found the combination that suits the dog's taste and meets its total nutritional requirements, you probably won't have to vary from it. If the dog begins rejecting the food at some later time, it will usually start eating it again when it becomes hungry and no other choice is offered. Should it still refuse, you can ex-

periment briefly to discover a more acceptable combination of flavors and types.

Adult dogs can get along on a single daily feeding. Still, it is preferable to feed them twice a day. Dogs fed only once always seem to be looking for something to eat.

To determine the proper portion for each meal you will have to consider such factors as the dog's size, age, general level of activity and whether it lives indoors or out. Be aware that most of these things are subject to change and the changes have to be provided for. During the winter months, for example, the outdoor dog must be fed more generously since it burns up more calories to keep itself warm.

The main thing to remember is that it is essential to the dog's health not to gain weight after it reaches maturity. Overweight dogs are invariably less active and often develop weight-related health problems as they grow older. It is a matter of record that they have a significantly shorter life-span than dogs maintained at the proper weight.

Obesity caused by steady overfeeding usually develops slowly, so it is not always apparent. The dog may only put on a pound or two a year. Nevertheless, you can easily estimate your pet's proper weight by examining the fat covering over its ribs:

• If you can't feel the individual ribs, the dog is too fat.

• If the ribs stick out so your fingers can go between them, the animal is too thin.

• If you can feel the ribs but can't stick your fingers between them, the dog is at the right weight.

In addition to giving your dog the right food, you should also make sure it always has access to fresh water. Water plays a vital role in maintaining health and can help prevent certain serious illnesses, particularly as the dog grows older. Place the water in a bowl near your pet's food dish and change it daily. To correct a common error, milk may be nearly the perfect food but it is no substitute for water in the dog's diet.

You should also add balanced vitamin and mineral supplements to the dog's diet several times a week. Unless your veterinarian recommends it, do not give your pet individual vitamins or minerals such as calcium. They can disturb its metabolic balance and impair its health. At one time owners of giant breeds such as Saint Bernards and Great Danes commonly fed their dogs enormous calcium supplements, causing many of them to develop bowed legs and other bone problems.

Take note of any significant increase or decrease in your dog's food and water intake, as well as such digestive irregularities as diarrhea, constipation and vomiting. If they persist, you should consult your veterinarian immediately, particularly if they are accompanied by other symptoms. (See the **SYMPTOM RECOGNITION INDEX** on page 83.) Although these conditions can be caused by dietary or environmental factors, they may also indicate the dog is infected with parasites or has some other illness.

TRAINING

A dog must be trained in three essential things for its own well-being and the safety and comfort of the other members of the family. It must be taught to relieve itself in the right place. It must be taught to be responsive to your commands. It must be taught to control its natural aggressive tendencies. Owners who fail to train their dogs in these respects often find themselves so frustrated that they feel they have to get rid of their pets, writing them off for their supposed stubbornness or stupidity. The blame, of course, should not be attributed to the dogs but to the owners themselves for their failure to meet the responsibilities of ownership.

HOUSEBREAKING

You can begin your efforts to housebreak the dog as soon as you get it home by taking it for a walk outside whenever it needs to perform its toilet functions. Until you become familiar with its own natural rhythms, you can only guess when that will be. As a general rule, it is advisable to walk your pet when it wakes up in the morning, after it eats or exercises and just before it goes to sleep at night. When it relieves itself on these walks, praise it immediately and give it a dog biscuit or some other small treat. Dogs have a generally cooperative nature, so they learn quickly when they understand what is expected of them.

The most effective way to help your pet understand is through a combination of rewards and punishments. The basic principle is simple enough. Reward your dog when it does the right thing. Punish it when it makes a mistake. The way the principle is applied is a bit more complicated, particularly with the punishment part of training.

If the dog makes a mistake and creates a mess in the house, respond immediately with a loud "No!" and then take it outdoors. It is neither necessary nor desirable to hit it. Striking your pet with a rolled up newspaper or heavy hand will only frighten it and may cause it to fight back to protect itself. Your hand should just be used to administer affection and reward. You will only confuse the animal if you also use it as an instrument of punishment. Dogs are so responsive to their owners that your tone of voice will soon be enough to communicate to your pet that you are upset with it. Not uncommonly, a dog that is beaten during housebreaking reacts so extremely that it comes to fear its stool and may even eat it rather than incur your anger.

To be effective, the praise or anger must come immediately so the dog can understand that it is a direct result of something it did. After only a few minutes go by, it will no longer sense any connection between the mess it created and the fact you are displeased with it. It is useless and confusing to the animal to punish it in the morning, for example, for an error it made during the night. The dog will know that something is wrong but cannot possibly comprehend what it is.

Housebreaking does not always go smoothly, but it will be easier to accomplish quickly and successfully if you keep your patience and remember that your pet is still under the stress of adjusting to a new home and new people, still recovering from its separation from friendly, familiar surroundings.

The process can be made a great deal easier in pleasant weather by letting the dog spend most of the day outside in its enclosed area and bringing it back in the house for only short periods when it can be closely supervised by a member of the family. By keeping it outdoors, you are in effect forcing it to do the right thing. When it performs its toilet functions outside the house and isn't punished, it will soon learn that this is the acceptable behavior. The lesson can be reinforced even further by bringing the dog back inside immediately afterwards and rewarding it with praise and a goody.

Whenever the dog is brought inside it should be supervised closely so that if it does make a mistake it can be disciplined immediately and returned to the outdoors. Close supervision is imperative because of the importance of immediate punishment. In the final stages of housebreaking when the dog becomes more reliable, indoor periods can gradually be extended until it spends most of its time in the house. Close, continuous control is the central point of this method.

In less-controlled situations where the dog spends most of its time inside before becoming housebroken, it is virtually certain to have an accident at some point.

No one can supervise a dog every minute of the day, so there is a good chance that the mess won't be discovered until later. To emphasize an earlier point, remember that delayed discipline is useless and if anything counterproductive. It may confuse the dog into thinking it is being punished because it performed its toilet functions, not because it did them in the house.

Keeping the dog indoors without close supervision before it is housebroken also creates the possibility of so confusing your pet that it gets the proper order of things reversed. In this common, extremely perplexing situation, the dog has an accident and is put outside, but when it is brought back in sometime later it promptly proceeds to make another mess. It is as if it had waited until it was inside to defecate or urinate. Unless this situation is quickly brought under control, it can drive the pet owner to distraction and create an oppressive condition of high anxiety in the dog.

Unquestionably, access to outdoor space facilitates the housebreaking process by making it easy for the dog to do the right thing. Close supervision at all other times is comparably important because it makes possible the immediate discipline necessary when the dog does the wrong thing.

Many owners who do not have an enclosed outdoor area or are too busy to walk their dogs often deal with the problem by training them to relieve themselves on newspaper. Paper training is not the most efficient way to housebreak a dog and should only be used if there is no real alternative. There are two major problems with this method. The first is that it prolongs the process by creating several separate and distinct steps for the dog to master. It must first learn to use the paper, then it must learn to go outdoors—a switch it may find confusing. The second problem is that it keeps the training situation from being fully under your control. Sooner or later the dog will make a mess in the house that goes unpunished because it is not discovered immediately. This sets up an inconsistent and confusing situation that can seriously impede the housebreaking process.

If you have no choice but to paper train your pet, here's how to do it:

• Limit the dog to one relatively small indoor area that you have completely carpeted with several thicknesses of newspaper. To keep it there, close off the doors leading to other parts of the house or block the entrances with expandable gates, but do not tie the dog up.

• Change the newspapers as they become dirty, removing all but the bottom sheets, which should still be clean. Place these sheets on top of the fresh paper you lay down. Since they carry the dog's own scent, they will help it understand what is expected of it.

• As the dog begins to get the idea, gradually reduce the size of the covered area. Supervise the dog as much as you can, praising it when it uses the paper and showing you are displeased when it goes off the paper.

• When the dog no longer makes mistakes, let it have free access to the rest of the house and begin to take it outside to perform its toilet functions. Walk it the first thing in the morning, after meals and exercise, before bedtime and whenever it seems to be preparing to relieve itself. Some owners have found that this last stage of housebreaking can be made easier by removing the newspapers from the floor, thereby forcing the dog to wait until it is taken out.

As an alternative to paper training, you might consider "crating" the dog, a housebreaking technique that has been found quite effective by many owners who don't have access to outdoor space or aren't home during the day.

This approach requires that the dog be placed in a cage with thick, rigid wire sides and bottom. The bottom of the cage should be lined with several thicknesses of newspaper, and the cage itself should be roomy enough to permit the pet to turn around and lie down but not so large that it can get away from its mess. The dog's natural aversion to lying in its own excrement, combined with the system of rewards and punishments described earlier, will encourage it to delay relieving itself until it is removed from the cage and taken outdoors. For crating to work, the owner must be committed to walking the dog regularly. If you aren't sure you will be able to meet this responsibility, it would be best not to use this method.

Unlike paper training, crating does not confine the dog to one place which may or may not be near the rest of the family. Since the cage can be picked up and moved from room to room, the pet can always be close to its owners. Fortunately, the confinement required by this method doesn't last very long, since the dog very quickly learns to wait until it is taken outside before urinating or defecating.

While housebreaking is proceeding and the dog still soils the floor, the soiled spots should be immediately cleaned to prevent the dog from returning to them. You can remove the odor that guides your pet to these spots by washing them thoroughly with white vinegar and water, then covering them over with a generous amount of baking soda. After three or four hours, the dry powder can be removed with a vacuum cleaner or broom.

OBEDIENCE TRAINING

The process of obedience training employs the same principle of reward and punishment used in housebreaking. The main objective here is to teach your dog to follow such basic voice commands as "come, heel,

"COME"   **"HEEL"**

"SIT"   **"STAY"**

sit" and "stay." Learning these things will make it a much more manageable, dependable and enjoyable pet.

Wait until the dog is at least six or eight months old before you start training it. When you are ready to begin, fit it with a training collar—a metal chain collar that tightens around the neck when pulled.

The first thing to teach it is to come when you call. This is the most basic and important of all commands. Remember that a dog can only absorb so much at once, so keep the training periods relatively short, to no more than a half dozen repetitions at one time. Two or three 15 minute sessions each day should be just about right.

• To begin, attach a leash to the dog's training collar, then holding the other end, squat down and encourage it to come to you by calling its name and telling it to "come" while offering it a dog biscuit or some other treat. Make sure to keep your voice playful, affectionate and encouraging rather than harsh and demanding. Do everything you can to make the dog take those first steps toward you willingly. If you succeed, you will be setting a more positive and constructive tone for all future training.

• If the dog does not come to you after the first few times you call, then tug sharply on the leash as you repeat its name and the command. Drag the dog toward you if it still doesn't respond, then when it finally does obey, praise it and give it its goody. Do not reprimand it or punish it. Being pulled on the leash is punishment enough. The dog should associate coming to you only with praise and reward. After a few times it will begin to understand that you want it to move to you

when you call and that it will receive something good when it does.

• Continue the process until the dog comes voluntarily without having to be jerked by the leash. As it responds more reliably, substitute a longer leash or rope and try to get it to obey from progressively longer distances.

• When the dog comes every time you call, it is ready to be trained without the tether. Take it to a small room, fenced-in yard or other enclosed space and continue calling to it and encouraging it to obey your command. At this stage of training it is important to pick a spot that is relatively free of distractions. If your pet isn't responsive, put it back on the tether and repeat the earlier steps until it obeys you without fail, then try this step again.

• Now move the training to a larger outdoor space where the dog's concentration may be deflected by people, noise and activity. As before, begin by tieing your pet to a short leash and gradually lengthen the tether until you have eventually worked up to the point where you can remove it altogether. Again, if the dog fails to obey when the tether is finally removed, put it back on and continue the training until it is able to respond freely. As in the earlier stages, encourage the dog to come to you and always praise and reward it when it does.

• When the dog is able to respond when it is off the tether, the final phase of training can begin. Now it must learn to obey you whether or not it is given a treat. To get to this point, start omitting the treat about half the time, then gradually cut back still further until its sole reward is your praise and approval.

When the dog has learned to come to you whenever you call, you can start training it to "heel," that is, remain close to your side as you walk along with it. The process involves essentially the same techniques as teaching it to come. The training periods should also be limited to a quarter hour or so.

• To begin, put on the dog's training collar and leash and take it outdoors for a walk. Have it stand close to your side, then as you start to step forward, say its name and the command "heel." At the same time, tug on the leash to get the dog moving along with you. If necessary, continue tugging on the leash as you walk so that it stays close to your side, neither behind nor ahead of you. Each time the dog returns to the correct position, praise it lavishly.

• Continue the training until the dog will walk by your side without being jerked by the leash.

• Using the same method, you can take the training a step further by teaching the dog to heel when it is not wearing a leash.

Training the dog to sit is usually a fairly simple process that can be accomplished at the same time it is learning to heel. With the dog at your side, say its name and the command "sit," then push down on its rump to force it into a sitting position. To keep it from lying down, hold up its head with the leash. Repeat the command each time you stop walking, and continue pressing down on its rump until it learns to sit without being forced. As before, praise the dog whenever it does what you tell it.

To teach the dog to stay still, get it to sit, then say its name and the command "stay." If necessary, keep it from getting up by pressing down on its rump each time it begins to move out of position. Gradually extend the time the dog remains still, increasing it from a few seconds to a minute or more. Continue the process until the dog responds reliably.

AGGRESSIVE BEHAVIOR

All dogs are instinctively aggressive to some degree, particularly males. Watch young puppies at play, and notice how they roll around growling and biting at one another, each trying to gain a clear advantage and force the others to surrender.

Such aggressiveness is both a natural and essential part of the animal's personality, one of the main reasons it survived as a species before it began to be domesticated. Without this trait it would not have been able to obtain food or defend itself from attack. Aggressiveness was also essential to the formation and maintenance of the pack, the animal's basic social unit. In the wild, undomesticated state, one dominant dog always emerges as the pack leader and maintains that position by defeating all challenges to its leadership. Most often, these challenges come from young males between six and eighteen months old who are maturing sexually and becoming more aggressive in their efforts to achieve dominance within the pack.

Domestication is the process by which the dog learns to live harmoniously with humans. By raising it from the time it is a puppy and giving it a secure home, good care, gentle handling and proper training, the owner can reduce the pet's natural aggressiveness to an acceptable level. It cannot, however, be eliminated altogether. Aggressiveness is one of the main reasons why people give up their dogs.

Taken as a whole, some breeds are more aggressive than others, but there is still a wide variation among dogs of the same breed and even within members of the same litter. The variation is even greater in mixed breeds. For this reason, you should always evaluate an individual dog's aggressiveness before bringing it into your home. Page 19 tells you how to go about making this evaluation.

You may, of course, want a certain amount of aggressiveness in your pet, depending on the purpose you want it to serve. It is a positive quality in a good watchdog or hunter, a strongly negative one in a family pet.

Some dogs respond aggressively to the slightest provocation. Others remain even-tempered in almost any situation. But given sufficient provocation, any dog will become aggressive. Even owners who have had their pets for years and never seen the slightest expression of violence may one day find their dogs reacting fiercely when placed in some particularly stressful set of circumstances.

To minimize this possibility, you should do your best to keep your dog from being provoked:

• Warn strangers that your pet may bite if it is bothered or feels threatened.

• If necessary, keep the dog away from people and animals you suspect may trigger a hostile response.

• Make sure it can always go someplace where nothing will bother it.

• Teach the children in your home that the dog is a living creature with feelings, not an inanimate toy. Youngsters who haven't learned this lesson will often tease or unintentionally hurt a family pet, forcing it to strike back to protect itself from some real or imagined threat. If necessary, keep your children from playing with the dog until they can comprehend that it must be treated with respect. If the children are too young to understand, you should probably postpone getting a dog until they are a bit more mature.

If you train the dog properly, warn people about your pet's limits and minimize the situations that provoke it, aggressiveness probably will never become a serious problem.

GROOMING

To keep your pet healthy and looking its best, you will have to groom it regularly. It is best to begin while the dog is still young. Puppies are far more tolerant than adult dogs of brushing and the like, and adapt to it much more readily. Once a regular routine has been established, they will accept it willingly and come to relax and enjoy it. You will have to expend a good bit more time and patience on a mature dog to bring it to this point, though eventually it too will come to accept grooming as an expected part of its daily routine.

BRUSHING

Since the dog's fur serves to protect it from the weather, its thickness normally varies with the seasons. The thickness of its coat is regulated by the temperature and the amount of sunlight to which it is exposed. Shedding is heaviest during the spring and summer months when there are the most hours of daylight. The fur is thickest during the winter months when the days are short. This explains why indoor dogs living in artificial light tend to shed more or less uniformly throughout the year.

Regular brushing provides much better care for the dog's coat than the animal can give itself. Here are some points to keep in mind to do it properly:

• Brush your pet's fur for at least five or ten minutes every day. Use a bristle brush for shorthairs and a wire brush for long-hairs. Matted hair should be combed, using the edge of the comb for particularly bad areas. Long-haired dogs should be brushed twice a day. This will untangle knots before they become matted and remove loose hairs that might otherwise be swallowed when the animal grooms itself with its tongue. It will also cut down on the number of unwelcome hairs you'll find scattered about your house and clothing. Hair longer than three-quarters of an inch should be combed before the final brushing.

• Brush the hair in the direction of growth. Go against the direction of growth before your final brushing to expose the underlayers to the brush and make the coat look attractively full and fluffy. Give as much attention to the stomach and inside of the legs as you do to the head, back and neck.

• Many long-haired dogs grow hair between their toes, which frequently becomes matted with asphalt, vegetation and foreign objects. To save your pet discomfort, inspect the area each time you give it a brushing and clean the material away whenever necessary. If the problem becomes recurrent, keep the hair between the toes trimmed short.

• Long hair around the anus should also be kept short to prevent anal plugs.

• Every time you brush, make a point of looking closely at the skin beneath the fur. It should be clean and pliable with a healthy pinkish color. Bald spots, redness and blotches are never normal and indicate that something is wrong. They may be caused by any number of conditions including parasites, skin diseases, allergies, poor diet and reaction to stress. Watch such symptoms closely. If they persist or worsen, bring them to your veterinarian's attention.

• Also be on the lookout for foreign substances that have become tangled in your pet's hair. Dogs are curious animals and often come home matted with paint, tar, chewing gum and the like. These substances can usually be dealt with best while they are still fresh and haven't yet become dried and crusted. Often they are water soluble and can easily be removed with soap and water.

• Areas matted with tar or other substances that are not soluble in water should be saturated with vegetable oil, then covered with bandages to keep the dog from licking at them. After about eight hours they ought to have softened enough to be removed with soap and water. It may be necessary to repeat the process if all the material doesn't wash away. When all of it finally has been removed, wash the entire area with soap and water, then rinse and dry it thoroughly.

• Never use cleaning fluid, turpentine or other strong solvents to clean matted fur. They will irritate the dog's skin and can poison the animal if absorbed into its body. If the fur is too badly matted to clean with soap and water or vegetable oil, have your veterinarian deal with it.

• It is never desirable and seldom necessary to remove matted hair by cutting it away. If it ever does become necessary, the matted area should be cut into small pieces in the direction of growth, not across it. This will take some time and patience, but these smaller pieces can then be combed or brushed from the coat without spoiling the dog's looks or depriving it of its natural protection. When large areas are affected, the dog should be brought to the vet.

• Occasionally, a dog's coat or feet may become soiled with toxic substances such as tar and paint. If they become absorbed into the animal's skin or enter the system through its mouth when it tries to clean itself, they may very well poison it. Should this happen, flush the poisons away as quickly as possible with large amounts of cool water. See **POISONING: CONTACT,** page 196, for the step-by-step procedure for dealing with this emergency.

BATHING

Dogs also require regular bathing. Even though they do groom themselves, they cannot really keep themselves clean. A grown dog should be bathed whenever necessary but not more than once a week. Long-haired breeds must be kept particularly clean, especially during the warm summer months when they are most susceptible to fleas, ticks and other external parasites. Puppies under three months old should not be bathed except when it is absolutely necessary. They are susceptible to many illnesses and don't yet have much resistance.

• Bathing should always be done indoors in a warm spot that is free of drafts.

• Try to get an assistant to hold the dog and keep it calm while you bathe it.

• Use a mild, non-detergent hand soap or a specially formulated dog soap available in pet shops.

• Wash the dog with a gentle stream of warm water. A hose or faucet is better than a spray, which may alarm the animal.

• Take special care to keep the soap out of the dog's eyes. If you don't have assistance, you may have to hold your pet down with one hand to prevent it from splashing soapy water into its eyes.

• After the fur has been cleaned, make sure to rinse away all traces of the soap to prevent irritation to the sensitive skin underneath.

• The dog should then be toweled down thoroughly and protected from drafts until it is completely dry. Keep it indoors while it is still wet. If you let it outside, it will probably want to roll around on the ground to dry itself. The hot summer sun can also cause heat exhaustion or sunstroke in a wet animal.

• When the dog is fully dry, give it a good brushing to remove all the loose hairs and restore the luster to its fur.

As an alternative to soap and warm water, the dog can be cleaned with a "dry bath." This is a commercial preparation available in pet shops that absorbs dirt and oil when applied to the skin, then is removed by brushing. It will do a reasonably good job of keeping the dog clean and is preferable for puppies under three months old. If you decide to try this method, you might consider using ordinary cornstarch rather than the commercial preparation. It does the same job at a substantially lower cost.

A healthy dog does not normally have a strong or offensive odor. If the dog does smell, it may have a disease or infection that should be treated by a veterinarian. An outdoor dog may have picked up the smell from its explorations or through an encounter with a skunk. Skunk smell is highly resistant to soap and water. The best way to remove it is by soaking the animal in tomato juice for several minutes, then bathing it as described above.

EARS

Once a week the dog's ears should be examined and, if necessary, cleaned. This is a relatively simple task, but there are a few important precautions to keep in mind: **Do not** use alcohol or other solvents on the dog's ears. **Do not** try to clean further inside the ear than you can actually see. The L-shape of the dog's ear canal offers natural protection to the delicate inner ear structures. For the same reason, **do not** pull on the ear flap while cleaning. This would straighten the ear canal and expose the inner ear structures to possible injury.

Before the cleaning begins, the dog must be restrained. It would be best to have an assistant hold down the dog for you, but if you are alone you should be able to do it yourself. The section on **RESTRAINTS,** page 209, details the procedures for both situations.

1. When the dog has been restrained, have your assistant grab its muzzle and steady its head against his chest. Lift the ear flap and hold it firmly without pulling on it. (If the dog's ears are cropped, just hold the ear.)

2. Carefully remove loose wax and debris from the ear and ear canal with dry cotton balls, then with cotton balls moistened in warm water.

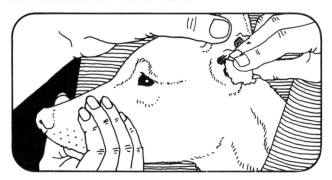

3. Using a gentle, rotating motion, clean loose wax and debris from the ear folds and crevices with dry cotton-tipped swabs. Repeat with cotton-tipped swabs moistened in warm water. Repeat the process on the dog's other ear.

EYES

The dog's eyes should also be cleaned whenever necessary to prevent scabs or ulcerations from accumulated debris. Keep in mind that the dog has an opaque third eyelid that is not normally seen but which may come up to protect an injured eye. Should this happen, **do not** try to remove it or otherwise interfere with it.

Again, the dog must be restrained before the cleaning begins, either by an assistant or yourself. See the section on **RESTRAINTS,** page 209, for the right procedures.

1. Facing the dog, grab its muzzle and steady its head.

2. Using a dry cotton ball, gently wipe away accumulated mucus and debris from the inside corner of the eye and the skin just below. **Do not** touch the eyeball.

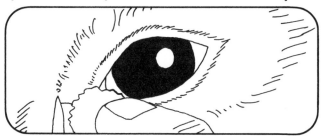

3. Remove any remaining mucus or debris with a cotton ball moistened in warm water. The lower lid may be pulled down slightly to facilitate cleaning. Repeat the process on the dog's other eye.

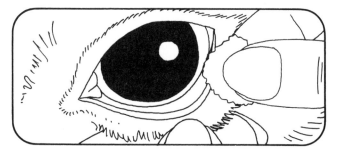

TEETH

The dog should also be inspected regularly for any signs of tooth decay or diseased gums. If you smell a strong, unpleasant odor when you open its mouth, something is probably wrong. Dogs with bad teeth don't seem to experience much pain and continue to bite and chew quite normally. But since abscesses, bleeding gums and lost teeth force the animal's body to fight constantly against infection, they have a seriously harmful effect and can eventually lead to anemia.

Make a particular point of checking that your pet's teeth are relatively free of tartar. If tartar is allowed to accumulate, the affected teeth may eventually fall out or have to be extracted. Look for the characteristic green stains, especially on the teeth toward the back of the mouth. If the stains are present, the dog should be taken to the vet to have its teeth cleaned. Some pets require a regular cleaning once a year to keep built-up tartar from becoming a problem.

Normally, counterpressure from the contact between the upper and lower jaws helps keep the dog's teeth in good condition. When there is no counterpressure because the bottom jaw overshoots or undershoots the top jaw, then the likelihood of tooth problems is considerable. This condition is particularly common in Pugs and Bulldogs and tends to affect the large incisors and other front teeth.

NAILS

The sturdy nails on the dog's paws grow constantly but are usually worn down by the dog's normal activities. Pets that spend a lot of time outdoors walking and running over rough ground aren't commonly bothered by overly long nails. However, indoor dogs and those that don't get very much exercise do require periodic trimming. Claws that become too long break easily and are likely to become snagged on carpets, furniture and clothing. If the dog has to struggle to break free, it can cause painful damage to itself and may even lose the nail.

Dogs that need it should have their claws clipped about once a month with professional clippers made for this purpose. You can ask your veterinarian to show you what to do or follow this relatively simple procedure:

Have someone help you restrain the dog on a plastic or metal tabletop. See **RESTRAINTS,** page 209.

1. Hold the paw in your hand, and taking each nail in turn, squeeze it at the base between your thumb and index finger. Leave just a slight excess of nail beyond your fingertips.

2. With your other hand, carefully clip the end of the nail, taking care not to clip the vein that enters the nail near the paw. If the dog's nails are translucent, a bright light will help you see this vein clearly. Should you have an accident, the bleeding can be stopped with direct pressure. See **BLEEDING: CUTS & WOUNDS,** page 153, for the proper procedure.

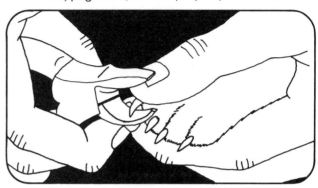

3. When you have finished the nails, trim the dewclaws. There may be more than one on each foot.

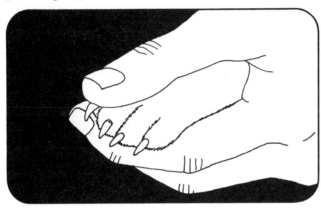

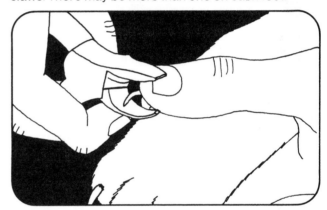

PARASITES

Fleas, ticks, lice and mites are among the common parasites that may infest your dog. Outdoor dogs are especially susceptible to these pests, particularly if they spend a lot of time in contact with cats and other dogs. These parasites attach themselves to the dog's hair or skin, then feed on the animal and begin to reproduce themselves. Some of them reproduce so quickly that they can seriously infest your pet in a very short time. Parasites are not only annoying to the dog but potentially dangerous. They can cause anemia and spread disease to the animal and the other members of your family.

Look closely for evidence of parasites on the skin and fur whenever you groom your pet. Even if you can't find anything, you should suspect the animal is infested if it constantly scratches at its fur, shakes its head vigorously or rubs its body against corners and other hard surfaces.

Parasites can neither be prevented nor eliminated

by regular bathing. If your dog is contaminated, you will have to treat it with the appropriate medication. Make sure the medicine is made specifically for use on dogs and follow the accompanying directions carefully. Do not use home remedies. They may contain injurious chemicals.

When the dog has parasites, you can assume that its bedding is also infested. Discard the bedding or wash it thoroughly and make a point of keeping the fresh bedding particularly clean until the parasites are gone. You will also have to decontaminate all the areas your pet frequents. Only a small percentage of the fleas, lice and mites in the dog's environment are on its body at any one time. Typically, these parasites will jump on the dog as it passes by, feed for awhile, then jump back off.

For more detailed instructions on how to treat specific parasites, see **PARASITES: EXTERNAL,** page 123.

TRAVEL

CARS

Most dogs don't have any difficulty traveling in cars once they become accustomed to being in a moving vehicle. If possible, start getting your dog used to it while it is still a puppy.

To begin, have the dog sit in your parked car for a few minutes at a time. Then gradually increase the time you leave it there. When your pet seems at ease, start running the engine while it sits there. Now begin taking it for short rides that gradually become longer. After a while, it should be perfectly comfortable and enjoy its outings thoroughly.

There are a number of precautions to keep in mind that will ensure your pet's safety and comfort:

• Dogs usually like to sit in the passenger seat next to the driver. This is all right for small pets, as long as they keep to their side of the car and don't interfere with the driver's operation of the vehicle. Large dogs should always ride in the back. For maximum safety, it would be best to put your dog in some sort of carrier.

• Don't let your pet travel with its head out the window. It may get something in its eye, or its nose or ears may become irritated.

• Make sure the dog always wears its license and identification tag when you take it driving. Should you somehow become separated, the person who finds your dog will need that information to get it back to you.

• Never leave the dog in a closed or even partially closed automobile on a sunny day. Even if the temperature is only moderate, the inside of a closed car can quickly heat up to 100°F. (37.7°C.) or more.

• On longer trips, try to bring along the dog's regular bedding and food dishes. They will help it feel more secure about being away from home.

MOTION SICKNESS

Younger dogs under about a year old are sometimes sensitive to motion and may start to salivate, drool, retch and vomit when taken out for a drive. These symptoms usually start slowly, but then progress more rapidly, continuing throughout the ride and for some time afterward. Some dogs outgrow this condition after awhile. Others do not.

If your dog is subject to motion sickness, your veteri-narian can prescribe Dramamine or some other medication that may keep it from becoming ill. Tranquilizers can also help a dog that is made anxious or frightened by travel. To be effective, the medication will have to be administered several hours before the trip. Withholding food and water doesn't usually keep a sensitive dog from feeling dizzy and nauseous, but it will reduce the mess if the animal becomes ill.

PLANES, TRAINS AND BUSES

All forms of public transportation that will accept dogs require that they be carried in a travel kennel or other suitable enclosure. This rule is necessary to prevent the dog from becoming a nuisance and to protect the other passengers from being harmed by an animal that turns suddenly vicious out of fright. It is also necessary to protect the dog itself from being hurt if the vehicle has to make an abrupt stop.

• Travel kennels come in all different sizes, from small boxes to large crates and cages. Make sure the one you choose is large enough to allow your dog to stand on all four legs and turn around comfortably.

• It should be sturdily constructed of easy to clean materials such as plastic, metal or wood.

• To keep it from opening in transit, it should be equipped with a sturdy hinged top or door that is held closed with several fasteners and a belt. The carrier for a smaller dog should have a rounded top and a strong carrying handle.

• Check that the enclosure is well-ventilated with small openings around the sides toward the bottom. Larger openings must be protected with screens or bars. The dog may harm itself if it is able to poke its paw through. Since dogs seem to feel more secure in potentially frightening situations if they cannot see or be seen, larger openings should be fitted with curtains to limit the animal's view of the outside and protect it from curious bystanders.

• Write your name and address clearly on the outside of the carrier in case you become separated from your pet.

• If the dog will be riding in the baggage compartment, also write any special handling or feeding instructions on the outside of the box, along with the words "LIVE ANIMAL" printed in large letters.

• When you take your pet on an extended trip that requires it to spend considerable time in the enclosure, line the bottom fully with shredded paper. The paper will give the dog a soft surface to lie on and also absorb its urine. To cut down on the amount of waste, don't give the dog food or water for several hours before the trip begins. Unless the weather is particularly hot or the ride lasts longer than 12 hours, withhold water until you reach your destination. On longer trips, limit the dog to small amounts of food and drink.

If you are going abroad and plan to take your dog with you, find out whether the country you will be visiting has any travel restrictions about pets. Regulations vary widely from one country to another. Some only require a health certificate stating that the dog has been recently inoculated against rabies and other infectious diseases. Others insist that it be quarantined for as long as six months.

LEAVING THE DOG BEHIND

If it isn't feasible to take the dog along with you on your travels, make early plans to leave it at a reliable kennel. Your veterinarian ought to be able to recommend one or may be able to board your pet in his own facility.

• The kennel you select should be operated by professionals who will provide clean and comfortable housing for your pet, feed and care for it properly, give it plenty of exercise and return it to you in good health. Don't make final arrangements until you visit the place and check its facilities yourself. If the dogs you see there don't look healthy and happy, find someplace else.

• Before leaving your pet at the kennel, make sure it has been immunized against infectious diseases within the past year. It will be in unusually close contact with many other animals while you are away and might be exposed to infection.

• Alert your veterinarian that you are leaving your dog at the kennel. Tell him that if an emergency arises he has your permission to treat the pet. Write down the vet's name, address and telephone numbers and give them to the kennel operator. Also give him a note detailing any special requirements about diet, medication and the like.

THE FACTS OF LIFE

SEXUAL MATURITY

The female dog usually reaches sexual maturity when she is about seven months old. From that time on she will usually come into season twice each year. Each heat cycle lasts about three weeks from start to finish and has several distinct phases:

• The first phase lasts about seven to nine days, during which time she is not receptive to the male. Several indications will tell you when this phase has begun. The dog's vulva swells, and she may lick at it constantly. You are also likely to find your floor spotted with drops of blood.

• During the ninth to thirteenth days, ovulation occurs and the female becomes fertile and receptive to the male. If she is bred during these four days, she will most likely conceive. A dog can breed numerous times during this period and may conceive more than once. The litter of puppies may have different fathers.

• From the thirteenth to the twenty-first day of the cycle, the female is less likely to be receptive to the male and less likely to conceive if she is bred. Her body returns to normal as the cycle comes to an end.

The heat period usually passes without any great changes in the dog's personality. She may be more likely to run out of the house, and since males will be attracted to her scent, she may be accidentally bred if you let her outside. She may also raise her tail and present herself in a receptive position when stroked or petted on the rump. But there is no radical alteration comparable to the female cat, who becomes loud and demanding during heat.

The male dog reaches sexual maturity at about 11 months. The signs are usually quite clear.

• He becomes highly territorial, marking out his area with his urine to attract females and warn other males away.

• He shows a greater tendency to roam and becomes much more aggressive with dogs encountered along the way, particularly other males.

• He will frequently mount pillows and other objects as well as children and adults. (This is common behavior in all puppies, but only the male continues it after reaching maturity.)

• Males also often show a preputial drip, a creamy yellow substance on the penis that may leave stains on upholstered furniture around the house.

THE DOG POPULATION EXPLOSION

Literally millions of unwanted puppies are born each year. A large number come from unaltered strays, but they are not the root of the problem. The majority are produced by household pets whose owners have allowed them to breed not because they wanted puppies but because they erroneously thought this was the "right" thing to do.

There is no evidence to suggest it is either more "natural" or desirable for a female dog to have at least one litter before she is altered. This view attributes highly questionable human-like feelings and emotions to the animal. From everything that is known, a dog's sexual behavior is strictly in response to instinct. Nor is there any basis for concluding that neutering a dog has a negative effect on its health or well-being. What is certain is that this one litter, multiplied by millions of dogs, produces a problem of enormous proportions.

Many owners also permit their females to breed because of the marvelous opportunity it gives their children to witness the miracle of birth. While there is no doubt that this can be an extremely worthwhile experience, it should not be provided at the expense of the puppies.

Before allowing your pet to mate, you should be prepared to find a good home for its puppies if you don't want to keep them yourself. This is often more difficult than you might expect.

Friends and neighbors who indicate they may be willing to take the puppies off your hands often change their minds by the time they are born, so you will need more than a few casual "maybes" to find them good homes. And you had better start looking early, as soon as you know the mother is pregnant. Ask your friends to ask their friends. Advertise in your local newspaper. Post notices on the public bulletin boards in your neighborhood. Have your youngsters tell their schoolmates. Keep in mind that the puppies will not be ready to leave their mother until they are six or eight weeks old and until then you will have to take care of them yourself.

If you are lucky, you may find responsible, loving homes for all your unwanted pups. If you aren't—and the enormous overpopulation of dogs makes this likely —then you may have a troublesome problem on your hands.

The Society for the Prevention of Cruelty to Animals (SPCA), Humane Society and other organizations devoted to the well-being of pets can offer only limited help. They simply don't have the facilities to house the enormous number of unwanted, lost and abandoned dogs and cats left at their doorstep. And despite their effective organizational and promotional resources, they succeed in placing only a small percentage of the animals they are able to shelter. For lack of a more satisfactory alternative, they are usually forced to put the remainder to a painless death. To illustrate the magnitude of the problem, of the 130,000 animals passing through one large animal shelter in a major city, only 15,000 were adopted or recovered by their owners. The remaining 115,000 had to be destroyed.

Many pet owners set their unwanted animals free, preferring to give them a chance at survival rather than subjecting them to euthanasia. This may seem to be a humane solution to the problem. It isn't. The facts are that few dogs thrust out on their own are able to feed and care for themselves and almost none live out their normal life expectancy. Those that aren't soon killed by automobiles gradually deteriorate and ultimately succumb to the effects of malnourishment, injury and illness.

Veterinarians and other animal health care specialists who see and treat these abandoned pets agree that releasing a dog to make its own way in the city, suburbs or country is both cruel and inhumane. Even though these specialists may be personally repulsed by the idea of euthanasia, many of them will tell you that it is, sadly, the lesser of two repugnant evils.

There is, of course, a better way. Don't let your pet breed if you don't want the puppies or won't be able to take care of them. A number of alternative methods are available.

If you think your female dog may have been bred because you found her with a male during her fertile period, you can consult your veterinarian immediately. If it is still early enough, the vet may be able to prevent or terminate the pregnancy. Unfortunately, this alternative isn't always effective. An owner may not realize the dog is pregnant until it is too late for anything to be done about it.

Conception can also be prevented by prescription medication that will temporarily postpone or end the heat cycle. This method is commonly used on pets whose fertile periods come into conflict with their owners' plans to enter them in dog shows. It is not intended as a lifelong form of birth control.

There are also intravaginal devices designed to prevent the male from entering the female. They are not reliable.

Almost all pet specialists agree that there is only one truly effective solution to the tragic overpopulation of unwanted puppies. Owners must be understanding and responsible enough to neuter any male or female dogs they do not want bred.

NEUTERING YOUR DOG

The veterinarian can neuter your dog at any age, but the best time would be before it reaches sexual maturity. Females should have the operation when they are around five and a half or six months old. Males ought to be slightly older.

The surgery is painless and relatively simple and safe. It involves castrating the male and removing the uterus and ovaries from the female. The dog will only have to stay in the hospital a day or two, then recover quietly at home for about a week.

Consult your veterinarian about his fee. Because the operation is somewhat more involved and time-consuming for a female, it usually costs somewhat more. It is also usually a bit more costly for larger dogs. But veterinarians have traditionally kept the expense down to as little as possible to encourage pet owners to have the procedure done. Some communities also have programs that make this surgery available to eligible pet owners at reduced cost. Your local SPCA or Humane Society should be able to tell you if such a program exists in your area.

Neutering the female ends the heat cycle but has no negative effect on the dog's personality. She should become an even nicer and more tranquil pet and no longer desire to run off every six months. As additional benefits, she is also likely to live longer and develop fewer of the health problems common to unaltered females during middle and later life.

The altered male will no longer mount people or objects, has less desire to roam and may even become less aggressive with other dogs. Only the preputial drip remains unaffected by neutering. He will also be less likely to have anal tumors and prostate disease. He may at first continue to show his usual sexual habits because of the hormones that temporarily remain in his system, but this will end within a month.

Some dogs, especially males, tend to gain weight after neutering. This can be controlled by providing sufficient exercise and adjusting the diet as necessary.

BREEDING YOUR DOG

If you decide you do want your female to have puppies, the ideal time to breed her is between the ninth and thirteenth days of her heat cycle.

Some time before then, have her examined by your veterinarian, so he can determine if she is in good health and begin any special care she may require.

Bring along a specimen of the dog's stool in a closed container. The vet will want to analyze it for evidence of internal parasites. If your pet is infected, she should be treated immediately. Many parasites can be passed to puppies while they are still inside the mother. It is difficult to do anything for infected newborn puppies because they don't have the strength to withstand the necessary medication.

Treatment for fleas and other external parasites should also be started before breeding. They can produce potentially fatal anemia in young pups that are heavily infested.

You should also have your female reimmunized against infectious diseases even if she has already had her regular series of vaccinations. The greater the mother's immunity, the greater the immunity of her puppies when they are born and during the crucial first weeks when they are still nursing.

The period of pregnancy lasts about 63 days. During most of this time the mother can be treated quite normally. You should, however, make a particular point of giving her adequate exercise and a properly balanced diet. They are essential both to her own health and the health of her puppies.

For the first month of pregnancy, maintain the mother on her normal portions of food. After that, put out extra food between regular meals so she won't become hungry. If you prefer, you can gradually increase the portions at each regular feeding so that she is getting about twenty-five percent more by the time the puppies are due. Also be sure to give her abundant amounts of fresh water throughout her pregnancy.

From 45 days after conception until their birth, the puppies are growing rapidly within the mother, drawing all their food from her as well as the vitamins, calcium and other minerals they need to develop properly. The mother can only supply them with what she receives in her diet along with whatever reserves she may have stored up in her body. If her food or calcium supply is inadequate, the puppies will begin to draw on this reserve and she will gradually lose weight and begin to look poorly during the last stages of pregnancy and right after the puppies are born.

For this reason, it is important to supplement the pregnant and nursing mother's diet with fresh milk and the vitamins and minerals prescribed by your veterinarian. If her calcium is not replaced as quickly as it is being used to form the puppies' bones and provide them with milk for nursing, the mother may develop eclampsia (milk fever), a serious disorder that can be fatal.

The symptoms of eclampsia are panting, anxiety, muscular tremors and twitches (particularly on top of the head) and an extreme fever that may reach as high as 110°F. (43.3°C.). If left untreated, it may quickly progress to convulsions and coma.

Should your female contract eclampsia and develop the characteristic high fever, you will have to reduce her body temperature at once to 103°F. (39.4°C.). Immerse or hose her in cold water, then wrap her in cold, wet sheets and pack her head in ice. As soon as the fever subsides, call your veterinarian for further treatment. Once the crisis has been passed, the mother will have to be removed from the litter and the puppies raised as orphans. Eclampsia tends to recur, so affected females should not be allowed to breed again.

During the last week or ten days of pregnancy, discourage your dog from running, jumping from high places and other strenuous exercise. Abortion can occur any time after the dog conceives as a result of hormonal, nutritional, or hereditary problems as well as from infection of the uterus, trauma or **BRUCELLOSIS** (see page 117), but it is especially likely to happen in the later stages.

Should your dog abort, fetal material will be expelled from the birth canal and you are likely to find blood and stringy mucus on her vulva or the ground. Always consult your veterinarian immediately if you suspect your dog has aborted. An incomplete abortion can lead to serious health problems.

WHELPING (DELIVERY)

A week of two before the puppies are due, prepare a whelping box for the mother to give birth in.

• It should be about twice as large as the dog's usual bed, so she will have enough room to lie down by herself on one side while the litter remains on the other.

• Make sure the sides are high enough to keep the puppies from falling or climbing out.

• Line the bottom with torn newspapers, and replace them as they become dirtied.

• Place the box somewhere in the house away from heavy traffic where it can still be closely watched. Select a spot that is relatively dark or that can be darkened. Dogs prefer to be secluded from the light when they have their young.

• Have the expectant mother spend some time in the box so she can become used to it. If she doesn't come to feel at home there, she will probably have the litter where she usually sleeps.

• Should this happen, do not move her to the box until she has completed delivery and all the puppies have been born. Interruptions should always be kept to a minimum. They can stop, inhibit or change the instinctive birth process.

Whelping commonly takes place at night and often begins with a period of anxiety and restlessness.

• The dog will seem unusually listless, fidgety and uncomfortable, then she will probably begin to dig in the box or try to hide in a closet or dark corner. This phase normally lasts from several hours to 24 hours.

• When active contractions begin, they will be evident by the way the dog strains and tenses her stomach muscles.

• After a quarter hour or so, she may deliver a fluid-filled sac, then stop her efforts and begin to walk around as if everything were normal. Eventually, she will return to active labor.

• The first puppy may be born in as little as 15 minutes or as long as an hour. Let the mother proceed at her own pace. Do not distract or interrupt her. Watch only from a distance.

• The puppy may come out either head first or tail first. Both ways are perfectly normal.

• It may be born bullet-shaped and enclosed in a sac of membranes filled with fluid. The mother's instinctive response is to chew the membranes open and lick the puppy to stimulate breathing. Once the puppy begins to move, the mother will probably chew the umbilical cord and eat the membranes.

• If the puppy is born free of membranes, they will come along right behind it with the umbilical cord. The mother will also eat the membranes after she licks the puppy.

• Between births, you may see a green discharge, possibly tinged with red or black blood. This is a natural part of the birth process and nothing to become alarmed about.

• The time between puppies can range from 30 minutes to two hours. Once the time pattern is established, the mother usually stays to it. While she is still actively involved in giving birth, she probably won't pay too much attention to the puppies that have already been born. If she does not resume active contractions following the normal period between births, it is usually safe to assume all the puppies have been delivered.

Whelping presents almost no danger to the mother, but certain complications may imperil the puppies if not dealt with properly.

Consult your veterinarian if contractions continue for several hours without a puppy being born or if they stop after one or two puppies are delivered and more still appear to be inside the mother.

Occasionally, a puppy may emerge only partially from the birth canal and the mother is unable to complete the delivery. Should this happen, restrain the mother (see **RESTRAINTS,** page 209), then grasp the puppy with a dry towel and pull it gently in a downward direction toward the mother's feet. As she strains during contractions, pull somewhat harder. As she relaxes between contractions, simply maintain your hold on the puppy so it is not pulled back in. The puppy can usually be delivered like this without harming the mother, although there is a good chance that it may be born dead.

Should the mother fail to free a puppy from the closed sac of membranes, you will have to do it yourself within five minutes to keep the puppy alive. Use dry paper towels to pull the sac open, then rub the puppy gently to stimulate breathing.

Within a day or two after delivery, place the mother and puppies in a proper carrier and bring them to the veterinarian to make certain the delivery was normal. The vet may give the mother injections to ward off infection, shrink the uterus, expel any material that is still there and bring down the milk so the puppies can feed without difficulty.

Watch the mother closely for two weeks after whelping and report any symptoms of serious illness to the veterinarian. Some vaginal bleeding is normal for one or two days after giving birth. Call your vet if the bleeding seems heavy or persists for more than a few days. The membranes she has eaten may take away her appetite for a day or so or cause a brief bout of vomiting or diarrhea. There is no cause for concern unless these symptoms continue.

The first milk that newborn puppies take from their mother is rich in colostrum, a substance that temporarily passes on to them her immunity to disease. It is very important that each puppy in the litter gets a share of this first milk. Watch the puppies as they nurse to make sure all have their turn. If any one of them doesn't, remove the other pups from the whelping box and put that one to the mother's breast.

It is also important to the mother's health that her mammary glands be adequately drained. They may not be if the puppies aren't taking enough of her milk, or if they become injured or infected or don't dry up naturally. (The breasts are a particularly fertile area for infection during and after pregnancy.) During the period when the mother is nursing her litter, feel her breasts every day to make sure they are still soft and pliable.

If they are hard and caked and you can feel a solid mass inside them, consult your veterinarian. He may tell you to apply warm compresses for 15 minutes three or four times a day.

Should the mother develop mastitis (an infection of the mammary glands), the breasts will be hot, red and painful when touched, and she may resist her puppies' efforts to nurse. In more advanced cases, the dog may develop a fever, lose her appetite and show other symptoms of systemic infection.

The glands may also form pus pockets and abscess to the outside of the breast. Call your veterinarian immediately at the first sign of any of these symptoms. The puppies will probably have to be taken away from the mother and raised as orphans.

In a normal situation where nothing goes wrong, the mother will continue to nurse her puppies for three or four weeks after they are born. Her need for food now will be even greater than it was during pregnancy. You may find it necessary to give her more than twice her usual portions. Make sure that extra food is always available to her during this period so she need never go hungry.

Breeds that have their tails cropped and dewclaws removed usually have it done when they are between two and four days old. At this age, the procedure is quick and easy and doesn't even require anesthesia. Boxers, Dobermans and other breeds that have their ears cropped should have it done at around seven or eight weeks.

TAKING CARE OF AN ABANDONED PUPPY

Occasionally, a new mother will move one of her puppies away from the other members of the litter and make a great point of keeping it there. This usually means she believes something is wrong with it. She is usually right. Unless the puppy is cared for separately, it will almost certainly die. You should make some attempts to place the puppy back in the litter, but don't be surprised if your efforts fail. If it is to survive, you will have to raise it yourself as an orphan. On those rare occasions when the mother shows no interest in caring for any of her pups, you will have to do the same thing with the entire litter.

The abandoned puppy should be placed in its own box in a draft-free room where the temperature can be maintained at a constant 85°F. to 90°F. (29.4°C. to 32.2°C.). If it is not kept at this temperature and becomes cold or chilled, it will inevitably die. Chilling is one of the most common causes of death in newborn pups because they are unable to regulate their own body temperatures.

Feed the puppy with a formula consisting of one egg yolk mixed in eight ounces of milk or a commercially prepared formula specifically made for orphaned pups. Warm the food and feed it to the puppy with an eye-dropper or dosing syringe. Give it as much as it will take five or six times a day. When it has had enough, its stomach will feel comfortably full but not distended or swollen. If it isn't getting enough to eat, it will whine and move restlessly about its box.

An abandoned puppy will also have to be stimulated to perform its normal toilet functions. This is best accomplished by rubbing a cotton swab dipped in mineral oil around its anus three or four times a day or inserting it about half an inch. After about four weeks the puppy should be able to take care of itself and the stimulation will no longer be necessary.

WEANING AND FEEDING PUPPIES

For the first three or four weeks of life, puppies are nourished exclusively by their mother's milk. After a month or so, the process of weaning can begin by giving them a little milk in a saucer. If it's necessary, you can encourage them to drink by gently pushing their faces toward the saucer. If that doesn't work, dip your finger in the milk, then place it in their mouths so they can suck on it. It won't take them long to learn to suck with their faces down, rather than up, and once they get the idea of sucking from the saucer, they will soon begin to lap.

Over the course of the next week or so, the milk can be gradually thickened with pablum or cereal grains to make it more solid. As the puppies adjust to their new food, it can be thickened still more with ground meat and egg yolks or a commercial puppy food. Puppies sometimes show an interest in what their mother is being given to eat. As long as this food is soft and moist, it is perfectly safe for them.

As the puppies take progressively less nourishment from the mother, her food portions should be gradually cut back to what they were before she became pregnant. Reducing the amount of the mother's food also reduces the amount of milk she produces. This will help wean the puppies by forcing them to find their food elsewhere.

By the time they are six to eight weeks old, the puppies should be fully weaned and on a solid diet. To ensure their proper growth, make certain their food is especially high in protein and rich in the necessary vitamins and minerals. Until they are about ten weeks old, feed them three or four times a day. After that, two or three meals a day will suffice.

THE BREEDS OF DOGS

This section provides basic information on the appearance, temperament and special needs of the most popular breeds of dogs in this country. It is intended to give the prospective buyer some general insight into each type of dog as it exists outside the show ring in its more characteristic role as family pet. This emphasis is more in keeping with the purpose of this book than the highly detailed "standards" formulated by experts to describe characteristics found in some hypothetically perfect specimen of a breed.

When you read these descriptions, keep in mind that the members of the same breed are far from identical. There are often substantial variations in size, color, hair length and texture and all the other physical characteristics. Although these variations can be crucially significant when it comes to championship breeding and show competition, they don't necessarily have any real bearing on whether or not a particular dog is suitable as a family pet.

Also keep in mind that there are wide variations in temperament among dogs belonging to the same breed. The personality of an individual dog is shaped by many things, including such circumstantial factors as the kind of home it came from, the kind it goes to and the early handling and training it has received. Very few valid generalizations can be made about temperament except in the broadest statistical sense. In fact, the variability **within** breeds may be even greater than that **between** breeds. Prospective buyers must always evaluate each dog's personality individually. After you have decided what breed you want and are looking at a particular dog, turn to page 19 and follow the procedure given there for assessing that animal's temperament.

HOUNDS

AFGHAN HOUND

APPEARANCE
A medium-sized, deep-chested dog given its distinctive appearance by its long, silky coat. The Afghan has a long, broad head with a topknot of hair and a long muzzle. Its long ears are heavily feathered and carried close to the head. It has powerful hindquarters, large feet and a long tail that curves upward.

COLOR
All colors.

HEIGHT
25 to 29 inches.

WEIGHT
50 to 60 pounds.

CHARACTERISTICS
An ancient breed from the Sinai Peninsula used thousands of years before Christ to hunt leopard and other game. It is not reliable around children, but for adults it is an excellent pet of exceptional speed and grace. Although the Afghan should have plenty of outdoor space to exercise, it is quite suitable as a house pet. Highly adaptable to extremes of temperature.

BASENJI

APPEARANCE
A lightly built, fine-boned dog, readily recognized by the "surprised" expression caused by its wrinkled brow. It has a wedge-shaped head with stiffly erect ears and slanted, dark, alert eyes. The lines of its body are clean and graceful. The tail curls tightly over its back. Its coat is short and silky.

COLOR
Reddish brown. Black with white markings. Tan with white markings.

HEIGHT
16 to 17 inches.

WEIGHT
22 to 24 pounds.

CHARACTERISTICS
An African breed originally used for hunting, the Basenji can be trained for tracking and retrieving but also makes a good, if active, house pet. It keeps itself exceptionally clean and requires only a minimum of grooming. Among its distinctive features are its keen sense of hearing and the fact that it "yodels" or "laughs" loudly rather than barks. It is a gentle and affectionate dog, but because it can be aggressive if provoked, it is probably not the best pet to have around young children. It should be exercised regularly outdoors.

BASSET HOUND

APPEARANCE
A compact, powerfully built dog that stands close to the ground on short but sturdy legs. Its long, powerful head is topped by a pronounced dome. Its long, velvety ears hang down loosely. The Basset's large dark eyes and hanging lips give it its characteristically "sad" appearance. The tail is quite long and carried gaily. Its coat is short and smooth.

COLOR
Usually in various combinations of white, tan and black.

HEIGHT
11 to 15 inches.

WEIGHT
About 50 pounds.

CHARACTERISTICS
Slow-moving but tireless, this hearty French hunting dog has been highly valued for centuries for its keen ability to follow the scent of game. It is a gentle, devoted animal with an excellent disposition, but often rather stubborn and difficult to train. In recent years Bassets have become popular as city dogs, but they are healthiest and most happy in the country.

BEAGLE

APPEARANCE
A compact, powerful hound with long thin ears that hang down the sides of its fairly long head. It has large, soft, dark brown eyes and a calm expression. Its fur is short and dense, shorter on the ears and legs than on the thighs and tail. The tail is moderately long and carried fairly high.

COLOR
Usually in various combinations of black, white and tan.

HEIGHT
13 to 15 inches.

WEIGHT
20 to 30 pounds.

An ancient hunting dog that may go back as far as the Third Century, the Beagle has been popular in England at least since the time of Queen Elizabeth I. It is an agile, fearless, independent animal, known for its distinctive baying sound when in pursuit of game. The Beagle makes a good pet both indoors and out, though is does have a stubborn streak and can be quite difficult to train. It should be exercised regularly outdoors.

BLACK AND TAN COONHOUND

APPEARANCE

A medium-sized dog with a long body, a straight, muscular back and a strong chest and neck. The head is moderately long with dark brown or hazel eyes and long ears that hang in folds. The lips also hang somewhat. Its coat is short but dense.

COLOR

Black with tan markings on the eyes, muzzle, legs, chest and toes.

HEIGHT

23 to 27 inches.

WEIGHT

45 to 60 pounds.

CHARACTERISTICS

The breed originated in the United States and has gained wide popularity as a hunter of raccoon and possum. Most at home in the country, it is a powerful, agile, alert dog with an excellent sense of smell.

BLOODHOUND

APPEARANCE

A large, heavy dog with a characteristically "sad" expression caused by the way the loose skin on its face falls into ridges and folds. It has a long head and muzzle with a distinct peak at the top of its skull. Its eyes are deep set, and the long ears are thin and low hanging. The long tail curves gradually upward. The coat is short and smooth.

COLOR

Usually black and tan or red and tan.

HEIGHT

23 to 27 inches.

WEIGHT

80 to 110 pounds.

CHARACTERISTICS

An ancient hunting dog developed in Belgium and England. The Bloodhound is well known for its keen sense of smell and its ability to track fugitives and lost children. It is a calm, mild mannered and affectionate animal, an excellent pet for children as well as adults. The Bloodhound is most at home in the outdoors, but it can also serve as a good house pet, provided your house is large enough.

DACHSHUND

APPEARANCE

Easily recognized by its short legs and long, low-slung, sausage-shaped body. Its long head is uniformly tapered to the nose, with long ears that reach just to the cheeks. The elongated body is muscular and compact, with relatively short forearms and a tapered tail that continues the line of the spine. The coat may be smooth (shorthaired), wirehaired or long-haired.

COLOR

Red, tan, yellow or brindle. May be dappled or marked with black, gray, white or dark brown.

HEIGHT

9 to 10 inches.

WEIGHT

About 18 to 20 pounds.

CHARACTERISTICS

Originally from Germany, the Dachshund is a courageous, intelligent, lively dog with an acute sense of smell. It has been widely used as a hunter, particularly of game that burrows underground. Although better with adults than with children, it makes an excellent house pet. It is an affectionate, companionable animal, very devoted to its owner, and is a good watchdog. The female has difficulty whelping and may require some assistance.

GREYHOUND

APPEARANCE

A sleek, streamlined, shorthaired dog with a long, narrow head and small ears. The Greyhound is deep-chested and muscular, particularly in the hindquarters, with long legs ending in strong claws. Its tail is long and thin and gradually curves upward.

COLOR

Black, white, red, blue, brindle—almost any color. Often white with black or tan markings.

HEIGHT

27 to 30 inches.

WEIGHT

60 to 70 pounds.

CHARACTERISTICS

Known from the time of ancient Egypt for its stamina and remarkable speed, this fastest of all dogs has been highly prized as a hunter and for its skill in racing and coursing. It is devoted to its owner but tends to be indifferent to others. This, plus its rather high-strung temperament make it less than an ideal pet if there are children in the home. Nor is it, because of its large size and great need for excercise, the best choice for a house dog.

IRISH WOLFHOUND

APPEARANCE

The tallest and perhaps most powerful of all dogs. It has a long, slightly tapering head and muzzle, with strong jaws, small dark eyes and small ears that are carried semi-erect. Its long back gives it a graceful but powerful appearance. The tail is long and thin, curving gracefully upward. The coat is wiry and hard.

COLOR

Gray. Red. Black. Tan. Brindle.

HEIGHT

30 to 34 inches.

WEIGHT

100 to 140 pounds.

CHARACTERISTICS

An ancient breed originally used for hunting wolf, elk and other large game as well as for military and guard purposes. For all its great size and strength, it is among the most gentle of dogs—affectionate, companionable and patient, especially with children. This highly intelligent animal needs the space and freedom of the outdoors, so it is not usually suitable as a house dog.

NORWEGIAN ELKHOUND

APPEARANCE

A powerfully built dog with a compact, square body. The head is broad and moderately long with small erect ears that come to a point. Its eyes are dark brown and express the dog's alertness. The tail curves tightly over the back. Its coat is dense and heavy, particularly on the neck, chest and the back of the thighs and legs.

COLOR

Various shades of gray.

HEIGHT

18 to 21 inches.

WEIGHT

About 50 pounds.

CHARACTERISTICS

An extremely old breed that goes back at least as far as the Vikings, the Norwegian Elkhound was originally used to hunt elk, bear and other large game. Over the years it has also served as a sled dog, farm dog and watchdog. Friendly, docile and highly intelligent, it makes an excellent, if active, family pet. It adapts easily to any climate and has great endurance. It should be exercised regularly outdoors.

WHIPPET

APPEARANCE

A slender, streamlined dog, surprisingly powerful for its slight build and apparent fragility. Resembling a miniature Greyhound, it has a large chest and a long body that arches over its hindquarters. The thin head has a flat skull and a long, fine muzzle. Its small thin ears are folded and carried semi-erect. Its eyes are dark and round. The Whippet's feet are small but strong, and its tail long and thin. The coat is short and dense.

COLOR

Gray, brown with white—almost any color.

HEIGHT

18 to 22 inches.

WEIGHT

18 to 22 pounds.

CHARACTERISTICS

Originally developed in England as a hunter, the Whippet gained great popularity as a racing dog because of its extraordinary speed. Gentle, intelligent, affectionate and obedient, it makes an excellent, if active, house and apartment pet for a family with older children. It should be exercised regularly outdoors, preferably in the country. An exceptionally robust, healthy animal, with clean habits and an easily groomed coat that doesn't require a great deal of care.

TERRIERS

AIREDALE TERRIER

APPEARANCE

The largest of the Terriers, the Airedale is a strong, squarely built dog of medium size with a long, flat skull, long muzzle and rather powerful jaws. Its coat is hard and wiry with a dense undercoat. Its tail is usually cropped to a length of several inches.

COLOR

Medium tan with black markings. Black with medium tan markings.

HEIGHT
22 to 24 inches.

WEIGHT
40 to 50 pounds.

CHARACTERISTICS

Originally bred in England for hunting fox, weasel, otter and other small game. Often used for guard work, to guide the blind and a variety of other purposes. Devoted and companionable, the Airedale makes a good pet, although it can often be quite difficult to dominate. It requires a great deal of outdoor exercise.

BULL TERRIER

APPEARANCE

The distinctive egg-shaped head of this breed makes it easily recognizable. The muzzle is long and particularly powerful. The eyes are small, deep-set and rather closely spaced. It has small, thin ears which are carried erect, and a short, thin tail. The body is short and powerful, with legs that are particularly heavy and strong. Its coat is short and close-fitting. The Bull Terrier is also bred in a miniature size.

COLOR

White. Brindle and white.

HEIGHT
Standard: 16 to 22 inches.
Miniature: under 14 inches.

WEIGHT
Standard: 30 to 55 pounds.
Miniature: under 20 pounds.

CHARACTERISTICS

A cross between the Bulldog and a Terrier, the Bull Terrier was originally bred in England as a fighting dog. Although it can still be a formidable adversary if provoked, it has lost most of its aggressive qualities. It is an affectionate, lively, companionable animal, although perhaps too playful for young children. It requires a great deal of exercise and can be quite difficult to dominate.

CAIRN TERRIER

APPEARANCE

A rugged, powerful little dog with short legs, a long head and a narrow muzzle. The ears are pointed and carried erect. It has a tough, shaggy, weatherproof outer coat and an undercoat that is short, soft and furry. The tail is relatively short and carried nearly upright.

COLOR

Red, sandy, gray, brindle, nearly black—almost any color but white. The coat is often marked with dark points on the muzzle, ears and tail.

HEIGHT
Under 10 inches.

WEIGHT
Under 14 pounds.

CHARACTERISTICS

A Scottish working and hunting dog used to pursue such game as otter and fox, the Cairn Terrier is a fearless, strong, agile animal adaptable to any situation. It is highly intelligent, and its gay, lively disposition makes it an excellent, if active, pet for a family with older children. It should be exercised regularly outdoors. The hard, short coat requires relatively little grooming.

FOX TERRIER

APPEARANCE

A small, muscular dog with a long, fairly thin head, dark, moderately small eyes and small, cropped ears folded forward. It has a short back and strong, straight legs. The tail is docked and upstanding. The coat may be smooth or wirehaired.

COLOR

White marked with black. Tricolor combinations of white, black and tan.

HEIGHT
14 to 16 inches.

WEIGHT
15 to 19 pounds.

CHARACTERISTICS

Once used for hunting fox in England, the Fox Terrier is an active, intelligent dog with considerable spirit and courage. Although somewhat independent in nature, it is easy to train and care for and makes an excellent indoor or outdoor pet for a family with older children. It should be exercised regularly outdoors.

APPEARANCE

The Irish Terrier has a long narrow head and muzzle, small dark eyes, extremely strong jaws and thin, V-shaped ears that hang close to the cheeks. Its back is long and straight, and its legs are powerful. The tail is docked and carried high. The thick, wiry coat is kept closely trimmed.

COLOR

Red. Yellow-red. Golden.

HEIGHT

About 18 inches.

APPEARANCE

A compact, powerful medium-sized dog with a long, narrow head and muzzle and flat cheeks. It has small dark eyes and fairly small V-shaped ears that are carried forward. The back is rather short, and the leg bones are heavy in structure. Its soft, wavy coat is usually kept clipped. The tail is commonly docked to a length of several inches.

COLOR

Various shades of blue-gray. The ears, muzzle and tail are darker than the rest of the body. (Its coat is black at birth and lightens as the dog matures.)

APPEARANCE

A squarely shaped, strongly built dog with a fairly long, narrow, rectangular head. The powerful muzzle is blunt in shape with a thick moustache and beard. Its dark eyes are heavily eyebrowed. Its ears are small and V-shaped and usually cropped. The Schnauzer has a relatively short back and deep chest, and its tail is usually cropped to a length of several inches. Its coat is hard, wiry and dense and commonly trimmed short. Schnauzers are bred in three sizes: Miniature, Standard and Giant.

COLOR

Black. Salt and pepper.

HEIGHT

Miniature: 11 to 14 inches.
Standard: 17 to 20 inches.
Giant: 21 to 26 inches.

IRISH TERRIER

WEIGHT

25 to 27 pounds.

CHARACTERISTICS

Originally bred in Ireland as a water retriever and hunter of large and small game, the Irish Terrier served in World War I as a messenger and guard dog. It is now used mostly as a pet. Quiet, whimsical and affectionate, it is good with people and particularly devoted to its owner. However, it does have an obdurate, strong-willed streak. It should be exercised regularly outdoors.

KERRY BLUE TERRIER

HEIGHT

18 to 19 inches.

WEIGHT

30 to 40 pounds.

CHARACTERISTICS

A versatile dog from Ireland originally used for herding sheep and cattle, hunting small game and water retrieving. This intelligent, alert, high-spirited animal makes an excellent watchdog and pet for a family with older children. It should be exercised regularly outdoors. The Kerry Blue is unusually long-lived.

SCHNAUZER

WEIGHT

Miniature: about 15 pounds.
Standard: about 35 pounds.
Giant: about 75 pounds.

CHARACTERISTICS

The Schnauzer was originally bred in Germany, where it served as a watch and guard dog, herded cattle and hunted rats on farms. It is a hearty, courageous, intelligent, loyal animal, particularly affectionate toward its master. Good-natured and willing to please, it can be trained easily if the process begins early enough to overcome the strong-willed, independent aspects of its personality. It should be exercised regularly outdoors. Some dog experts caution that the Schnauzer is not usually suitable for homes with young children. The miniature version is popular as a family pet and watchdog.

SCOTTISH TERRIER ("SCOTTIE")

APPEARANCE
A small, compact, solidly built dog with a short back, broad hindquarters and rather short legs. Its head is very long, with a distinctive blunt, heavily whiskered muzzle and small, deep-set, almond-shaped dark brown eyes. The ears are small and erect. The tail is naturally short. Its soft undercoat is topped by a wiry-textured outer coat, which should be kept clipped.

COLOR
Black. Gray. Brindle. Wheaten.

HEIGHT
10 to 11 inches.

WEIGHT
17 to 21 pounds.

CHARACTERISTICS
An ancient breed originally developed in Scotland, where it was used as a hunter. It has an independent, spunky nature and tends to select a favorite person as master. The Scottie is a good watchdog and an excellent, if active, pet for apartment dwellers. It should be exercised regularly outdoors. Some may be unreliable around children.

WELSH TERRIER

APPEARANCE
A small dog with a short, muscular back and strong hindquarters. It has a wide head, a fairly long and heavily whiskered muzzle and powerful jaws. Its eyes are small and dark, and its V-shaped ears are folded over and carried close to the cheeks. The hard, wiry coat should be kept trimmed. The tail is usually docked to several inches.

COLOR
Black and tan. Grizzle and tan.

HEIGHT
14 to 15 inches.

WEIGHT
18 to 21 pounds.

CHARACTERISTICS
Developed as a hunter of badger, fox and otter, this alert and vigorous dog responds well to training if it is begun early. Although it requires considerable exercise outdoors, its affectionate, obedient nature and small size make it an ideal, if active, house pet. It plays particularly well with children and will serve as an excellent watchdog.

WEST HIGHLAND WHITE TERRIER

APPEARANCE
Resembling the Scottish Terrier in all but color, the West Highland White Terrier is a small but strong dog with a medium-long muzzle, wide-set dark eyes and small ears that are carried erect. Its muscular hindquarters are offset by a short, upright tail. It has medium long, straight fur.

COLOR
White.

HEIGHT
10 to 11 inches.

WEIGHT
14 to 19 pounds.

CHARACTERISTICS
Bred several centuries ago in Scotland to hunt fox. It is a cheerful, generally friendly dog, if somewhat independent in nature, and makes a good pet and alert watchdog for a family with older children. It should be exercised regularly outdoors.

WORKING DOGS

ALASKAN MALAMUTE

APPEARANCE

A large, exceptionally strong dog with a medium-sized head tapering to a powerful muzzle. The eyes are slanted and the ears slightly rounded and erect. It has a long tail, which is carried over the back. The coat is medium long, with a dense, oily undercoat and a thick, hard outer coat.

COLOR

Wolf gray to black, with white or dark markings. Usually has cap and mask markings on its face.

HEIGHT

22 to 25 inches.

WEIGHT

50 to 90 pounds.

CHARACTERISTICS

An Alaskan breed of unusual endurance and strength originally used as a sled and pack dog. Despite its Arctic heritage, it adapts well to all climates. Calm, affectionate and especially attached to its master, it makes an excellent pet. Be aware, though, that it is often aggressive with other dogs and may be unreliable around young children. It requires a great deal of outdoor exercise. The Malamute is a clean, odorless animal and doesn't bark. It does have something of an independent streak, so it is best to train it as early as possible.

BOXER

APPEARANCE

A medium-sized, muscular dog with a smooth coat. The head is powerfully built, with the lower jaw protruding past the upper jaw. The general shape of the head and body is squarish, with a fairly wide chest and strong hindquarters. The ears and tail are usually cropped.

COLOR

Various shades of fawn, from light tan to mahogany. Brindle, with a dark muzzle and black stripes on a fawn background. May have white markings.

HEIGHT

21 to 25 inches.

WEIGHT

60 to 80 pounds.

CHARACTERISTICS

Developed in Germany at the end of the Nineteenth Century for guard, military and police work, the Boxer is a hardy, alert, strong, active animal. It has an even-tempered, docile, companionable disposition, which makes it an excellent family pet. It is particularly good with children—gentle, tolerant and playful. The Boxer's acute hearing and sense of attachment to its household also make it a superb watchdog. It should be exercised regularly outdoors.

BULL MASTIFF

APPEARANCE

A large dog with a compact, powerful body. The head is large and square with a wrinkled brow, short muzzle and slightly undershot jaw. The dark eyes are small and set wide apart. The small ears are V-shaped and carried close to the head. It has a rather short back and powerful shoulders and hindquarters. The coat is short and dense. The tail is long and tapering.

COLOR

Red. Fawn. Brindle. With dark ears and a black muzzle and face mask.

HEIGHT

24 to 27 inches.

WEIGHT

100 to 130 pounds.

CHARACTERISTICS

A cross between the Bulldog and Mastiff, the Bull Mastiff was bred in England in the Nineteenth Century for the specific purpose of protecting estate properties from poachers. Its intelligence, courage and exceptional night vision make it an excellent guard dog. It is a faithful, dependable pet, usually good with children. It requires a great deal of outdoor exercise.

COLLIE

APPEARANCE

A strong, graceful dog of medium size with a long, narrow muzzle and head. Its eyes are almond-shaped. Its small ears droop slightly at the tips. The tail is carried low but curves up slightly at the end. It is bred in two varieties: the shorthaired Smooth Collie and the more popular long-haired Rough version, with its long, thick, rather roughly textured coat.

COLOR

Sable and white. White. Blue merle. Tricolored.

HEIGHT

22 to 26 inches.

WEIGHT

50 to 75 pounds.

CHARACTERISTICS

Originally used in Scotland to herd sheep. The Collie's alert, reliable, protective nature makes it a fine watchdog. Although it does have a somewhat independent nature, it is easily trained and can be an excellent pet for a family with children. It requires a great deal of outdoor exercise. The long-haired Rough Collie is an especially beautiful animal, but its coat requires considerable grooming to look its best.

DOBERMAN PINSCHER

APPEARANCE

A beautifully streamlined, powerful dog of medium size. It has a long, flat head and a long muzzle with tight lips and extremely powerful jaws. The eyes are dark and oval. The ears are set high on the head and docked. The tail is also closely docked. Its smooth, sleek coat hugs its powerful body.

COLOR

Black. Brown. Red. Blue. Fawn. With tan markings.

HEIGHT

24 to 28 inches.

WEIGHT

60 to 75 pounds.

CHARACTERISTICS

Developed in Germany to herd sheep and cattle, this intelligent, courageous animal is widely used for police, military and guard work. A good watchdog and hunter, it usually also makes a devoted pet. The Doberman is easy to train but does require firm handling and strong discipline. It tends to be loyal to its owners and protective of their property but often favors one family member over the others. It requires a great deal of outdoor exercise.

GERMAN SHEPHERD

APPEARANCE

A medium-sized dog with a distinctive wolflike appearance. Its body is lean and muscular, with a deep chest and strong, well-angulated legs. The strong, handsome head has a long, wedge-shaped muzzle and powerful jaws. The large eyes are dark and almond-shaped. The broad ears taper to a point near the tips. The long tail is carried in a slight upward curve. The dog has a fairly long, straight, close topcoat that covers a soft undercoat.

COLOR

Black with tan markings. Gray and black.

HEIGHT

22 to 26 inches.

WEIGHT

60 to 85 pounds.

CHARACTERISTICS

One of the world's most popular breeds, originally developed in Germany for hunting, sheepherding and guard work. It is a hardy, graceful, intelligent animal that can make an excellent family pet if it is trained properly at an early age and given the outdoor space it requires. Good with children, this versatile animal also makes a fine guard dog and guide for the blind.

GREAT DANE

APPEARANCE

A true giant of a dog with a powerful, muscular well-formed body and long, arched neck. The massive head has a long, narrow muzzle and a wide-bridged nose. The medium-sized eyes are round, dark and deep set. The small, high-set ears are usually cropped. It has a medium long tail that hangs straight or curves slightly. Its coat is very short and smooth.

COLOR

Gold. Blue. Black. White and black. Gold and white.

HEIGHT

30 inches or more.

WEIGHT

120 to 150 pounds.

CHARACTERISTICS

Originally bred in Germany, not Denmark, where it was used to hunt boar. Despite its huge size and formidable appearance, it is a generally friendly and playful animal. It is affectionate with its family, particularly the youngsters, although it may inadvertently knock down small children who get in its way. A good watchdog, the Great Dane tends to be rather cool toward strangers and may become aggressive if it thinks itself threatened. It requires a great deal of outdoor space for exercise.

MASTIFF

APPEARANCE

A massively large and powerful dog with a large head and blunt, strong muzzle. The forehead is slightly wrinkled. The small, dark eyes are set well apart. Its ears are V-shaped and droop close to its head. It has a strong, powerful body, with muscular hind legs and a long tail that hangs straight down. Its coat is short, close and shiny.

COLOR

Fawn. Apricot. Silver-brindle. Fawn-brindle. The ears, nose and muzzle are black.

HEIGHT
27 inches or more.

WEIGHT
165 to 185 pounds.

CHARACTERISTICS

An ancient breed probably originating in Asia, the Mastiff was used in England for dogfighting, bullbaiting, hunting large game, and guard and military work. For all its huge size, it is a calm, gentle, affectionate animal, a good pet for families that have the outdoor space it requires. Intelligent and protective, it also serves as a good watchdog.

OLD ENGLISH SHEEPDOG

APPEARANCE

A medium-sized fairly large dog with a long, shaggy coat of straight hair that covers its dark eyes. The head is rather square, with small ears that are carried flat. Its body is short and compact, with round, muscular hindquarters and a tail that is usually docked. The dog makes a characteristic ambling movement when it walks or runs.

COLOR

Gray. Blue. Grizzle. Often marked with white.

HEIGHT
21 to 25 inches.

WEIGHT
75 to 90 pounds.

CHARACTERISTICS

Developed at least as early as the Eighteenth Century, this intelligent animal was once used to guard flocks and herd sheep and cattle. Even-tempered and affectionate, it makes an excellent house pet as long as it has enough space to exercise outdoors. Its thick coat provides protection against severe cold but requires considerable grooming. Shedding may be a problem in warm weather.

PEMBROKE WELSH CORGI

APPEARANCE

A strong, long dog with short legs that place it close to the ground. The head is long and wedge-shaped with dark eyes and erect ears. The tail is naturally short or docked to a short length. Its thick coat is moderately long.

COLOR

Red. Black and tan. Tan. May have white markings.

HEIGHT
10 to 12 inches.

WEIGHT
18 to 25 pounds.

CHARACTERISTICS

A very old breed brought to Great Britain from Flanders in the early years of the Twelfth Century. Originally used to herd cattle, it is an alert, intelligent, companionable animal that makes a good, if active, pet and guard dog. It should be exercised regularly outdoors.

SAINT BERNARD

APPEARANCE

An immensely large and heavy dog with muscular legs and a broad, powerful head and back. The small, dark, deep-set eyes have a characteristically warm, gentle expression. The ears are set high on the head and hang close to the cheeks. The tail is long and heavy and usually hangs down. Some Saint Bernards have dense, short, smooth coats; others have medium-length coats of slightly curling hair.

COLOR

Usually brown or red with white markings.

HEIGHT
25 to 29 inches or more.

WEIGHT
165 to 175 pounds.

CHARACTERISTICS

Legendary for its skill at rescuing lost travelers in the Swiss Alps, this intelligent, powerful dog makes a good family pet and guard. Because it grows quickly, it must be trained at the earliest possible age. And it does have an appetite to match its prodigious size. It requires a great deal of outdoor exercise.

SAMOYED

APPEARANCE

A squarely built, powerful dog distinguished by the beauty of its heavy, weather-resistant coat, which stands out from its body. The head is broad and wedge-shaped. The eyes are almond-shaped, slanted and well-separated. The ears are rounded at the tips and stand erect. Its heavily furred tail is carried curled over the back.

COLOR

White. Biscuit and white. Cream.

HEIGHT

19 to 24 inches.

WEIGHT

35 to 60 pounds.

CHARACTERISTICS

An ancient Siberian breed of great strength and endurance, the Samoyed was used to herd cattle and pull sleds. It is a particularly good guard dog and an affectionate, gentle and loyal pet. Early training can help overcome its independent nature. It requires a great deal of outdoor exercise.

SHETLAND SHEEPDOG ("SHELTIE")

APPEARANCE

Looking like a scaled-down version of the Collie, the Shetland Sheepdog is a small, graceful animal with a long, narrow muzzle and head. It has almond-shaped eyes and small ears that droop slightly at the tips. The outer coat is long, thick and straight; the undercoat, thick and close. The tail is carried low but curves slightly upward at the end.

COLOR

Sable. Black. Blue merle. With white or tan markings.

HEIGHT

14 to 16 inches.

WEIGHT

About 16 pounds.

CHARACTERISTICS

An agile, swift, intelligent working dog originally used in Scotland to herd sheep. The Sheltie combines the good looks and easy temperament of the Collie with a smaller size that appeals to apartment dwellers and others with limited space. It is obedient, companionable and easy to train, but requires affection and frequent grooming. It should be exercised regularly outdoors.

SIBERIAN HUSKY

APPEARANCE

A powerful medium-sized dog with heavily muscled shoulders and hindquarters. The head is wedge-shaped, with the ears well-separated and erect. The eyes are commonly brown but are sometimes blue or mixed brown and blue. The Husky's dense undercoat is covered by a thick, soft, moderately long outer coat. Its well-furred tail may curl over the back or droop down.

COLOR

All colors and markings. Most commonly gray or light brown marked with white.

HEIGHT

20 to 24 inches.

WEIGHT

35 to 60 pounds.

CHARACTERISTICS

The Husky was developed in Siberia as a sled dog, then imported to Alaska in the early Twentieth Century, where it was used for sled racing and rescue work. For all its great strength and endurance, it is a gentle, friendly, affectionate pet, particularly good with children and notably unaggressive with other dogs. It needs the open spaces to run and dig, and its thick coat makes it well-suited to outdoor living in even the coldest climate. It also adapts well to more moderate temperatures, but it does shed heavily. The Husky is an intelligent, versatile animal with a strong tendency to independence.

SPORTING DOGS

AMERICAN COCKER SPANIEL

APPEARANCE
An attractive dog with a short, compact body that is covered with a wavy, medium-long profuse coat. The abdomen, chest, legs and ears are heavily feathered. The broad, round head has a rather short muzzle, long ears and dark, gentle eyes. It has a short back and well-rounded hindquarters with a docked tail.

COLOR
Black. Light brown. Cream. Black and brown. Patches of colors.

HEIGHT
14 to 15 inches.

WEIGHT
22 to 28 pounds.

CHARACTERISTICS
The smallest of the sporting dogs, originally developed from the larger English Cocker Spaniel. Once used mainly for hunting birds, this sprightly, sturdy animal has become one of the most popular American house dogs. It is a gentle, affectionate, loyal pet. It requires considerable grooming to look its best.

AMERICAN WATER SPANIEL

APPEARANCE
A medium-sized, sturdily built dog with a moderately long head and square muzzle. Its long, wide ears are covered with curls. Its eyes are widely separated and either dark or hazel in color. The coat is thick and closely curled. The medium-long tail is heavily feathered.

COLOR
Liver. Dark chocolate.

HEIGHT
15 to 18 inches.

WEIGHT
25 to 45 pounds.

CHARACTERISTICS
One of the few dogs originally bred in the United States. It is an intelligent, friendly animal of great strength and endurance, popular with sportsmen for its skill at hunting field and waterfowl. Although the Water Spaniel tends to favor its master, it makes a good pet for a family with older children. It requires a great deal of outdoor exercise.

BRITTANY SPANIEL

APPEARANCE
A squarely shaped, lightweight dog with considerable strength for its fairly small size. The medium-long head has a wedge-shaped muzzle, deep-set gray eyes and ears that hang down close to the cheeks. Its chest is full and its back fairly short. The tail is generally docked to four inches or less. The coat is either flat or wavy, with some feathering on the forelegs, chest and ears.

COLOR
White with reddish-brown or orange. Liver and white.

HEIGHT
17 to 20 inches.

WEIGHT
30 to 45 pounds.

CHARACTERISTICS
Originally bred in France as a hunting dog, it is the only Spaniel that points as well as retrieves. Tireless, fast, with an acute sense of smell, it has become one of the most popular hunting dogs in the United States. Because of its small size and gentle, friendly, lively disposition, it also enjoys a reputation as a good family pet.

CHESAPEAKE BAY RETRIEVER

APPEARANCE
A fairly large, particularly hardy dog with a broad, rounded head, short muzzle and small ears that hang loosely to the side of the head. It has distinctive yellow or light-colored eyes. Its hindquarters are slightly higher than its front. The medium length coat is very dense, with an oily, woolly undercoat and harsh outer coat. The tail is long and thick.

COLOR
Dark brown to light tan.

HEIGHT
21 to 26 inches.

WEIGHT
55 to 75 pounds.

CHARACTERISTICS
A native American breed adept at retrieving ducks and other game birds in icy water and snow. Its coat sheds water readily, and its webbed feet make it a powerful swimmer. This courageous, alert, intelligent animal makes an excellent family pet. It requires a great deal of outdoor exercise.

ENGLISH SETTER

APPEARANCE

A graceful, particularly beautiful dog with a long, silky, flat coat that feathers the ears, legs and tail. It has a long, lean, oval-shaped head, moderately long, rounded ears and a long, square muzzle with large nostrils. The medium-sized eyes are dark brown in color. The tail is set low.

COLOR

Black, white and tan. Black and white. Lemon and white. Orange and white.

HEIGHT

22 to 26 inches.

WEIGHT

55 to 65 pounds.

CHARACTERISTICS

Developed in England about four centuries ago. Originally used as a hunter, especially of birds, it also makes an excellent house pet. It is even-tempered, devoted and quiet, good with children and gentle with other dogs. Adaptable and easily trained, this companionable animal adjusts readily to a large or small environment. It is alert but not vicious, and also serves as a fine watchdog. It requires a great deal of outdoor exercise.

ENGLISH SPRINGER SPANIEL

APPEARANCE

A medium-sized, compact dog with a fairly short, strong body. The head is medium in length and rather broad, with a square muzzle, flat cheeks and deep lips. It has dark hazel eyes and long, fairly wide ears that are rounded at the ends and heavily feathered. Its tail, which is also feathered, is set low, carried level and docked short. The weather-resistant coat is close and straight.

COLOR

Liver and white. Black and white. Tricolored.

HEIGHT

18 to 20 inches.

WEIGHT

45 to 55 pounds.

CHARACTERISTICS

The oldest of the Spaniels, the English Springer is the progenitor of almost all the other Spaniel breeds. It is an intelligent, fast-moving animal, an excellent bird hunting dog with good resistance to cold weather. Its animated, happy disposition makes it an affectionate, loyal family pet, though it does have something of an independent streak and should be trained at the earliest possible time. It requires a great deal of outdoor exercise.

GERMAN POINTER

APPEARANCE

A heavy, powerful dog of medium size, modeled on rectangular lines. It has a clean-cut, domed head with a powerful muzzle. The long nose bows slightly upward in the center. Its eyes are either light or dark brown. Its long ears hang close to the cheeks, reaching the corners of the mouth. The tail is docked to about half an inch. The German Pointer is bred with two kinds of coats: The Shorthaired version has a close, tight coarse coat. The Wirehaired Pointer, which is about an inch taller, has a coarse, water-resistant outer coat and a soft, dense undercoat.

COLOR

Liver. Liver and white. White with liver.

HEIGHT

21 to 25 inches.

WEIGHT

45 to 70 pounds.

CHARACTERISTICS

Developed in Germany in the late Nineteenth Century as an all-around hunting dog, it is both a pointer and a retriever. Although it has a tendency to wander, it makes a good family pet, easily trained and particularly affectionate toward its master. It is best off in the country rather than the city.

GOLDEN RETRIEVER

APPEARANCE

A medium-sized dog with a fairly short, strong body, broad head and powerful muzzle. Its eyes are dark, and its medium long ears are wide set and carried close to the head. The long tail is heavily feathered. The dense, short, shiny coat is water-repellent and can be either flat or wavy.

COLOR

Golden to light cream.

HEIGHT

20 to 24 inches.

WEIGHT

55 to 70 pounds.

CHARACTERISTICS

This lively, intelligent dog was developed slightly more than a century ago in Scotland, where it was used for hunting. A highly versatile animal, it is now also popular as a guide for the blind and a family pet. Friendly and kind, it is especially gentle with children. It requires a great deal of outdoor exercise.

IRISH SETTER

APPEARANCE

A strong, graceful dog of medium size, with medium-long, straight, silky fur. Its head and muzzle are long and lean, its brow well-defined. The eyes are dark hazel or dark brown. The moderately long ears hang close to the head. Its long tail is carried fairly low and curves slightly upward.

COLOR

Mahogany. Deep chestnut red.

HEIGHT

23 to 27 inches.

WEIGHT

50 to 70 pounds.

CHARACTERISTICS

Developed in Ireland almost two hundred years ago, it is currently one of the most popular dogs in the United States. Its speed, endurance and acute sense of smell make it an excellent bird hunter. Lively and intelligent, it can also be rather temperamental and stubborn, so it needs to be skillfully trained. Although it may be too active for many families, it is often chosen as a family pet. It requires a great deal of open space for exercise.

LABRADOR RETRIEVER

APPEARANCE

A strong, muscular, compact dog with a well-rounded body and straight back. The wide, clean-cut head has a long, powerful muzzle, brown or black eyes and medium-long ears carried alongside the head. The thick tail is long and tapering. The coat is short and thick.

COLOR

Black. Chocolate. Yellow.

HEIGHT

21 to 24 inches.

WEIGHT

55 to 75 pounds.

CHARACTERISTICS

Brought to England from Newfoundland in the early years of this century, this intelligent, highly trainable dog has become the most popular of retrievers. Valued for its skill at retrieving waterfowl, it is also a good family pet, especially gentle with children. This versatile dog is also used for police and guard work and as a guide for the blind. It requires a great deal of outdoor exercise.

VIZSLA

APPEARANCE

A lightly built but powerful dog of medium size, with a short back and deep chest. The clean-cut head has a broad nose and long ears that hang close to the head. Its tail is docked to slightly more than half its normal length. The coat is short, smooth and dense and lies close to the body.

COLOR

Golden rust. Light red.

HEIGHT

21 to 24 inches.

WEIGHT

40 to 60 pounds.

CHARACTERISTICS

An ancient hunting breed traced back as early as the Tenth Century. This Hungarian hunting dog is both a retriever and pointer, equally adept at hunting hare, upland game and waterfowl. It adapts very well to any climate and is gentle, affectionate and easy to train. The Vizsla makes a lively, companionable family pet. It should be exercised regularly outdoors.

WEIMARANER

APPEARANCE

A medium-sized, strongly built dog with a fairly short back, muscular chest and well-developed hindquarters. The lean head has a long muzzle, generous lips and distinctive blue-gray or amber eyes. Its long, wide ears hang close to its cheeks. The coat may be short and smooth, wirehaired or moderately long. The tail is docked.

COLOR
Various shades of gray.

HEIGHT
23 to 27 inches.

WEIGHT
55 to 85 pounds.

CHARACTERISTICS
This brave, fast-running dog originated in Germany, where it was used to hunt large game. An intelligent, affectionate animal that makes a good pet, it does require substantial space outdoors and has a somewhat uncertain reputation with children.

NON-SPORTING DOGS

BOSTON TERRIER

APPEARANCE
A cross between the Bulldog and Bull Terrier. It has a large, flat head with a flat nose and somewhat undershot lower jaw, and a short, compact, square body. Its ears are small and erect, its eyes large and round. The silky coat is short, close and smooth. The short tail is carried either straight or tightly curled.

COLOR
Brindle with white. Black with white.

HEIGHT
14 to 16 inches.

WEIGHT
15 to 25 pounds.

CHARACTERISTICS
Originally bred in Boston for pit fighting, this intelligent, energetic dog has lost most of its aggressive qualities. Although it may not be good around young children or in noisy, active environments, it makes a lively, companionable house pet. Because of the large head size, puppies usually have to be delivered by Caesarean surgery. It should be exercised regularly outdoors.

BULLDOG

APPEARANCE
A low-slung, powerful dog with a massive head, short nose and undershot lower jaw. Its forehead is broad and wrinkled, and its rather small ears fold over backward. The dark eyes are round and moderately large. The Bulldog has extremely powerful shoulders and chest, and short, strong legs. Its coat is smooth and short. Its short tail is carried either straight or tightly curled.

COLOR
White. Brown. Fawn. Patches of colors. Brindle. Almost any color but black.

HEIGHT
14 to 16 inches.

WEIGHT
40 to 50 pounds.

CHARACTERISTICS
A courageous, tenacious dog used in England as early as the Thirteenth Century to bait bulls for sport. With the banning of bullbaiting in the Nineteenth Century, its original ferocity was bred out of it. Despite its forbidding appearance, it is now one of the most affectionate, good-natured dogs, splendid with children and a devoted, fun-loving family pet. It should be exercised regularly outdoors. The short coat requires a minimum of grooming. The female tends to have whelping difficulties.

CHOW CHOW

APPEARANCE
A compact, medium-sized dog given its characteristic lionlike appearance by the heavy ruff that surrounds its neck. Its flat, broad head has a broad muzzle, small, dark, almond-shaped eyes and small, slightly rounded ears that are carried erect. Its unusually straight back legs give it its distinctive gait. The coat has a profuse, dense, straight outer coat and a woolly undercoat. The tail is heavily feathered and carried curved over the back. The Chow Chow is the only dog with a blue-black tongue.

COLOR
Red. Black. Rust. Blue. Tan. Cream.

HEIGHT
18 to 20 inches.

WEIGHT
50 to 60 pounds.

CHARACTERISTICS
An ancient breed known in China from before the time of Christ. For all its powerful, dignified bearing, it is an affectionate, devoted pet for families with older children. Rather standoffish with strangers, it makes an excellent guard dog as well as a good hunter. It should be exercised regularly outdoors.

DALMATION

APPEARANCE
Easily recognized by the distinctive markings on its short, thick, glossy coat, the Dalmation is a strong, active, muscular dog of medium size, with a long muzzle and broad skull. Its round, bright, wide-set eyes are either dark or amber and outlined with either black or brown. It carries its wide ears close to the sides of its head. The medium-length tail curves slightly upward.

COLOR
White with well-defined black or liver spots.

HEIGHT
19 to 23 inches.

WEIGHT
50 to 55 pounds.

CHARACTERISTICS
Originating in what is now part of Yugoslavia, the Dal- mation was used first for hunting, then later to accompany and protect horse-drawn carriages. Best known in the United States as a firehouse dog, this intelligent, versatile animal makes a loyal, protective pet and guard for families with older children. It does require substantial exercise outdoors and should be trained as early as possible. The short coat requires relatively little grooming.

LHASA APSO

APPEARANCE
This small, distinctive-looking dog has a relatively long body with short, muscular legs and catlike feet. It is covered from head to toe with a thick, long heavy coat which beards its face and forms a mane around its neck. Its dark eyes are also covered by fur. Its heavily feathered tail is carried over the back.

COLOR
Golden. Sandy. Honey. Dark gray. Grizzle. Brown. Black. White.

HEIGHT
10 to 14 inches.

WEIGHT
15 to 16 pounds.

CHARACTERISTICS
This "Lion Dog" of Tibet was originally bred by Tibetan monks and used inside the house to warn against intruders. Brought to the West less than half a century ago, its beauty, intelligence and small size have also made it popular here as a house pet. Assertive and independent, it does tend to be rather difficult to train and may not be good with young children. Despite its small stature, it is a rugged animal, able to adapt to heavy snow and extreme cold. It should be exercised regularly outdoors.

POODLE

APPEARANCE
A distinctive, elegant-looking animal with a dense, harsh, woolly coat. It has a long, narrow head with flat cheekbones, wide-set oval or almond-shaped eyes and long, wide ears that hang down close to the face. The shoulders, hindquarters and short, strong back are smoothly muscular. The paws are small and oval-shaped. Its straight tail is docked to about half its natural length. The Poodle is bred in three distinct sizes: Standard, Miniature and Toy.

COLOR
Black. Blue. Gray. Brown. White. Cream. Apricot.

HEIGHT
Standard: Over 15 inches.
Miniature: Between 10 and 15 inches.
Toy: Under 10 inches.

WEIGHT
Standard: 45 to 55 pounds.
Miniature: About 16 pounds.
Toy: About 7 pounds.

CHARACTERISTICS
An ancient breed thousands of years old, this intelligent, active, alert animal is one of the most popular dogs in the United States. Good-natured, affectionate and easily trained, it has served as a hunter and circus performer as well as a family pet. The Standard Poodle is good with children; the Miniature and the Toy may be too excitable. The Poodle's coat does not moult, but it does require considerable care, including regular clipping.

SHIH TZU

APPEARANCE
Similar in look to the Lhasa Apso, this small dog has a relatively long body and short, muscular legs. Its thick, long, heavy coat covers its entire body, bearding its short face and forming a lionlike mane on its neck. Hair also covers its dark eyes. The tail is heavily feathered and carried over the back.

HEIGHT
9 to 11 inches.

WEIGHT
12 to 15 pounds.

CHARACTERISTICS
An ancient Tibetan breed that served as the royal dog of China, it was first brought to the United States after World War II. It is excellent in snow and extreme cold, and makes a happy, friendly, if active and somewhat independent, house pet.

COLOR
Almost any color. Often marked with white on the forehead and tip of the tail.

TOY DOGS

CHIHUAHUA

APPEARANCE
An extremely small dog with a finely boned, compact body. The head, which is well-rounded on top, has a short, pointed muzzle, large flaring ears and prominent shiny eyes. The medium-long tail curves upward. The Chihuahua is bred with two different coats: The Long-coated variety is soft and either flat or slightly wavy. The more popular Smooth-coated version is close and glossy.

COLOR
Any color. May be either solid or marked.

HEIGHT
About 5 inches.

WEIGHT
1 to 6 pounds.

CHARACTERISTICS
This tiniest of all dogs originated in Mexico among the Toltecs and Aztecs. It is an intelligent, alert and friendly animal that responds well to training. Clean and easy to care for, it makes a good, if active, house pet as well as a loyal, courageous watchdog.

MALTESE

APPEARANCE
A small, elegant dog with short legs, long head, straight muzzle and dark, close-set eyes. The long, feathered ears hang down close to the head. Its profuse, long silky coat is parted straight down the spine.

COLOR
Pure white.

HEIGHT
5 to 7 inches.

WEIGHT
2 to 7 pounds.

CHARACTERISTICS
An ancient lapdog that probably originated on the island of Malta. It is a loyal, graceful, intelligent animal that makes a lively, devoted companion. Not nearly as fragile as its appearance suggests, it can be quite aggressive. The Maltese requires a good bit of grooming and careful feeding.

PEKINESE

APPEARANCE
A sturdy, strong little dog with a heavy, full chest and large bones for its size. The head is broad and massive, with a very short muzzle that places its large black nose almost squarely between its large, dark eyes. The ears are heavily feathered and carried close to the head. It has a profuse mane and a long, straight coat with a thick undercoat.

COLOR
Various solid colors. White marked with various colors. Often has a black face mask.

HEIGHT
6 to 10 inches.

WEIGHT
7 to 10 pounds.

CHARACTERISTICS
Originally bred in China, where it was considered sacred and could be owned only by emperors, the Pekinese was introduced into the West following the sack of Peking in 1860. A courageous little animal with great stamina, it makes a loyal and companionable pet. There is an independent, sometimes stubborn side to its nature, so it is not generally recommended for families with children.

POMERANIAN

APPEARANCE
A small, compact dog with a long, coarse, straight outer coat and a thick, soft undercoat. The head is thin and fox-like, with a short muzzle and thick mane of hair around the neck. It has dark eyes and small, erect ears. The plumed tail is carried over the back.

COLOR
Orange. Red. Black. Cream. Brown.

HEIGHT
5 to 7 inches.

WEIGHT
3 to 7 pounds.

CHARACTERISTICS
Originating in Germany, the Pomeranian was bred down from a much larger dog that weighed about 30 pounds. It is a robust little animal that does particularly well in cold weather and snow, and often lives to a ripe old age. Spirited, intelligent and alert, it benefits from early training and gentle handling. It is not generally regarded as good around young children.

PUG

APPEARANCE

A distinctive-looking dog with a massive head, a short, broad square muzzle and a deeply wrinkled brow. The prominent large dark eyes have a characteristic "worried" look. The small ears hang down close to the head. Its body is short, square and compact, and is covered by a soft, glossy, short coat. The short tail curls tightly over the hip.

COLOR

Black. Apricot fawn. Silver. With a black face mask and black marking down the spine.

HEIGHT

10 to 12 inches.

WEIGHT

14 to 18 pounds.

CHARACTERISTICS

First bred in China, this alert, companionable dog is now highly valued in the West as a house pet. Devoted and intelligent, it does have a decided stubborn streak. Because of its short, squat face, stress often produces labored breathing. It does very poorly in hot weather. The coat doesn't shed, so is quite easy to care for.

YORKSHIRE TERRIER ("YORKIE")

APPEARANCE

An extremely small dog with beautiful, long, straight, silky hair that parts straight down the back and touches the ground. It has a compact body and a small, flat head with dark eyes and pointed ears that are carried erect or semi-erect.

COLOR

Blue with tan or blond.

HEIGHT

7 to 8 inches.

WEIGHT

5 to 8 pounds.

CHARACTERISTICS

Originally developed from much larger Terriers that served as hunting dogs, the Yorkie evolved into one of the smallest of breeds. Intelligent, high-spirited and friendly, it has become a highly popular house and lapdog.

HOUNDS

BLOODHOUND

GREYHOUND

BASENJI

BLACK AND TAN COONHOUND

BEAGLE

AFGHAN HOUND

BASSET HOUND

DACHSHUND

IRISH WOLFHOUND

NORWEGIAN ELKHOUND

WHIPPET

TERRIERS

AIREDALE TERRIER

BULL TERRIER

CAIRN TERRIER

FOX TERRIER

IRISH TERRIER

KERRY BLUE TERRIER

SCHNAUZER

SCOTTISH TERRIER ("SCOTTIE")

WELSH TERRIER

WEST HIGHLAND WHITE TERRIER

WORKING DOGS

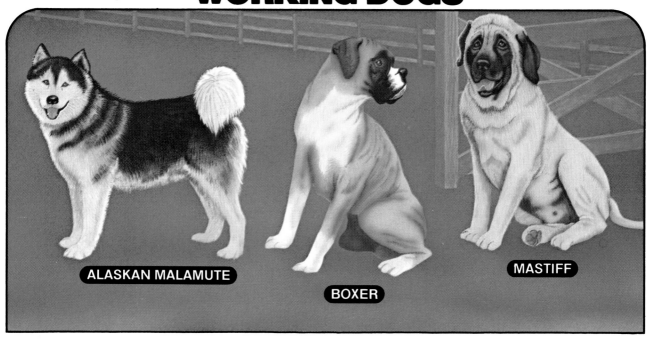

ALASKAN MALAMUTE

BOXER

MASTIFF

DOBERMAN PINSCHER

BULL MASTIFF

COLLIE

OLD ENGLISH SHEEPDOG

GERMAN SHEPHERD

SAINT BERNARD

GREAT DANE

PEMBROKE WELSH CORGI

SAMOYED

SHETLAND SHEEPDOG ("SHELTIE")

SIBERIAN HUSKY

SPORTING DOGS

AMERICAN WATER SPANIEL

BRITTANY SPANIEL

CHESAPEAKE BAY RETRIEVER

AMERICAN COCKER SPANIEL

GOLDEN RETRIEVER

GERMAN POINTER

ENGLISH SPRINGER SPANIEL

ENGLISH SETTER

VIZSLA

IRISH SETTER

LABRADOR RETRIEVER

WEIMARANER

NON-SPORTING DOGS

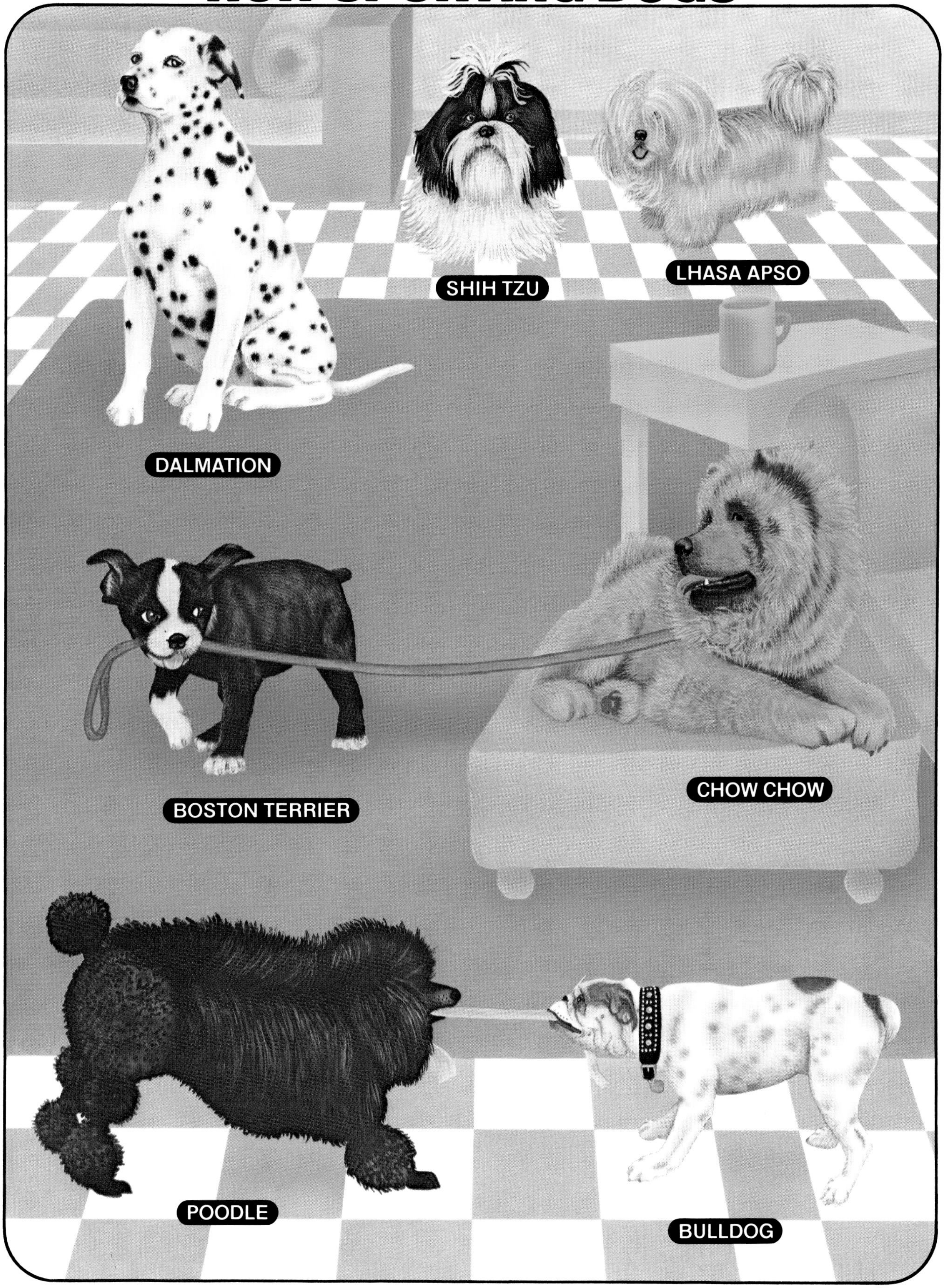

SHIH TZU

LHASA APSO

DALMATION

BOSTON TERRIER

CHOW CHOW

POODLE

BULLDOG

TOY DOGS

YORKSHIRE TERRIER ("YORKIE")

PEKINESE

POMERANIAN

MALTESE

PUG

CHIHUAHUA

ALPHABETICAL INDEX OF BREEDS

RECORDS AND SUPPLIES

PUPPY GROWTH AND DEVELOPMENT

AGE	STAGE OF DEVELOPMENT
Birth	Eyes closed. Deaf.
12 to 15 days	Eyes open. Vision limited. (Keep in soft light.)
15 to 18 days	Dog begins to hear. (Keep sounds soft.)
3 to 5 weeks	Weaning begins. Drinks from saucer. Begins to get baby teeth. Vision normal.
6 to 8 weeks	Eats 2 to 3 times a day. First trip to veterinarian. Housebreaking can begin. Weaning complete. Begins to eat solid food. May go outdoors. Old enough to be adopted. Has all of 28 baby teeth.
4 to 7-1/2 months	Gets 42 permanent teeth.
5-1/2 to 6 months	Females old enough to be neutered.
6 to 8 months	Obedience training can begin.
6-1/2 to 7 months	Males old enough to be neutered.
7 to 10 months	Females reach sexual maturity.
6 to 11 months	Males reach sexual maturity.
12 months	Eats once or twice a day. Growth complete. Old enough to be mated.

IMMUNIZATION SCHEDULE AND RECORD

Dog's Name _____ Date of Birth _____

COMBINED CANINE DISTEMPER-HEPATITIS-LEPTOSPIROSIS

1st Dose (6 Weeks Old) Date _____ Veterinarian _____
2nd Dose (9 Weeks Old) Date _____ Veterinarian _____
3rd Dose (12 to 16 Weeks Old) Date _____ Veterinarian _____
Booster Shot (Annually) Date _____ Veterinarian _____
Date _____ Veterinarian _____

HEARTWORM

Test (Each Spring or beginning of mosquito season.)
Date _____ Veterinarian _____   Date _____ Veterinarian _____
Prescribed Medication
Date _____ Veterinarian _____   Date _____ Veterinarian _____

RABIES

1st Dose (12 Weeks Old) Date _____ Veterinarian _____
Booster Shot (Annually) Date _____ Veterinarian _____
Date _____ Veterinarian _____

Dog's Name _____ Date of Birth _____

COMBINED CANINE DISTEMPER-HEPATITIS-LEPTOSPIROSIS

1st Dose (6 Weeks Old) Date _____ Veterinarian _____
2nd Dose (9 Weeks Old) Date _____ Veterinarian _____
3rd Dose (12 to 16 Weeks Old) Date _____ Veterinarian _____
Booster Shot (Annually) Date _____ Veterinarian _____
Date _____ Veterinarian _____

HEARTWORM

Test (Each Spring or beginning of mosquito season.)
Date _____ Veterinarian _____   Date _____ Veterinarian _____
Prescribed Medication
Date _____ Veterinarian _____   Date _____ Veterinarian _____

RABIES

1st Dose (12 Weeks Old) Date _____ Veterinarian _____
Booster Shot (Annually) Date _____ Veterinarian _____
Date _____ Veterinarian _____

Dog's Name _____ Date of Birth _____

COMBINED CANINE DISTEMPER-HEPATITIS-LEPTOSPIROSIS

1st Dose (6 Weeks Old) Date _____ Veterinarian _____
2nd Dose (9 Weeks Old) Date _____ Veterinarian _____
3rd Dose (12 to 16 Weeks Old) Date _____ Veterinarian _____
Booster Shot (Annually) Date _____ Veterinarian _____
Date _____ Veterinarian _____

HEARTWORM

Test (Each Spring or beginning of mosquito season.)
Date _____ Veterinarian _____   Date _____ Veterinarian _____
Prescribed Medication
Date _____ Veterinarian _____   Date _____ Veterinarian _____

RABIES

1st Dose (12 Weeks Old) Date _____ Veterinarian _____
Booster Shot (Annually) Date _____ Veterinarian _____
Date _____ Veterinarian _____

GENERAL HEALTH RECORD

Dog's Name _____ Date of Birth _____
Veterinarian: Name _____ Office Phone _____ Home Phone _____

Dates Wormed
Type _____ Date _____ Type _____ Date _____
Type _____ Date _____ Type _____ Date _____
Type _____ Date _____ Type _____ Date _____
Date Neutered _____ Veterinarian's Name _____

Present Medical Problems & Chronic Conditions _____
_____
_____

Medicines Taken Regularly _____

Special Precautions & Other Information _____

	NATURE	DATE	VETERINARIAN	PHONE
Hospitalizations				
Surgery				
Major Injuries				

Dog's Name _____ Date of Birth _____
Veterinarian: Name _____ Office Phone _____ Home Phone _____

Dates Wormed
Type _____ Date _____ Type _____ Date _____
Type _____ Date _____ Type _____ Date _____
Type _____ Date _____ Type _____ Date _____
Date Neutered _____ Veterinarian's Name _____

Present Medical Problems & Chronic Conditions _____
_____
_____

Medicines Taken Regularly _____

Special Precautions & Other Information _____

	NATURE	DATE	VETERINARIAN	PHONE
Hospitalizations				
Surgery				
Major Injuries				

Dog's Name _____ Date of Birth _____
Veterinarian: Name _____ Office Phone _____ Home Phone _____

Dates Wormed
Type _____ Date _____ Type _____ Date _____
Type _____ Date _____ Type _____ Date _____
Type _____ Date _____ Type _____ Date _____
Date Neutered _____ Veterinarian's Name _____

Present Medical Problems & Chronic Conditions _____
_____
_____

Medicines Taken Regularly _____

Special Precautions & Other Information _____

	NATURE	DATE	VETERINARIAN	PHONE
Hospitalizations				
Surgery				
Major Injuries				

STOCKING UP

- [ ] Absorbent Cotton Balls
- [ ] Activated Charcoal
- [ ] Adhesive Tape, 1 & 2 inches wide
- [ ] Antacid Liquid (Pepto-Bismol, etc.)
- [ ] Antibiotic Ointment
- [ ] Antihistamine Syrup (contained in many cough & cold preparations)
- [ ] Antihistamine Tablets (check for veterinarian's recommendation)
- [ ] Bandages, Elastic & Nonelastic
- [ ] Calamine Lotion
- [ ] Cotton Batting
- [ ] Cotton-Tipped Swabs
- [ ] Kaopectate
- [ ] Measuring Cup
- [ ] Measuring Spoons
- [ ] Medicinal Hydrogen Peroxide (3%), U.S.P.
- [ ] Nail Clipper (professional type)
- [ ] Nose Drops (Neosynepherine or the like)
- [ ] Petroleum Jelly
- [ ] Plastic Eyedropper or Dosing Syringe (available from veterinarian)
- [ ] Rectal Thermometer
- [ ] Rubber Gloves
- [ ] Rubbing Alcohol
- [ ] Safety Pins
- [ ] Scissors (with rounded edges)
- [ ] Sterile Gauze Pads, 2 x 4 inches
- [ ] Sterile Gauze Roll, 2 & 3 inches wide
- [ ] "Tamed" Iodine or Other Antiseptic
- [ ] Tourniquet: A short, sturdy stick and a clean cloth 1 inch wide. See **BLEEDING: TOURNIQUET,** pages 154-156, before using.
- [ ] Tweezers or Forceps
- [ ] Wooden Tongue Depressors

ADHESIVE TAPE

ANTIBIOTIC OINTMENT

Nose Drops

Calamine Lotion

COTTON BATTING

Bandage

Petroleum Jelly

COTTON TIPPED SWABS

STERILE GAUZE PADS

1 TEASPOON

1 TABLESPOON

½

ANTIHISTAMIN TABLETS

QUART LIQUID   .50 8

1 CUP LIQUID   8 OZ.

HOME PET VET GUIDE FIRST-AID KIT

- [ ] Collar (round for long-hairs, flat or round for shorthairs)
- [ ] Comb (medium fine, smooth teeth)
- [ ] Food Dish (shallow, non-corrosive, easy to clean)
- [ ] Hairbrush (natural bristle for shorthairs, wire for long-hairs)
- [ ] Harness
- [ ] Large Rawhide or Fiber Bone
- [ ] Leash
- [ ] Rubber Ball
- [ ] Travel Kennel
- [ ] Toys
- [ ] Water Dish (weighted base, deep)

Do not let your dog play with thread or string, plastic bags, small beads or anything brittle or small enough to be swallowed.

PART TWO

THE ANATOMICAL DOG

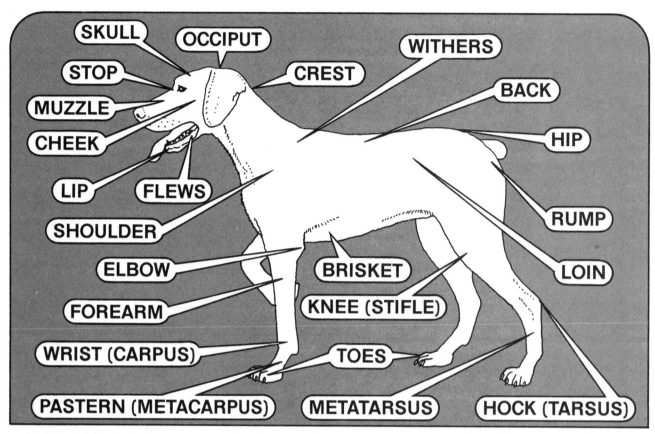

SKULL OCCIPUT CREST WITHERS BACK HIP
STOP MUZZLE CHEEK LIP FLEWS SHOULDER
ELBOW FOREARM WRIST (CARPUS)
PASTERN (METACARPUS) BRISKET KNEE (STIFLE) TOES
METATARSUS RUMP LOIN HOCK (TARSUS)

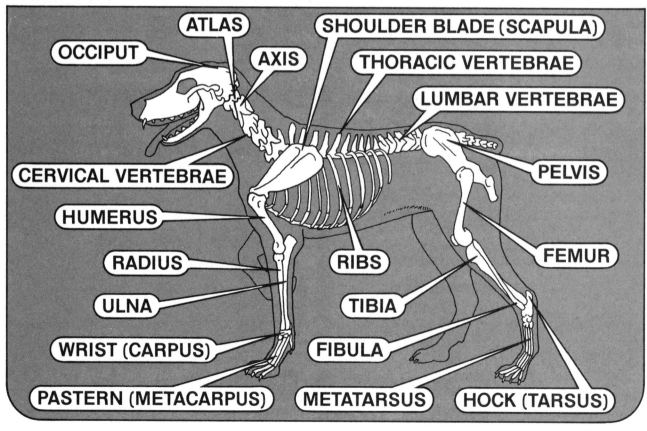

OCCIPUT ATLAS AXIS SHOULDER BLADE (SCAPULA)
THORACIC VERTEBRAE LUMBAR VERTEBRAE
CERVICAL VERTEBRAE HUMERUS RADIUS ULNA
WRIST (CARPUS) PASTERN (METACARPUS) RIBS TIBIA FIBULA
METATARSUS PELVIS FEMUR HOCK (TARSUS)

SYMPTOM RECOGNITION INDEX

Most of the responsibility for determining whether your dog is ill necessarily falls on you and the other members of your household. Only a small percentage of health disorders are discovered by the veterinarian during routine examinations. The rest are brought to his attention by owners who recognize, from their more or less continuous contact, that their pets aren't reacting normally and something is wrong.

Virtually any change in your dog's physical appearance or behavior can be an indication of impaired health. The symptoms presented here are the most familiar signs of the common disorders described in the two sections that follow on illnesses and health emergencies. The symptoms are arranged alphabetically. Under each symptom you will find listed the various disorders with which it is associated, along with the relevant page references.

A given symptom can usually have any number of causes. Rarely is it so unique that it is seen in one and only one illness. Most illnesses also have more than one symptom. By turning to the cited pages and comparing these other symptoms with what you observe in your dog you will be able to narrow down what is probably wrong with it and find out what to do.

As a general rule, it is best to consult your veterinarian whenever you find any symptoms of ill health in your dog, even if you are uncertain about them or they seem mild or appear only occasionally. Depending on the cause, some symptoms come on suddenly and are entirely obvious, but others may develop slowly and subtly and be only intermittent. Nor does the apparent severity of the symptom necessarily signify the seriousness of the underlying cause. Minor disorders sometimes produce dramatic symptoms, while far more serious illnesses may have symptoms that are scarcely evident. Your veterinarian would certainly prefer a false alarm to the unnecessary delay that may lead to complications or permit the disorder to worsen and perhaps even threaten the dog's life.

Ⓑ

BACK

BALANCE IMPAIRED

BARK IS ABNORMAL

BEHAVIOR CHANGES

BIRTH PROBLEMS

BITES, CHEWS OR LICKS AT SELF

BLEEDING

EYES

JERKY MOVEMENTS

JOINTS

Enlarged

LEGS

Dragging

Elbows Are Swollen & Painful

Extended

Front Wrist Joints Are Swollen & Painful

Hopping: See HOPPING

Limping Or Lameness: See LIMPING OR LAMENESS

Muscle Spasms

Paddling Motions

Pain

Paralysis

Poor Conformation ("Cow Hocks")

Reduced Use

Stiffness

Make Grating Or Rubbing Sound

Pain

L

Weak Or Wobbly

LETHARGY

LICKS AT SELF: See BITES, CHEWS OR LICKS AT SELF

LIMPING OR LAMENESS

LIPS

Blue

Charred Or Burned

Reddened

Sores Or Ulcerations

Swollen Or Thickened

T

TAIL IS LIMP

TEETH

TEMPERATURE: See FEVER

TESTICLES

U

WORMS

In Stool Or Vomit

In Wounds

WOUNDS

Bites & Stings

Bleeding

ILLNESSES AND DISORDERS

This section describes the illnesses and disorders that are most likely to beset your dog. Each is discussed in terms of its common symptoms, underlying cause and, most importantly, what you as the dog's owner should do about it. Special precautions and recommendations for prevention are also indicated whenever they are appropriate. For infectious diseases, you will also find information about incubation, communicability and duration.

The section is designed to be used as a reference guide to help you understand and cope with conditions that may impair your pet's normal good health. It is not a substitute for a veterinarian, though in those rare situations where veterinary care is inaccessible or delayed, it may indeed enable you to preserve your dog's life until professional help can be obtained.

Keep in mind that a dog afflicted by a given disorder may show some, all or none of the listed symptoms. And to stress an earlier point, it is usually best to tell your veterinarian about any indication of illness, no matter how minor it may seem. By the same token, if your dog is hit by a car or subjected to some other severe blow, it should be examined by the vet even if no symptoms are evident.

Dogs are hardy animals, and with proper veterinary treatment and home care they usually recover from most illnesses. Sometimes, however, they do not. The responsibilities of ownership are never quite so troublesome as when a cherished pet is painfully debilitated by a serious illness and has little or no chance of recovering. Some owners deal with the problem by letting nature take its course. Others make the difficult decision to end the pet's suffering through euthanasia and submit it to a painless and peaceful death.

Should you ever have to confront this disturbing choice, your veterinarian will be able to give you some approximate idea about the dog's chances for getting better as well as how long it will take and what it will cost. He can provide you with the best available information and advice, but of course the ultimate decision has to rest with you yourself. If it seems best to have euthanasia performed on your dog, the vet can give it a quick, painless death through an overdose of anesthetic. He can also arrange to dispose of the remains. In some communities, it is possible to have a dog cremated and buried in a pet cemetary.

CANCER

LYMPHOSARCOMA

SYMPTOMS

Swollen, enlarged lymph nodes can be felt on both sides of the neck under the jaw, in front of the shoulders and behind the knees of the rear legs. Weakness. Loss of appetite. Loss of overall physical condition. Pale gums, tongue and inner linings of eyelids. A malignant cancer of the lymph nodes caused by the dramatic and unexplained reproduction of lymphocytes, a type of blood cell important in fighting infection.

WHAT TO DO

• Consult your veterinarian. Symptoms lessen for a period following treatment, but then recur. Spontaneous cures can occur.

MAMMARY TUMORS

SYMPTOMS

Hard, knot-like swellings can be clearly seen and felt within the breast. As these tumors grow—and they can become very large—the skin covering them becomes thin, then ulcerated and bloody. The dog chews or licks at the affected area. The tumors can be either benign or malignant. Occur only in female dogs. Most common in those that develop false pregnancy. The precise cause is unknown, although related to the female hormone.

WHAT TO DO

• Consult your veterinarian. Early treatment is important. Malignant tumors can spread and affect other areas of the body. Surgery is usually required. To reduce occurrence in the dog's other breasts, spaying is often recommended.

• Can be effectively prevented by neutering the dog when it is about 6 months old.

SKIN CANCER

SYMPTOMS

A solid lump can be clearly seen and felt on the skin. If left untreated, the lump continues to grow. May be benign or malignant. Usually seen in older dogs. Particularly common in Boxers.

WHAT TO DO

• Consult your veterinarian. Early treatment is important. Malignant skin cancer can spread and affect other areas of the body.

SQUAMOUS CELL CARCINOMA

SYMPTOMS

A sore or ulcer that does not heal on the mouth, lips, tongue, eye, eyelid or elsewhere on the body where mucous membranes meet the skin. The affected area grows in size, becomes angry, inflamed and rough, and emits a foul odor. In later stages, it may increase in thickness and take on a fatty, cauliflower-like appearance. A very serious, fast-growing cancer.

WHAT TO DO

• Consult your veterinarian. Early care is essential. Squamous cell cancer tends to spread and affect regional lymph nodes and other areas. Surgery is required.

• After treatment, an affected animal should be watched closely for symptoms of recurrence.

TESTICULAR TUMORS

SYMPTOMS

Firm enlargement of one of the testicles. May or may not be painful. (Not evident if the testicles haven't descended.) The dog may or may not develop female sexual characteristics such as enlarged nipples and breasts, perhaps containing milk. Caused by a tumor in the testicle. Most common in males with an undescended testicle.

WHAT TO DO

• Consult your veterinarian. Early treatment is important.

• As a precaution, inform your veterinarian if there is any significant change in the relative size of your dog's testicles.

TUMORS OF THE SPLEEN

SYMPTOMS

Sudden weakness. Inability to stand. Pale gums, tongue and inner linings of the eyelids. Fluid-filled "potbelly." No visible bleeding. Symptoms develop suddenly in an apparently healthy, vigorous dog in less than 24 hours. Caused by the sudden rupture of a tumor that has been slowly growing in the spleen. May be benign or malignant. Usually affects large dogs, particularly German Shepherds.

WHAT TO DO
• **Consult your veterinarian. Early diagnosis and treatment are important.** Requires surgery. Other areas of the body may be affected.

CIRCULATORY DISORDERS

ANEMIA

SYMPTOMS

Progressive weakness and fatigue. In advanced cases, the mucous membranes of the gums, mouth and inner linings of the eyelids look pale and whitish rather than a normal healthy pink. A consequence of any condition that results in an inadequate supply of circulating red blood cells. Various causes include reduced production of red blood cells (inadequate diet, leukemia in the bone marrow, etc.), increased rate of destruction of red blood cells (poisoning, diseases such as leptospirosis, etc.) and blood loss (trauma, acute hemorrhage, parasites, etc.).

WHAT TO DO
• **Consult your veterinarian.**
• As a precaution, check your dog's gums for paling if it shows weakness and fatigue.

AUTOIMMUNE HEMOLYTIC ANEMIA

SYMPTOMS

A sudden or gradually developing paleness of the tongue, gums and inner linings of the eyelids. Weakness. Loss of appetite. Dehydration. Caused by the production of antibodies that destroy the red blood cells. Can develop slowly or rapidly. May recur after treatment.

WHAT TO DO
• **Consult your veterinarian. Early treatment is important.**

CONGESTIVE HEART FAILURE

SYMPTOMS
Very resonant coughing, usually at night or early morning or after exertion or excitement. Phlegm, with or without blood. In advanced cases: The dog may not cough but has difficulty breathing, carries its head elevated, refuses to lie down and seems anxious. Obvious respiratory distress. The lips, gums and inner linings of the eyelids become blue. Results from an accumulation of fluid in the lung tissue due to interference with the normal blood flow. Usually affects dogs over 6 years old. Develops slowly and increases in severity over a period of months or years.

WHAT TO DO
• **Consult your veterinarian. Early treatment is important.** Advanced symptoms indicate that the condition is already critical. Lifetime medication is usually required.
• **For home care:** Place your dog on a low salt diet. Do not exercise it strenuously.

HEART MURMUR

SYMPTOMS
IN OLDER ANIMALS: Coughing. Difficulty breathing. Fluid-filled "potbelly." IN PUPPIES: May be without apparent symptoms, or a "hum" or "purr" may be felt in the chest. A result of any interference with the normal flow of blood through the heart. Can be present

from birth or acquired with age. In puppies, can be caused by the failure of fetal heart openings to close fully when the animal is born or by defects in the shape of the heart or its valves.

WHAT TO DO
- **Consult your veterinarian.**
- If your older dog is severely affected, observe for **CONGESTIVE HEART FAILURE,** page 106.

HEART MUSCLE (MYOCARDIAL) DISEASE

SYMPTOMS

Fluid-filled "potbelly." Loss of appetite. Gradual weight loss. The dog may or may not have difficulty breathing. The condition slowly worsens. In advanced cases: Weight loss may become extreme within just a few weeks. Quickly worsening breathing difficulties. Coughing. A common disease of unknown cause in which the heart muscle fails to function properly and the heart becomes enlarged. Can affect one or both sides of the heart. Most common in large and giant dogs. Tends to occur in young animals.

WHAT TO DO
- **Consult your veterinarian. Early care is essential.** Ongoing medication is usually required. The medication can improve the functioning of the heart and slow the progress of the disease, but cannot effect a complete cure.

DIGESTIVE DISORDERS: ANUS

ANAL PLUG

SYMPTOMS

Accumulated stool and matted hair around the anus, which blocks defecation. Pain in the affected area. The dog scoots or rubs its rear end on the ground. Straining during futile attempts to defecate. Foul odor. The skin under the matted hair is irritated and inflamed. A common condition in long-haired puppies and dogs.

WHAT TO DO
- **Consult your veterinarian.**
- **For home care:** Restrain the dog; see **RESTRAINTS,** page 209. Gently cut away the hair that holds the plug against the skin and remove the mass. Clean the area with hand soap and warm water.
- To prevent recurrence, keep the hair around the anus trimmed short and check the area frequently.

ANAL SAC ABSCESS

SYMPTOMS

Hot, painful swelling to the sides of the anus or just below it. The dog may rub, lick or bite at the area. The abscess may eventually open a small hole, through which pus and blood may drain. Caused by an infection of the anal sacs. These sacs are normally emptied of their secretions by the pressure of the dog defecating. For unknown reasons, the secretions can thicken and block the openings in the sacs, causing inflammation and abscess.

WHAT TO DO
- **Consult your veterinarian.** Surgery is usually required.
- As a prevention, examine your dog's anus regularly and clear the anal sacs if necessary; see **ANAL SAC IMPACTION,** page 143.

PERIANAL FISTULA

SYMPTOMS

The anus is red and angry, and surrounded by many small holes that exude pus. The dog may lick, bite or scratch at the area. Pain, especially during efforts to defecate. Unpleasant odor. A chronic disease. Most commonly affects male German Shepherds.

WHAT TO DO
- **Consult your veterinarian.** Surgery is usually required to remove all affected tissue.
- Closely observe the dog for 3 or 4 months after surgery to make sure all affected tissue has been removed.

PERIANAL TUMORS (ADENOMAS)

SYMPTOMS

Small, firm lumps or clusters of lumps inside or around the anus. The dog may lick or scratch at the area. Advanced cases may include: Larger and more numerous lumps. The anus becomes distorted and makes defecation difficult. A progressive, hormone-related disease most common in males and older dogs.

WHAT TO DO

• **Consult your veterinarian.** Surgery may be required in advanced cases to remove large masses. In males, the condition is usually helped by castration, which reduces the growths and permits the anus to return to normal.

• Can be prevented by neutering the dog when it is about 6 or 7 months old.

RECTAL PROLAPSE

SYMPTOMS

A small or large cylindrical red mass protrudes from the anus. It is very inflamed and may also be bloody. Most common in puppies with severe diarrhea, but also found in older dogs after a long period of straining to defecate. Common causes include chronic constipation or obstipation, urinary obstruction or infection, prostate disease and birth difficulties.

WHAT TO DO

• **Consult your veterinarian. Early care is important.**

• If a vet isn't immediately available, apply cold moistened cloth compresses against the exposed tissue. This will prevent further exposure, hold down the swelling, keep the tissue clean and prevent it from drying out.

• As a precaution, tell your veterinarian if your dog strains frequently while defecating.

DIGESTIVE DISORDERS: ESOPHAGUS

DILATATION OF THE ESOPHAGUS

SYMPTOMS

Weight loss, particularly in a young puppy. Loss of overall physical condition. The dog vomits immediately or shortly after it eats. May develop coughing. A condition in which the esophagus forms a pouch or "balloon" just above an abnormal narrowing of the passage. The constriction may be the result of many causes, including congenital malformation and scar tissue from an injury.

WHAT TO DO

• **Consult your veterinarian.** In some cases, surgery may be required. In other cases, the dog's condition may be improved by frequently feeding it small portions of food while it stands on its hind legs.

FOREIGN OBJECTS IN THE ESOPHAGUS

SYMPTOMS

Drooling and persistent gulping from bones, fishhooks, metal objects, etc. that have been swallowed and become stuck in the esophagus. The dog tries to vomit or does vomit. The vomit contains some blood. Anxiety. If there is a partial obstruction, the appetite may be unaffected, or the dog may be able to drink liquids but attempts to throw up solids. A condition commonly caused by the dog's habit of gulping rather than chewing its food. May be recurrent in some dogs.

WHAT TO DO

• **Consult your veterinarian. Early treatment is essential** to prevent damage to the esophagus or pneumonia from inhaled food caught behind the object. **Do not** give the dog food or water.

• As a prevention, try to keep your dog from playing with small objects or bones that can be swallowed.

DIGESTIVE DISORDERS: INTESTINES

ACUTE ENTERITIS

SYMPTOMS

Diarrhea, with or without blood. Often follows bouts of vomiting within 24 hours. An acute inflammation of the intestines from various causes including foreign material, bacteria, virus infection, toxic agents and chemicals. Can lead to dehydration if severe or pro-longed. Bloody diarrhea can be serious because of the possibility of substantial blood loss.

WHAT TO DO
- **Consult your veterinarian.**
- **For home care:** See **DIARRHEA,** page 174.

COLITIS

SYMPTOMS

Frequent, often strained bowel movement. Diarrhea, with or without blood. The dog passes bloody mucus. A result of an inflammation of the colon. Can have numerous causes including parasites, bacteria and allergy to certain foods. Can be chronic or intermittent. Frequently recurrent.

WHAT TO DO

- Consult your veterinarian.

- When caused by an allergic reaction to particular foods, they must be eliminated from the dog's diet to prevent recurrence.

INTESTINAL OBSTRUCTION AND INTUSSUSCEPTION

SYMPTOMS

Vomiting. Loss of appetite. Swollen or painful stomach. Arching of the back. The dog passes bloody mucus or dark, tar-like stool. A condition in which the intestinal tract is partially or totally blocked, slowing or stopping the normal passage of food. Most commonly caused by foreign objects such as stones and bones. Occasionally, a section of intestine may begin to fold like a telescope, producing an obstruction called "intussusception." Usually acute, but can be chronic or intermittent. Severity is determined by the degree of the blockage and where it occurs.

WHAT TO DO
- **Consult your veterinarian. Early treatment is important.**
- Withhold food and water until your vet sees the dog.

MALABSORPTION SYNDROME

SYMPTOMS

Persistent diarrhea. Normal appetite but chronic weight loss. Lack of overall physical condition. Poor coat. Stool may be gray, fatty or foul smelling. Caused by a variety of conditions that prevent the intestines from absorbing or properly utilizing the nutrients in food. Often mistaken for heavy parasitic infestation or chronic pancreatitis. To be suspected in a dog that has been wormed or tested free of parasites yet continues to lose weight.

WHAT TO DO
- **Consult your veterinarian.** He may prescribe a special diet of low residue highly nutritious food, along with special vitamin supplements and enzyme products.

OBSTIPATION

SYMPTOMS

Frequent, largely futile efforts to defecate. Straining, with or without pain. The dog stands in a defecating position for long periods. A condition resembling constipation. The dog is unable to move its bowels because the normal passage of feces is obstructed. Common causes include prostatitis, tumors and deformities that obstruct the intestines. Can lead to perineal hernias or prolapse of the rectum.

WHAT TO DO
- **Consult your veterinarian. Prompt treatment is important.** The underlying cause must be found and treated. (True constipation is rarely a problem in dogs unless they are fed an all beef diet.)

PANCREATITIS

ACUTE PANCREATITIS: Vomiting. Severe abdominal pain that prevents the dog from lying down. Pacing. Diarrhea, with or without blood. Can range from mild to severe. In a severe case, the dog may suddenly hemorrhage and collapse. **CHRONIC PANCREATITIS: Ravenous appetite with no gain in weight, or actual weight loss. Loss of overall physical condition. Stools are foul smelling, grayish in color and fatty. Stool eating.** A life-threatening inflammation of the pancreas that can destroy its ability to produce the enzymes necessary for normal digestion. Most commonly affects obese females about 5 to 7 years old, particularly those with high fat diets. Acute episodes can lead to the chronic condition and to diabetes.

WHAT TO DO
- **Consult your veterinarian. Early treatment is important.** Following treatment, enzyme replacement may be necessary throughout the dog's life.
- Observe for **SHOCK,** page 202.
- Observe for **DIABETES MELLITUS,** page 120.
- As a prevention, keep your dog on a low-fat diet.

DIGESTIVE DISORDERS: MOUTH

FOREIGN OBJECTS IN THE MOUTH

SYMPTOMS

Violent pawing at the face. Rubbing the mouth along the floor. The dog may not be able to close its mouth. Futile attempts to dislodge the object with violent tongue movements. Commonly caused by biting down on sticks, pieces of bone or plastic, etc. that then become stuck between two teeth or across the roof of the mouth. Usually, but not always, involves the upper teeth.

WHAT TO DO
- Restrain the dog; see **RESTRAINTS,** page 209. Open its mouth and carefully check the upper and lower teeth and the roof of the mouth. Grasp the object firmly with pliers or your fingers, and gently remove it. (Usually, no additional care is required. Small cuts in the mouth heal quickly.)
- If you can't locate a foreign object and the symptoms persist, consult your veterinarian.

INFLAMMATION AND ULCERS

SYMPTOMS

Red, angry areas on the lips, tongue or inside the cheeks. Profuse salivation. Unwillingness to eat. Pain. The dog may paw at its mouth. Common causes include accumulated tooth tartar, irritation from tooth infection, burns from chemicals and biting an electrical cord.

WHAT TO DO
- **Consult your veterinarian.**

- To avoid further inflammation, give the dog only bland food and drink served at room temperature.
- Watch the dog closely. Consult your veterinarian again if the inflammation and ulcers haven't disappeared within 1 week.
- The accumulation of irritating tartar can be slowed by vigorously brushing the dog's teeth every week with a moist toothbrush.

PYORRHEA (TOOTH INFECTION)

SYMPTOMS

Inflammation and infection of the gums around the teeth. Bleeding. Lost or loose teeth. Foul breath. Ulcers on the lining of the cheek near the affected teeth. A result of tooth tartar and gingivitis.

WHAT TO DO
- **Consult your veterinarian. Early treatment is important** to prevent tooth loss, weakened bone structure, more serious infection and systemic damage from chronic infection in the mouth.

RETENTION OF PUPPY (DECIDUOUS) TEETH

SYMPTOMS

The small puppy teeth do not fall out as the larger permanent teeth grow in but remain in the mouth next to or behind the permanent teeth. Normally, puppy teeth are replaced before the dog is 6 months old.

WHAT TO DO

• **Consult your veterinarian.** If not removed, the puppy teeth may distort the shape or location of the permanent teeth or cause the jaw to close improperly.

STOOL EATING

SYMPTOMS

The dog eats its own stools or those of another animal. Thin or scrawny appearance. Recurrent infestation of internal parasites following prescribed treatment. Usually affects young dogs. The cause is not known but may be related to inadequate digestive chemicals, vitamin and mineral deficiencies, or boredom. The major concern is chronic thinness and re-infestation by internal parasites.

WHAT TO DO

• **Consult your veterinarian.**
• A teaspoon of meat tenderizer mixed with each serving of food may help some dogs by supplying the needed digestive chemicals.
• Vitamin and mineral supplements to the regular diet are often recommended.
• To keep your dog from being bored, try not to leave it alone for long periods of time.

TOOTH TARTAR AND GINGIVITIS

SYMPTOMS

Tan or brown discoloration of the teeth, starting at the gum line and progressing under the gums and over the teeth. Inflammation or infection of the gums around the teeth. Receding gums. Lost or loose teeth. Foul breath. May lead to more serious tooth infection.

WHAT TO DO

• If necessary, have your vet clean the dog's teeth once a year. This will remove accumulated tartar and reduce the likelihood of inflammation, infection and abscess.

• Some dogs accumulate tartar quickly. You can slow this accumulation between regular visits to the veterinarian by vigorous weekly brushings with a moist toothbrush.

UPPER P4 SYNDROME

SYMPTOMS

An infection of one of the fourth premolars (P4), the large upper teeth directly under the dog's sinuses. (The infected tooth may appear normal.) The cheekbone directly under the eye protrudes from the pus that fills the sinus cavity and distorts the dog's face. In advanced cases, a small opening develops under the eye and pus drains down the dog's cheek.

WHAT TO DO

• **Consult your veterinarian. Early treatment is important.**

DIGESTIVE DISORDERS: STOMACH

BLOAT

SYMPTOMS

Dramatic swelling of the stomach and chest to an enormous size within a very short period of time, as little as an hour. The stomach sounds hollow and drum-like when tapped with the fingers. Futile attempts to vomit. Progresses rapidly to: Difficulty breathing. Blue gums, tongue and inner linings of the eyelids. Agitation. Coma. Possible death. A potentially fatal condition that occurs when an enormous amount of stomach gas is produced in a very short time and the dog is unable to relieve itself. Most common in large, deep-chested dogs, particularly after eating. Twisting of the stomach may complicate the condition.

WHAT TO DO

• **Consult your veterinarian. Prompt treatment is crucial. Bloat can be quickly fatal.**

- To prevent recurrence, which is common, add anti-gas medication to the dog's food, and feed it smaller meals several times a day, when you can observe it for several hours afterward.

FOREIGN OBJECTS IN THE STOMACH

SYMPTOMS

Sudden brief episodes of vomiting or diarrhea. The vomit or diarrhea may contain blood. Caused when indigestible objects such as bones, stones or pieces of metal are swallowed and remain in the stomach. A common condition because of the dog's habit of gulping rather than chewing its food. May be recurrent in some dogs.

WHAT TO DO

- **Consult your veterinarian. Early treatment is essential** to prevent the object from passing into the intestines where it may present a more serious problem. May require surgical removal. Some foreign objects can be passed with the use of prescribed lubricant-type laxatives.
- As a prevention, try to keep your dog from playing with small objects that can be swallowed.

HEMORRHAGIC GASTROENTERITIS

SYMPTOMS

Sudden bloody vomiting and diarrhea containing jelly-like blood clots. Shock. In severe cases, coma and death may follow within 24 hours of the onset of symptoms. An acute inflammation of the digestive system that results in severe internal bleeding. The cause is unknown. Often affects Schnauzers and Poodles.

WHAT TO DO

- **Consult your veterinarian. Early treatment is crucial.**
- Observe for **SHOCK**; see page 202.

EARS

HEMATOMA

SYMPTOMS

A large or small painful soft swelling on the ear flap. Caused by accumulated blood from a broken blood vessel in the cartilage of the flap. Often a result of head shaking and ear scratching due to otitis externa.

WHAT TO DO

- **Consult your veterinarian.** Failure to treat will cause a knotting and constriction of the cartilage and result in a permanently disfigured "cauliflower" ear.

Treatment involves draining the blood from the ear flap and binding it tightly to prevent disfiguration. May recur if the underlying cause is not eliminated.
- Always check with your veterinarian if your dog scratches its ears frequently or shows other symptoms of **OTITIS EXTERNA**; see below.
- As a prevention, clean your dog's ears regularly to keep them free of accumulated wax, debris and matted hair; see **CLEANING THE DOG'S EARS**, page 35.

OTITIS EXTERNA

SYMPTOMS

Shaking the head or tipping it to one side. Scratching at ears. Discomfort or pain when the ear or ear flap is touched. The skin in the ear canal is red and angry. Discharge from the ear. Foul odor. A common inflammation of the ear canal due to irritation caused by accumulated wax and debris. The inflammation allows various bacteria to infect the area. Can progress to ulceration of parts of the ear canal. Dogs that grow hair in their ear canals are especially likely to be affected.

WHAT TO DO

- **Consult your veterinarian** if there are signs of infection. You may have to administer long-term care to keep the dog's ears clean and medicated until they heal.
- You may be able to treat a less serious case yourself by keeping your dog's ears clean; see **CLEANING THE DOG'S EARS**, page 35.
- To prevent otitis, clean your dog's ears regularly to keep them free of accumulated wax, debris and matted hair. As an additional precaution, thin the hair inside the ears.
- Prolonged scratching and head shaking can result in **HEMATOMA**, see above.

EYES

CATARACTS

The pupil of the eye becomes whitish-blue, then gradually turns milky white and opaque as the disease progresses. Indications of reduced vision, particularly in dim light. May affect one or both eyes. Can occur at any age. (Older dogs sometimes have a whitish-blue haze in their eyes that resembles cataracts but does not affect their vision.)

- **Consult your veterinarian.** Surgery is usually recommended when vision is lost. An affected dog may also have other eye diseases or diabetes mellitus.
- A dog that has undergone cataract surgery will have less than normal vision but will be able to function quite well. You should, however, carefully plan its environment to protect it from new dangers arising from its partial loss of sight.

CONJUNCTIVITIS

Pink or red inflamed eyes, eyeballs or inner linings of the eyelids. Squinting and sensitivity to light. Discomfort. Possible pus-like discharge. Possible exposure of the opaque third eyelid, which is not normally seen. May be accompanied by fever. Common causes include direct irritation, injury and infectious diseases. Can affect one or both eyes. If seen in one eye, it is most likely a local problem from irritation or injury. If seen in both eyes, it might be a local problem or an indication of a serious systemic illness such as distemper.

- **Consult your veterinarian. Prompt treatment is important.**
- Keep the eyes clean and free of debris; see **CLEANING THE DOG'S EYES,** page 36.
- Depending on the cause, conjunctivitis can sometimes be contagious through direct contact. An affected dog should be isolated until it has been properly diagnosed.
- Should the opaque third eyelid come up to protect the injured eye, **do not** try to remove it or otherwise interfere with it.

CORNEAL ULCER

Extreme pain in the eye. Tearing. Squinting and sensitivity to light. The surface of the eyeball is roughened and dished out rather than smooth and mirror-like. Caused by a loss of substance of the transparent membrane covering the eye, a result of any chronic irritation such as hair in the eye, folds of facial skin in contact with the cornea, foreign bodies caught under the eyelid, etc. A serious problem that can lead to blindness if not treated. In severe cases, the ulcer may actually penetrate the cornea, resulting in extreme damage that threatens the eyeball. Dogs with prominent eyes are more subject to chronic irritation because their eyes are more exposed.

- **Consult your veterinarian. Early care is important.** May require extended treatment or surgery.
- Unless the underlying cause is eliminated, the condition can recur.
- Early treatment of eye irritation and **CONJUNCTIVITIS,** see above, can help prevent this condition.
- As a further precaution, examine your dog's eyes regularly, particularly if they are in contact with long hairs or folds of facial skin. Trim hair if necessary.

EPIPHORA

Dark tear-staining of the fur and skin in the corner of the eye closest to the nose. In chronic cases, the tears may mat the hair and cause a crust to form in the corner of the eye, which can progress to an ulceration in the skin just below it. Caused by an excess production of tears resulting from an irritation of the eye or an obstruction or blockage of the tear duct. Commonly affects Poodles.

- **Consult your veterinarian.**
- **For home care:** Keep your dog's eyes clean; see **CLEANING THE DOG'S EYES,** page 36. Medicinal hydrogen peroxide applied with a cotton-tipped swab can be used to bleach out stains caused by tears on the hair below the eye. Take care not to get hydrogen peroxide in the dog's eye.

EXPOSURE OF THE THIRD EYELID

SYMPTOMS

An opaque film rises from the lower corner of the eye nearest the nose and covers some portion of the eyeball. The eyeball may seem to have moved upward out of its normal position. The third eyelid serves as a protective device for the eye and is not normally seen unless the eye is injured, irritated or inflamed, or the dog has an upper respiratory illness. Often occurs with conjunctivitis. If seen in both eyes, may be a symptom of upper respiratory illness.

WHAT TO DO

• **Consult your veterinarian.**
• **Do not** try to remove the third eyelid or otherwise interfere with it.
• As a prevention, keep the eyes clean and free of debris; see **CLEANING THE DOG'S EYES,** page 36.

FOLDED EYELID

SYMPTOMS

If the edge of the eyelid folds inward toward the eyeball: Tearing. Pain. Squinting and sensitivity to light. Possible exposure of the third eyelid, which is not normally seen. If the edge of the eyelid folds outward away from the eyeball: The eye is chronically red and angry. Conjunctivitis, with or without pus in the sac formed by the eyelid. May result from a birth defect or can occur at some later time. May affect either the upper or lower lid in one or both eyes. An outward-folding eyelid more often affects the lower lid.

WHAT TO DO

• **Consult your veterinarian.** Can progress to **KERATITIS,** see below, or **CORNEAL ULCER,** page 113. Surgery is usually required.
• Should the opaque third eyelid come up to protect the injured eye, **do not** try to remove it or otherwise interfere with it.

GLAUCOMA

SYMPTOMS

Any signs of decreased vision, particularly in dim light. There may or may not be an obvious enlargement of the eyeball, with or without red and enlarged surface blood vessels. The eye appears hazy. Caused by increased pressure within the eye. May be a result of increased production of the normal fluid in the eye or some interference with the normal flow of excess fluid from the eye. Usually develops slowly over a long period of time, but may appear quite suddenly. Some vision may be permanently lost before the disease is discovered. May affect one or both eyes. Cocker Spaniels, Beagles and Basset Hounds are most prone to this disease.

WHAT TO DO

• **Consult your veterinarian. Early treatment is important.** Surgery may be recommended.

KERATITIS

SYMPTOMS

Tearing. Pain. Squinting and sensitivity to light. The cornea is covered by a blue haze. Possible exposure of the third eyelid, which is not normally seen. The result of an inflammation of the cornea, the transparent covering of the eye. May affect one or both eyes. Common causes include direct irritation of the cornea by ingrowing lashes, infectious diseases and injury. In dogs with protruding eyes and short muzzles, folds of skin may cause chronic irritation and recurrent bouts of keratitis.

WHAT TO DO

• **Consult your veterinarian. Early treatment is important.** If not treated promptly and effectively, may lead to more serious eye conditions, such as **PANNUS,** page 115, **CORNEAL ULCER,** page 113, or the deposit of black pigment in the cornea, which produces partial or total blindness.
• Should the third eyelid come up to protect the injured eye, **do not** try to remove it or otherwise interfere with it.
• As a prevention, keep the eyes clean and free of debris; see **CLEANING THE DOG'S EYES,** page 36.

KERATOCONJUNCTIVITIS SICCA (DRY EYE)

SYMPTOMS

The eye appears dry. Stringy, thick mucus in the eye. Squinting and sensitivity to light. A blue haze may cover the cornea. **Possible exposure of the third eyelid, which is not normally seen. Pink or red inflamed eyeball or inner linings of the eyelids.** A slowly developing condition in which the tear glands do not produce enough fluid to keep the eye constantly moist. Usually a result of inflammation from any number of causes. Typically affects one eye but may occur in both.

WHAT TO DO
- **Consult your veterinarian.** If left untreated, the condition can progress to **KERATITIS,** page 114, or

CORNEAL ULCER, page 113. If the eye does not respond to treatment, you will have to administer ongoing medication; see **APPLYING LIQUID MEDICINE TO THE EYES,** page 225. Surgery is sometimes recommended.
- Should the opaque third eyelid come up to protect the injured eye, **do not** try to remove it or otherwise interfere with it.

PANNUS

SYMPTOMS
A grayish veil-like haze of blood vessels and other cellular elements can be seen gradually creeping across the cornea. Usually moves from the temple side toward the nose. A progressive condition that can lead to blindness. Very common in German Shepherds.

WHAT TO DO
- **Consult your veterinarian. Early treatment can slow the progress of this condition.** May require extended treatment or surgery.
- As a prevention, examine your dog's eyes regularly.

PROLAPSE OF THE GLAND OF THE THIRD EYELID (CHERRY EYE)

SYMPTOMS
Possible exposure of the opaque third eyelid, which is not normally seen. Protruding from this eyelid is a small, bright red growth.

WHAT TO DO
- **Consult your veterinarian.** Although surgery is usually required, this condition is not as serious as its dramatic appearance might suggest.
- **Do not** try to remove the third eyelid or otherwise interfere with it.

RETINAL DISEASES

SYMPTOMS
Sudden or progressive loss of vision, often beginning with loss of night vision. An impairment of the light-sensitive materials that line the inner surface of the rear of the eye. Many possible causes, including a congenital or metabolic defect, infectious disease, inflammation or injury. Sometimes occurs as a result of distemper.

WHAT TO DO
- **Consult your veterinarian.**

SUBCONJUNCTIVAL HEMORRHAGE

SYMPTOMS
A diffuse blood-red discoloration in the white of the eye. In more severe cases, the transparent membrane covering the eye may bulge out and look like a red growth. The result of ruptured small blood vessels. Most commonly caused by trauma or severe straining.

WHAT TO DO
- **Consult your veterinarian.** Only severe cases usually require treatment.
- Continue to observe an affected dog. If the condition was caused by straining, it may recur if the cause of straining is not eliminated.

HERNIA

ABDOMINAL HERNIA

SYMPTOMS
Large swelling under the skin of the abdomen. Caused by a rupture or break in the abdominal muscles, which allows abdominal organs and other structures to pro-

trude. Commonly the result of some trauma to the abdomen such as being hit by a car or kicked by a horse.

WHAT TO DO
- **Consult your veterinarian. Early treatment is important.** Will require surgery.

DIAPHRAGMATIC HERNIA

SYMPTOMS

Great difficulty breathing. Distress. The abdomen rises and falls as the dog tries to breathe. The dog resists being handled and may not lie down. In severe cases, the gums, tongue and inner linings of the eyelids become progressively more blue. Caused by a hole or break in the diaphragm (the muscle separating the abdomen from the chest), which allows the abdominal organs to pass into the chest and press on the lungs, preventing them from expanding when the dog tries to breathe. If it is small, the symptoms may not develop for several days or longer. Usually the result of a hereditary defect in the diaphragm or a trauma. To be suspected if the dog has recently experienced an injury involving a sharp blow to the body.

WHAT TO DO
- **Consult your veterinarian. Early treatment is important.** Surgery is required.
- Try to keep the dog calm. Any excitement can cause death.

EVENTRATION

SYMPTOMS

Internal organs protrude through a surgical incision. If the skin sutures remain closed, the organs will form a large soft lump under the skin resembling a hernia and the dog will experience moderate pain. If the skin sutures are open, the internal organs will protrude completely out of the incision and the dog will experience severe pain. In both cases, the dog may lick and chew at the affected area. Can be caused by a breakdown of the tissues around the incision or by the dog biting at its stitches. Most commonly occurs in abdominal surgery and involves the intestines or other abdominal organs. Usually happens within one week of surgery.

WHAT TO DO
- **Consult your veterinarian. Early treatment is important.** Surgery is required to replace the organs and restore sutures.
- To protect exposed organs, cover them immediately with a moistened towel. Tie the towel around the dog and keep it moistened so the exposed tissues will not become dry.
- As a prevention: Observe the incision closely after your dog has undergone surgery. Consult your veterinarian if there is swelling or the dog licks at the incision. Do not let it chew at exposed organs. This seriously complicates repair and recovery. Try to restrict exercise for 2 weeks following surgery.

INGUINAL HERNIA

SYMPTOMS

A bulge can be seen in the dog's groin, most noticeably when it stands on its hind legs. Caused by intestines and other internal structures passing through a defect in the closure of the inguinal canal, a small hole in the abdominal muscles where the nerves and arteries leave the abdomen and enter the hind legs in the groin area. The intestinal structures that come through are likely to become squeezed and twisted, cutting off the blood supply to these structures and causing them to die. A major problem that may affect one or both sides of the groin. Tends to be hereditary. May be present from birth, but often is not noticed until the dog is at least one year old. The size of the bulge varies according to what has come through, but it tends to be fairly large.

WHAT TO DO
- **Consult your veterinarian. Early treatment is important.** Usually requires surgery.

PERINEAL HERNIA

SYMPTOMS

Large, soft, protruding swelling on one or both sides of the anus or circling the anus completely. Severe difficulty defecating. The dog remains in the defecating position longer than usual. Straining. The dog may defecate in the house. It may also have difficulty urinating. Severe distress. Caused by a breakdown of the tissues around the anus that hold the abdominal structures in place, permitting these structures to shift their position. The resulting swelling around the anus may contain fatty tissue, the bladder or parts of the rectum or intestine. The consequence of any condition that makes the dog strain while defecating over a long period of time, such as obstipation, prostatitis, tumors, urolithiasis or cystitis.

WHAT TO DO

- **Consult your veterinarian.** Surgery is required. Castration is often recommended.
- As a prevention, consult your veterinarian if you observe your dog straining to defecate, particularly if it has a known history of prostate disease. Straining is never normal and must not be allowed to continue for any extended length of time.

SCROTAL HERNIA

SYMPTOMS

One or both sides of the scrotum become enlarged. The scrotum may seem to contain more than two testicles. Caused by a loop of intestine or other abdominal structure entering the male scrotum through the tract normally followed by the testicles when they descend from the abdomen. The abdominal structures that come through are likely to become squeezed and twisted, cutting off the blood supply to these structures and causing them to die. A major problem that can occur when the opening from the abdomen to the scrotum is unusually large. Tends to be hereditary.

WHAT TO DO

- **Consult your veterinarian. Early treatment is important.** Usually requires surgery.

UMBILICAL HERNIA

SYMPTOMS

A "bubble" at the umbilicus (belly button) containing fatty abdominal tissue, a section of intestine or other abdominal structures. Caused when internal structures pass through an abnormal opening in the muscles that form the abdominal wall at the umbilicus. The intact outer skin holds these structures in place and prevents them from becoming exposed. If these structures become squeezed or twisted, their blood supply may be cut off and they may die. Tends to be a hereditary defect in which the abdominal wall does not close fully following birth. Most common in puppies. The hernia can vary in size but is usually small.

WHAT TO DO

- **Consult your veterinarian.** Small umbilical hernias are generally not serious and may not require treatment. Hernias that are large, constricted or contain abdominal structures should be surgically repaired.

INFECTIOUS DISEASES

BRUCELLOSIS

SYMPTOMS

This bacterial infection tends to affect males and pregnant females. In the pregnant female, symptoms may include: Sudden abortion during the last 3 weeks of pregnancy. The puppies are stillborn or die within a few days of birth. Recurrent abortions or stillbirths. Swollen lymph nodes. Painful swollen joints. In the male, symptoms may include: Infection of the prostate gland. Swelling, extreme sensitivity and possible infection in the testicles. Infertility. Swollen lymph nodes. Painful swollen joints.

INCUBATION

Unknown.

DURATION

Extended.

COMMUNICABILITY

Highly contagious to dogs. Humans can also be infected. Passed by direct contact with infectious placental and uterine discharges or by sexual contact with an infected animal.

WHAT TO DO

- **Consult your veterinarian immediately.** An infected animal may have to be neutered or destroyed to keep the disease from spreading.
- Keep the infected dog isolated from the other dogs in the household.

- Since brucellosis can be passed to humans, infected animals and their discharge should not be handled.
- As a prevention, if there is an epidemic of the disease in your area, ask your vet to give your dog a negative

brucella test before allowing it to breed. Also make sure that the animal your dog is to breed with has had the test.

DISTEMPER

SYMPTOMS

Sneezing. Coughing. Vomiting. Diarrhea. Loss of appetite. Conjunctivitis. The eyes and nose exude pus. Depression. Moderate fever. Gradual weight loss and dehydration. In the advanced stage, the brain and spinal cord may be affected, and further symptoms can include twitching, chomping of the jaws, progressive weakness in the legs and convulsions. A common, very severe viral infection. One of the most devastating canine illnesses, particularly if it affects the brain or spinal cord. Usually occurs only in unvaccinated dogs. Most frequent and serious in unvaccinated puppies.

INCUBATION

7 to 10 days.

DURATION

Can be quickly fatal to young puppies or last for months in older dogs.

COMMUNICABILITY

Highly contagious to other dogs. Passed by airborne droplets or contact with infected vomit, stool or urine. The virus may live for up to 3 months in moist indoor areas.

WHAT TO DO

- **Consult your veterinarian. Early treatment is important.** May require hospitalization.
- When the dog gets back home, it will have to be nursed with care until it fully recovers. Be sure to give it nourishing food when it will eat and to keep it warm and dry.
- To keep the disease from infecting the other dogs in your home, be sure to wash your hands thoroughly and change your clothes after handling an affected dog or coming into direct contact with its surroundings.
- Can be prevented by inoculation and annual boosters.
- If you suspect distemper in a dog, isolate it from the other dogs in the household and vaccinate any that have not been inoculated in the previous 12 months.

INFECTIOUS HEPATITIS

SYMPTOMS

Loss of appetite. High fever. Excessive thirst. Conjunctivitis. Tenderness or severe pain in the abdomen. Vomiting and diarrhea, sometimes containing blood in advanced cases. The dog may show few symptoms in the early stages. Advanced symptoms are often mistaken for acute poisoning. A viral infection that usually occurs only in unvaccinated dogs. Most common and severe in unvaccinated puppies.

INCUBATION

2 to 9 days.

DURATION

Usually 5 to 14 days, but varies according to severity. Can be quickly fatal to young puppies.

COMMUNICABILITY

Highly contagious to other dogs. Passed by airborne droplets or contact with infected urine or stool. The virus remains present in the urine of affected dogs for up to 6 months following infection. Survives 3 to 11 days on solid objects.

WHAT TO DO

- **Consult your veterinarian. Early treatment is important.**
- To keep the disease from infecting the other dogs in your home, be sure to wash your hands thoroughly and change your clothes after handling an affected dog or coming into direct contact with its surroundings.
- Can be prevented by inoculation and annual boosters.
- If you suspect infectious hepatitis in a dog, isolate it from the other dogs in the household and vaccinate any that have not been inoculated in the previous 12 months.

KENNEL COUGH (INFECTIOUS TRACHEOBRONCHITIS)

SYMPTOMS

Dry, hacking cough. Gagging, as if something were caught in the throat, sometimes producing small amounts of fluid. Occasional diarrhea, fever or loss of appetite. A mixed infection of the upper respiratory system caused by viruses and virus-like particles. Severity varies.

INCUBATION
5 to 10 days.

DURATION
3 to 5 weeks.

COMMUNICABILITY
Highly contagious to other dogs. Passed through direct contact with infected dogs or contaminated objects or droppings. Often contracted after a dog has been boarded or groomed at a kennel or been walked in a contaminated area.

WHAT TO DO
- **Consult your veterinarian.**
- To control coughing and gagging, give the dog a cough suppressant made for people (child's dosage for a small or medium dog; adult's dosage for a large or giant dog). See **ADMINISTERING LIQUID MEDICINE,** page 220.
- To keep the other dogs in your home from being infected, be sure to wash your hands thoroughly and change your clothes after handling an affected dog or coming into direct contact with its surroundings.
- Inoculation may prevent the illness or reduce its severity.
- If you suspect kennel cough in a dog, isolate it from the other dogs in the household and vaccinate any that have not been inoculated in the previous 12 months.

LEPTOSPIROSIS

SYMPTOMS
Vomiting. Loss of appetite. Conjunctivitis. Excessive thirst. Labored breathing. Muscle stiffness and reluctance to walk. Bloody diarrhea. High fever. Frequent urination. Red patches in the mouth. Symptoms come on rapidly and may vary from mild to severe. A common infectious disease caused by a spirochete.

INCUBATION
5 to 15 days.

DURATION
Varies according to severity.

COMMUNICABILITY
Highly contagious to other unvaccinated dogs. Can be passed to humans. Communicable through direct contact with affected animals, airborne droplets or urine. May be passed through the skin and affect unborn puppies.

WHAT TO DO
- **Consult your veterinarian.**
- To keep the disease from infecting other unvaccinated dogs in your home or yourself, be sure to wash your hands thoroughly and change your clothes after handling an affected dog or coming into direct contact with its surroundings.
- Can be prevented by inoculation and semi-annual boosters.

RABIES

SYMPTOMS
May include: Severe changes in the dog's personality; it may show vicious, aggressive behavior, become unusually affectionate, keep itself hidden or take to roaming long distances away from home. Unusual subdued, hoarse cry. The dog's jaw hangs open and it drools saliva. (May be mistaken for a foreign object in the mouth.) The dog cannot drink and becomes dehydrated. In advanced cases, further symptoms include progressive paralysis and convulsions. A viral disease that only affects dogs that have not been vaccinated against it.

INCUBATION
Varies widely. Symptoms develop anywhere from 12 days to 1 year after infection.

DURATION
Always fatal, usually within 4 days after symptoms appear.

COMMUNICABILITY
Communicable to all warm-blooded animals that have not been vaccinated against it, including human beings. Passed by the saliva of an infected animal in a bite, open wound or scrape. Under certain conditions, can also be passed by airborne droplets.

WHAT TO DO
- **Consult your veterinarian immediately.**
- If you suspect rabies in your dog, confine or isolate it without handling it. Use extreme caution. Remember that rabies can be passed to humans.
- As a further precaution, confine any pets that have come into contact with a dog you suspect may be rabid.
- Rabies can be prevented by inoculation and annual booster shots.

METABOLIC AND HORMONAL DISORDERS

DIABETES MELLITUS

SYMPTOMS

Develop slowly and may include: Increased thirst and urination. Ravenous appetite with weight loss or no gain. Weakness. Cataracts. Advanced cases may include: Loss of appetite. Vomiting. Depression. Coma. An inadequate production of insulin by the pancreas, causing an improper use of sugar and other metabolic problems. May also result from the body's inability to utilize insulin. Most commonly occurs in female dogs over 7 years old.

WHAT TO DO

- **Consult your veterinarian. Early treatment is essential.**
- Usually requires ongoing daily injections of insulin at home. To determine the proper dosage, you will have to test the dog's urine daily to discover the current level of glucose.
- To balance the daily doses of insulin, you will also have to regulate the dog's food intake and activity level.

HORMONAL HAIR LOSS

SYMPTOMS

Symmetrical hair loss on both sides of the body, particularly on the back, rump and torso. Usually, the dog does not scratch at itself. Caused by deficient or excessive hormonal production.

WHAT TO DO

- **Consult your veterinarian.** Hormones or surgery may be required.

HYPOGLYCEMIA

SYMPTOMS

Occur within 1 to 4 hours after the dog has been in a stressful situation. May include: Loss of energy or "fading." The dog's legs are weak and wobbly, and it cannot stand. Exhaustion. In extreme cases, coma and death. Caused when the dog's blood sugar drops significantly below normal levels. Often a reaction to stress, such as being wormed or vaccinated by the veterinarian. Commonly occurs in young puppies that refuse to eat because of a radical change in diet. Most common in small dogs, particularly toys, under a year old. Usually outgrown after the first year.

WHAT TO DO

- **Consult your veterinarian.**
- If you suspect hypoglycemia, immediately give your dog 2 or 3 tablespoons of honey, sugar water or Karo syrup. See **ADMINISTERING LIQUID MEDICINE,** page 220. The dog should recover completely within an hour, but repeat the treatment daily for 3 days.
- Consult your veterinarian if the dog does not recover within 2 hours after you have first treated it. The symptoms may be caused by some other condition.

HYPOTHYROIDISM

SYMPTOMS

Develop and progress slowly. May include: Gradual decline in vigor and physical activity. Increased sleep. Weight gain or obesity. Changes in the facial features. Thinning of the hair on the back and stomach, progressing to bald spots. The dog seeks warmth and resists going out into the cold. It becomes increasingly more lethargic. Caused by a lowering of the metabolic process resulting from an inadequate supply of thyroid hormone. Most common in dogs over 6 years old. Often mistaken for the deteriorations of old age.

WHAT TO DO

- **Consult your veterinarian.** Hormone replacement generally results in improved activity level and new hair growth.

PSEUDOCYESIS (FALSE PREGNANCY)

SYMPTOMS

May include: Enlarged abdomen (not as enlarged as in a true pregnancy). Enlarged breasts. Production of milk. In the later stages, may also include symptoms of impending whelping such as agitation, panting and preparing a nest in a dark closet or under a bed. **The**

condition usually develops about 2 months after the female's last heat period and lasts around 2 or 3 weeks. Believed to be caused by a hormone imbalance. Affected dogs are also likely to develop other hormone-related illnesses such as mammary tumors, pyometra and uterine cancer.

WHAT TO DO
- **Consult your veterinarian.** Most dogs recover without treatment.
- Unless puppies are desired, the dog should be spayed to prevent recurrence and the possible development of other hormone-related illnesses.

NEUROLOGICAL DISORDERS: BRAIN

BRAIN TUMOR

SYMPTOMS

Vary according to the size and location of the tumor. May include: Personality changes. Weakness. Seizures. Paralysis. Unconsciousness. Changes in bodily functions. If the breathing or heart functions are affected the dog may die. An abnormal growth of cells within the skull that causes pressure on the brain. The underlying cause is unknown. Usually develops slowly, with symptoms progressing from mild to severe as the resulting pressure increases. Can occur at any age but most common in older dogs.

WHAT TO DO
- **Consult your veterinarian.**

IDIOPATHIC EPILEPSY

SYMPTOMS

Vary according to severity. Mild seizures may involve just a short period of body stiffening and confusion. In more severe cases, symptoms may include: Falling. Stiffening of the body. Chomping of the jaws. Paddling motion of the legs. Jerky, uncontrollable movements, usually lasting 2 to 3 minutes. Voiding of the bladder and bowels. The dog is conscious but unresponsive. Caused by a sudden discharge of electrical impulses anywhere in the brain. The size and location of the affected area determine the kinds of symptoms seen and their severity. The underlying cause is unknown but thought to be hereditary. Not usually seen in dogs under 1 year old, but can occur at any age. Symptoms can be brought on by any kind of excitement, such as a ringing doorbell or a visit to the veterinarian. The disease is lifelong, although some dogs have only 1 or 2 seizures a year, while others have more frequent, even daily episodes.

WHAT TO DO
- **Consult your veterinarian.** Seizures can usually be controlled by anticonvulsive medications, which will allow the affected dog to lead a reasonably normal life.
- **For emergency treatment:** See **CONVULSIONS & SEIZURES,** page 173.
- Be aware that an affected dog may show fright and disorientation for 15 minutes or more following a seizure. **Do not** handle it during this period.
- Although convulsions are rarely fatal unless repetitive, tell your veterinarian about all of them, no matter how brief or infrequent. If left untreated, they tend to become more frequent and severe.

TRAUMA TO THE BRAIN

SYMPTOMS

Vary with the severity and exact location of the injury to the brain. Symptoms may appear immediately or not until hours later. They are not usually localized in a particular part of the body. May include: Semiconsciousness or unconsciousness. Disorientation. Difficulty breathing or moving parts of the body. Bleeding from the ears, nose or mouth. Convulsions. Wild, uncontrollable movement. Frenzied, aimless running. A sudden injury to the brain caused by a severe blow to the head, a car accident or a collision with a fixed object (common in puppies). The symptoms are commonly produced by a depressed fracture of the skull or bleeding within the skull which causes pressure on the brain.

WHAT TO DO
- **Consult your veterinarian. Early treatment is important.**
- As a precaution, if your dog is hit by a car or subjected to a serious head blow, try to keep it calm and still until seen by the veterinarian.

VESTIBULAR DISEASE

SYMPTOMS

Sudden severe twisting of the head and neck to one side. Apparent dizziness. The dog may lose its balance, fall down and roll in one direction like a barrel. Rapid eye movements. Vomiting. An inflammation of the inner ear, nerves or areas of the brain that control the sense of body position. Very often mistaken for a stroke.

WHAT TO DO

• **Consult your veterinarian. Early treatment is important.** Some dogs are left with a slight permanent head tilt but still function normally.

NEUROLOGICAL DISORDERS: SPINE

INTERVERTEBRAL DISC DISEASE

SYMPTOMS

Vary according to severity and the exact place on the spine that is affected. Can be mild or severe, sudden or progressive. May include: Shaking. Panting. Anxiety. The dog doesn't jump, climb stairs or move. It holds its neck inflexibly or drags its rear toes, feet or legs. Paralysis. Loss of sensation. Interference with normal bladder or bowel functions. The dog may howl in pain when approached or moved. A degenerative process within the doughnut-like shock-absorbing discs between the bones of the spine. The tough outside of the discs breaks down and allows the jelly-like inner material to press against the spinal cord or nerves. The pressure is increased when this material causes the spinal cord to become inflamed. Can occur anywhere along the spine. Most common in Dachshunds, Lhasa Apsos, Shih Tzus, Beagles, Bassets and Cocker Spaniels.

WHAT TO DO

• **Consult your veterinarian. The disease responds best to early treatment.**
• Transport the dog to the vet with a minimum of movement. See **TRANSPORTING A DOG,** page 204.
• Until you transport it, keep the dog as immobile as possible, preferably in a cage or box. Unnecessary movement can cause sudden partial or total paralysis of the hind legs.
• To relieve its pain, give the dog buffered aspirin with its food (one 5 grain tablet for a small dog; two tablets for a larger dog). See **ADMINISTERING PILLS,** page 221.
• Since this is a recurrent condition, a dog with known disc problems should be watched closely. At the first sign of any pain, immobilize it until your veterinarian can see it.
• As a precaution, limit jumping and other vigorous exercise in an affected dog.

TRAUMA TO THE SPINAL COLUMN

SYMPTOMS

Vary according to severity and the exact location of the spinal injury. Symptoms usually affect parts of the body behind the point of the injury. May include: Pain. Weak and wobbly rear legs. Muscle spasms in the rear legs. Partial or total paralysis of the rear legs. Limp tail. Loss of sensation. Depression of the backbone at the point of injury. In severe cases, symptoms may also include: Stiff, fully extended front legs. Loss of bowel and bladder control. Usually caused by a car accident or being hit violently on the back with a stick or other object. Usually involves a fracture or dislocation of the spinal bones and pressure against the spinal cord.

WHAT TO DO

• **Consult your veterinarian. Early treatment is important.** Depending upon their severity, the symptoms may be temporary or permanent. Recovery is slow.
• Transport the dog to the vet with a minimum of movement. See **TRANSPORTING A DOG,** page 204.
• Until you transport it, keep the dog as immobile as possible, preferably in a cage or box. Unnecessary movement can worsen the injuries.

PARASITES: EXTERNAL

EAR MITES

APPEARANCE
Virtually invisible to the naked eye.

SYMPTOMS
Affect the inside of the ear. Often difficult to detect. May include dark soil-like material. The dog may or may not scratch at its ear or shake its head with agitation.

WHAT TO DO
• Treat the dog at home with commercial ear mite medication made especially for use on dogs. See **APPLYING MEDICINE TO THE EARS,** page 223. After each application, vigorously massage the outside of the ear, then clean the inside carefully with a cotton-tipped swab. See **CLEANING THE DOG'S EARS,** page 35. Continue applications until the dog has recovered. May require extended treatment.
• Consult your veterinarian if the dog does not respond to treatment.
• Ear mites are easily passed to cats and other dogs. As a precaution, treat the unaffected animals in your home once a week until the affected dog is cured. (Treat a cat with medication made especially for use on cats.)
• To help prevent ear mites, treat your dog regularly over its entire body with mite, flea or tick insecticide made especially for use on dogs. Also apply the insecticide to the dog's bedding and the other areas it frequents.

FLEAS

APPEARANCE
Small, dark, flat, hard-shelled and wingless. Quick-moving. When seen off the dog, they jump rather than crawl. Dark specks of flea excrement on the dog's fur will turn red when moistened with water.

SYMPTOMS
Often infest the back, abdomen and the base of the tail. Bald or reddened areas may indicate flea allergy, a common problem. The dog probably will scratch at itself. In advanced cases, the dog may chew at the infested areas.

WHAT TO DO
• Treat the dog at home with flea powder, collar, bath or spray made especially for use on dogs. Follow the accompanying directions carefully. If you give the dog a flea collar, **do not** also treat it with a flea bath. Using both can cause serious poisoning. Always restrain the dog before administering treatment. See **RESTRAINTS,** page 209.
• Discard or thoroughly wash the dog's bedding, and make sure to keep the bedding clean.
• For 4 to 6 weeks following treatment (or as long as necessary), apply flea powder weekly to the dog's bedding and the other areas it frequents.
• **Consult your veterinarian** if the dog does not respond to treatment or if it shows an allergic reaction to fleas. See **FLEA ALLERGY DERMATITIS,** page 131.
• As a precaution, treat all dogs and cats in the household for fleas. Fleas can be passed to other pets and humans and can cause anemia in very young puppies and kittens. Only use dog medication for dogs and cat medication for cats.
• If repeated treatment of animals and animal areas does not end the problem, you may have to decontaminate the entire house, particularly if it is winter.

LICE

APPEARANCE
Extremely small, white, flat and wingless. Move by crawling. Eggs attached to the dog's hairs may appear silver or white.

SYMPTOMS
Scratching. Biting at self. Restlessness.

WHAT TO DO
• Treat the dog at home with parasite bath or powder made especially for use on dogs. Follow the accompanying directions carefully. Always restrain the dog before administering treatment. See **RESTRAINTS,** page 209.
• **Consult your veterinarian** if the dog does not respond to treatment.
• Lice can be passed to other dogs and to cats. They most commonly infest pets living on a farm. As a precaution, treat the unaffected animals in your home until the affected dog is cured. (Treat a cat with medication made especially for use on cats.)

MAGGOTS

APPEARANCE

Light yellow carrot-shaped worms about 1/2 inch long. Worm-like movement. May be mistaken for tapeworms. Maggots are the hatched larvae of flies that have laid their eggs in dead or decaying tissue.

SYMPTOMS

Flies seen around open wounds or dead tissue, particularly around the anus. Maggots crawl in and under the dog's flesh.

WHAT TO DO

• **Consult your veterinarian.**

• As a precaution, try to keep flies away from old or weakened dogs, particularly in warm weather.

TICKS

APPEARANCE

Relatively large, dark, flat or grape-like, and wingless. Move by crawling. The legs can be seen if you move the tick with your finger. Only the mouth is embedded below the surface, not the entire body. The body looks like a mole or wart on the skin.

SYMPTOMS

Few symptoms, so it is important to examine your dog regularly. Ticks often affect the ears but may appear anywhere on the body. The dog may lick at embedded ticks.

WHAT TO DO

• Treat the dog at home with tick spray, powder, collar or medicated bath made especially for use on dogs. (Follow the accompanying directions carefully. If you give the dog a flea collar, **do not** also treat it with a flea bath. Using both can cause serious poisoning.) Always restrain the dog before administering treatment. See **RESTRAINTS,** page 209. Wait about half an hour, then remove the dead ticks with tweezers. Apply "tamed" iodine or other antiseptic to the bites.

• Apply tick powder or spray to the dog's bedding and the other areas it frequents. If the dog has ticks in cold weather, your home may be contaminated and a professional exterminator may be necessary.

• **Consult your veterinarian** if the dog does not respond to treatment.

• As a precaution, be sure to wash your hands thoroughly after you handle your dog. Ticks can be passed to other animals and humans, as can some of the diseases they carry.

PARASITES: INTERNAL

COCCIDIOSIS

SYMPTOMS

Diarrhea, with or without dark tar-like blood. Weight loss. The parasite is passed by contact with contaminated stool. Frequently affects puppies, to whom it can be fatal, particularly after contact with many other puppies and following periods of high stress.

WHAT TO DO

• **Consult your veterinarian.** Administer the follow-up treatment he prescribes. Responds well to treatment and usually does not recur.

• As a precaution, have the veterinarian analyze a specimen of your dog's stool once a year. Also have the analysis made before you buy a puppy or breed a female. If necessary, have the dog wormed. Coccidiosis is often overlooked by commercial breeders in routine wormings.

HEARTWORM DISEASE

SYMPTOMS

Coughing and tiring during exercise, progressing to a chronic cough with labored breathing. Symptoms develop slowly, sometimes over a period of years, as the **worms multiply and increase the parasitic load on the dog. In an advanced case, the dog may develop a fluid-filled "potbelly."** Caused by the larvae of a parasite worm that have been transmitted to the dog by the bite of an infected mosquito. Mature worms, usually between 6 and 12 inches long, live in the chambers of the heart and its major blood vessels but mainly affect the lungs.

WHAT TO DO
- **Consult your veterinarian.** The treatment, which is aimed at killing the worms, can be dangerous to the dog.

- As a precaution, have the veterinarian check your dog for heartworm before the mosquito season begins.
- If the dog is unaffected, you can easily prevent this disease by administering heartworm medication throughout the mosquito season and for the following 60 days.
- As a further precaution, try to protect your dog from mosquitos as much as possible.

HOOKWORMS

SYMPTOMS
May include: Diarrhea, with or without dark or tar-like blood. (The parasite is not visible in the stool.) In advanced cases, the gums, tongue and inner linings of the eyelids become pale and whitish. Affects all ages but particularly dangerous to puppies. May be passed to a puppy before birth or through its mother's milk. Can also be contracted by contact with contaminated stool or surroundings.

WHAT TO DO
- Consult your veterinarian. Early treatment is important.

- Back home, administer the prescribed follow-up treatment and give the dog nourishing food to maintain its strength.
- To prevent reinfestation, maintain particularly good sanitation of all areas the dog frequents, especially if it is a paper-trained puppy or a stool eating dog. See **STOOL EATING,** page 111.
- As a precaution, have the veterinarian analyze a specimen of your dog's stool once a year. Also have the analysis made before you buy a puppy or breed a female. If necessary, have the dog wormed.

ROUNDWORMS

SYMPTOMS
Stool or vomit may contain whitish, spaghetti-like coiled worms from 2 to 6 inches long. Other symptoms may include: "Potbelly." Dull coat. Listlessness. Restlessness. Diarrhea, in advanced cases. The parasite may be passed to a puppy before birth, or through its mother's milk. Can also be contracted by contact with an affected dog or contaminated surroundings.

WHAT TO DO
- Consult your veterinarian. Early treatment is important.
- Back home, administer the prescribed follow-up treat-

ment and give the dog nourishing food to maintain its strength. Be sure to wash your hands thoroughly whenever you handle the dog.
- To prevent reinfestation, maintain particularly good sanitation of all the areas the dog frequents, especially if it is a paper-trained puppy or a stool eating dog. See **STOOL EATING,** page 111.
- As a precaution, have the veterinarian analyze a specimen of your dog's stool once a year. Also have the analysis made before you buy a puppy or breed a female. If necessary, have the dog wormed.

TAPEWORMS

SYMPTOMS
Flat, rice-like white or cream-colored segments 1/2 inch long may be seen around the dog's tail or in its droppings or bedding. (May be mistaken for MAGGOTS; see page 124.) The dog may scoot on its rear end. It may develop a ravenous appetite but does not gain weight or may actually lose it. The parasite can be passed to the dog when it eats infected fleas, prey or raw meat or fish. Routine stool analysis may fail to reveal the presence of tapeworm eggs.

WHAT TO DO
- Consult your veterinarian.
- Back home administer the prescribed follow-up treatment and give the dog nourishing food to maintain its strength. Also treat the dog for **FLEAS;** see page 123. (Tapeworms are difficult to get rid of permanently because infected fleas can reinfest the dog and medications are not as potent as those used for other parasites.)
- As a precaution, do not let the dog eat prey or raw meat or fish.

TOXOPLASMOSIS

SYMPTOMS
May include: Difficulty breathing. Diarrhea. Loss of coordination. In advanced cases, there may be a wide range of other symptoms, depending on the part of the body that has been infected. (The parasite affects the intestines initially but then spreads to other areas of the body including the brain, liver, eyes and lungs. Toxoplasmosis should be suspected whenever an illness in any part of the body does not respond to the appropriate treatment.) The parasite can be passed to a dog before birth by an affected mother. It can also be contracted by direct contact with contaminated cat feces or by eating infected raw meat, fish or prey. Most severe in puppies.

WHAT TO DO
- **Consult your veterinarian.** Requires prolonged treatment.
- As a precaution, do not let the dog eat prey or raw meat or fish. Also try to keep it away from areas that may be contaminated by infected cat stool. The parasite eggs can live in soil for many months.

WHIPWORMS

SYMPTOMS
May include: Loss of condition. Weight loss or chronic thinness. Periodic or chronic bouts of foul-smelling diarrhea, with or without dark or tar-like blood. In advanced cases, the gums, tongue and inner linings of the eyelids become pale and whitish. Contracted by eating soil contaminated by whipworm larvae.

WHAT TO DO
- **Consult your veterinarian.**
- Back home, administer the prescribed follow-up treatment and give the dog nourishing food to maintain its strength.
- To prevent reinfestation, maintain particularly good sanitation of all the areas the dog frequents, especially if it is a paper-trained puppy or a stool eating dog. See **STOOL EATING,** page 111. Continue to observe the dog closely. Particularly in stool eating dogs, whipworms often become a chronic problem, requiring worming twice a year.
- As a precaution, have the veterinarian analyze a specimen of your dog's stool once a year. Also have the analysis made before you buy a puppy or breed a female. If necessary have the dog wormed. Routine analysis of normal stool may fail to reveal the presence of whipworm eggs, although they will be found in an affected dog's diarrhea.

RESPIRATORY DISORDERS

BRONCHIAL ASTHMA

SYMPTOMS
Severe dry, hacking cough. Wheezing. May progress to severe difficulty breathing. Symptoms may not be present continually.

WHAT TO DO
- **Consult your veterinarian.**

COLLAPSED TRACHEA

SYMPTOMS
Brief periods of difficult breathing. Coughing. When the dog pulls against its leash or becomes excited, it makes a dry honking noise that sounds like a duck or goose. During these episodes, the gums, tongue and inner linings of the eyelids may become somewhat blue. When the episodes pass, the dog seems to return to normal. Caused by a malformation of the trachea so that it loses its round, cylindrical shape and becomes flattened, making it partially closed as the dog breathes in. The cause is unknown but may be hereditary. Seems to be most common in toy and miniature breeds.

WHAT TO DO
- **Consult your veterinarian.**
- Affected dogs should wear harnesses rather than collars and be kept from excessive exercise and excitement.
- Since this condition may be hereditary, it may be preferable not to breed affected dogs.

OBSTRUCTION OF THE NASAL PASSAGES

SYMPTOMS

Pawing at the nose. Sneezing. Nasal discharge or blood from one or both nostrils. The dog may shake or throw its head violently in an effort to dislodge the obstruction to its breathing. The obstruction may be caused by a tumor, infection or a foreign object lodged in the nasal passage.

WHAT TO DO

• **Consult your veterinarian.** Foreign objects can usually be removed. Tumors require difficult surgery.

PNEUMONIA

SYMPTOMS

Loss of appetite. Severe depression. Fever. Dehydration. Extreme weakness. Deep, moist cough, sometimes with gagging. In severe cases: Rapid, shallow, difficult breathing. The dog may carry its head elevated and show pain if lifted by the chest. The tongue, gums and inner linings of the eyelids become progressively more blue. Caused by an inflammation of the lungs resulting from an inhalation of swallowed or vomited material, or from bacteria, fungi or a viral infection.

WHAT TO DO

• **Consult your veterinarian.** Early treatment is important.

• Your dog will require good nursing care at home. Keep it comfortable and quiet and avoid putting it in stressful situations that may cause it to breathe heavily.

• Coughing is never normal in a dog and should always be brought to the veterinarian's attention.

PNEUMOTHORAX

SYMPTOMS

Severe labored breathing. The gums, tongue and inner linings of the eyelids may become progressively more blue. The dog's abdomen may rise and fall as it tries to breathe. Caused by air entering the chest from a ruptured lung or a puncture or laceration in the chest. The air surrounds and presses against the lungs, preventing them from expanding fully as the dog tries to breathe.

WHAT TO DO

• **Consult your veterinarian.** Early treatment is important.
• After treatment, watch the dog closely for recurring symptoms that indicate air is still leaking into its chest.

PULMONARY EDEMA

SYMPTOMS

Coughing. Difficulty breathing. Shallow, rapid breathing through the mouth. Wheezing. Severe anxiety. The dog may refuse to lie down. Caused by an abnormal accumulation of fluid in the lungs. Usually a complication of other conditions such as congestive heart failure, heart muscle disease and brain tumor. Depending on the cause, may develop suddenly or slowly. May occur suddenly as a result of an allergic reaction, electric shock, drowning, or a snake or spider bite.

WHAT TO DO

• **Consult your veterinarian.** Early treatment is important.

• Carefully transport the dog to the vet, making sure it has plenty of cool, fresh air. See **TRANSPORTING A DOG,** page 204.

• Additional stress will worsen the symptoms, so try to keep the dog from becoming excited, particularly while you are taking it to the vet.

REVERSE SNEEZE SYNDROME

SYMPTOMS

Recurrent episodes of what sounds like sneezing, snoring or snorting, except that the dog is drawing air in rather than expelling it out. May last between 15 seconds and 1 minute. The dog may also show some respiratory difficulty. Can be caused by a throat spasm or postnasal drip.

WHAT TO DO

• **Consult your veterinarian** if the condition occurs frequently or lasts for extended periods.

SKELETAL DISORDERS

ELBOW DYSPLASIA

SYMPTOMS

Pain. Reduced use of the limb. Chronic or intermittent limping. A hereditary condition of the small bones in the elbow that prevents them from fusing together at the appropriate stage of maturity to form a normal, functioning joint.

WHAT TO DO

• **Consult your veterinarian.** Surgery is usually required.

• To reduce stress on the joint, keep the dog's weight as low as possible and avoid vigorous or extended exercise.

• Because the condition is hereditary, an afflicted dog should not be allowed to breed.

• As the animal gets older, watch for the onset of arthritis in the elbow joints; see **OSTEOARTHRITIS**, below.

HIP DYSPLASIA

SYMPTOMS

May first be noted in puppies as poor conformation of the hind legs or "cow hocks." As the dog matures, symptoms may include: Weakness and pain in the hind legs when the dog tries to stand or climb stairs. Limping. Chronic lameness or malfunctioning of the hind legs. Rabbit-like hopping. A hereditary, progressively degenerative joint disease that affects the way the bones of the hind legs fit into the hip socket. Present from birth but often difficult to detect in puppies. Most common and pronounced in large and giant dogs.

WHAT TO DO

• **Consult your veterinarian.** Surgery may be required.

• Give the dog buffered aspirin to relieve its pain (one 5 grain tablet for a small or medium dog; two tablets for a large or giant dog). See **ADMINISTERING PILLS**, page 221.

• To reduce stress on the joint, keep the dog's weight as low as possible and avoid vigorous or extended exercise.

• Because the condition is hereditary, an afflicted dog should not be allowed to breed.

• Arthritic changes usually occur in the hip joint as the distress progresses; see **OSTEOARTHRITIS**, below.

NUTRITIONAL SECONDARY HYPERPARATHYROIDISM

SYMPTOMS

Painful, swollen elbows and front wrist joints. The toes are widespread and splayed outward. Fractures, with little or no reason. A major disease of puppies in which calcium is drawn from the bones, causing them to become progressively thin and fragile and subject to fractures. Caused by an imbalance of calcium and phosphorus in the diet. A common result of an all meat diet, especially if it consists of heart, liver and kidneys.

WHAT TO DO

• **Consult your veterinarian.** He may prescribe calcium supplements or recommend a diet that contains a proper balance of calcium and phosphorus.

• As a prevention, avoid feeding your puppy an all meat diet, particularly one made up of heart, liver and kidneys.

OSTEOARTHRITIS (DEGENERATIVE JOINT DISEASE)

SYMPTOMS

Tenderness and pain. Limping. Enlargement of the joint. A rubbing or grating sound may be heard when the joint is moved. A common chronic disease of the moveable joints involving deterioration of the cartilage. To protect itself, the joint makes structural changes such as growing excess bone. Can be the result of injury, a poor fit in the joint or misuse of the joint. May affect more than one joint. The condition often worsens as the dog grows older.

WHAT TO DO

• **Consult your veterinarian.** Treatment is aimed at relieving pain, restoring the function of the joint and preventing further degeneration. Ongoing medication may be required.

• Give the dog buffered aspirin to relieve its pain (one 5 grain tablet for a small or medium dog; two tablets for a large or giant dog). See **ADMINISTERING PILLS**, page 221.

• To reduce stress on the joint, keep the dog's weight as low as possible and avoid vigorous or extended exercise.

OSTEOCHONDRITIS DISSECANS

SYMPTOMS

Vary according to severity but may include: Lameness. Pain when the shoulder joint is extended. Gradual wasting away of the shoulder muscles. A disease that affects the large bones during the period of rapid growth. Causes pieces of cartilage overlying the bone at a joint to chip and break away, leaving a defect in the normally smooth cartilage surface. May affect one or more limbs.

WHAT TO DO

• **Consult your veterinarian.** Surgery may be required to repair the defects in the cartilage and bones.

• Confine the dog in a small area to limit the use of the affected limbs and provide rest and relaxation.

• Give the dog buffered aspirin to relieve its pain (one 5 grain tablet for a small or medium dog; two tablets for a large or giant dog). See **ADMINISTERING PILLS,** page 221.

• After treatment, continue to observe the dog closely for the onset of arthritis, which may beset the affected joints. See **OSTEOARTHRITIS,** page 128.

OSTEOMYELITIS

SYMPTOMS

The dog has a bone wound that does not heal. The wound drains fluid and pus and may develop a foul odor. The area around the wound is hot, swollen and painful. A bacterial infection within a bone commonly caused by bite wounds, compound fractures, bone surgery or other conditions where bacteria can reach the bone and the blood circulation in the area has been disturbed. Occasionally caused by a fungus. Usually affects the long bones. As the infection progresses, it begins to eat away the calcium and weaken the bone.

WHAT TO DO

• **Consult your veterinarian.** Surgery is usually required to clean out all the infected material. Long-term hospital and home treatment will probably be necessary.

PANOSTEITIS

SYMPTOMS

Sudden painful lameness, sometimes shifting from one leg to another. The affected area is extremely painful when touched. A disease of unknown cause that affects the long bones of growing dogs between 5 and 12 months old. Occasionally seen in older dogs. Most common in males. It is outgrown with age.

WHAT TO DO

• **Consult your veterinarian.** Treatment is aimed at reducing the pain and inflammation.

TRAUMA

SYMPTOMS

Less severe cases may include: Sprains, strains and bruises. Soreness. Reduced use of the affected part. Limping. More severe cases may include: Fractures or dislocations, most commonly in the leg or thigh. Acute, severe pain. Swelling. The dog carries its leg lame. Severe fractures may make a grating sound when the affected parts are moved. A sudden injury to the bones caused by car accidents, falls or severe blows.

WHAT TO DO

• **Consult your veterinarian.**

• **For emergency treatment of a severe trauma:** See **BREAKS: FRACTURES & DISLOCATIONS,** page 161.

• As a precaution, always consult your veterinarian in cases of prolonged mild or intermittent lameness.

SKIN DISORDERS

ABSCESS

SYMPTOMS

Soft swelling on the limbs or elsewhere on the body. The affected areas are tender and painful. The dog objects to being touched there but does not otherwise appear to be ill. In advanced stages, the swollen areas become open draining sores. A localized, encapsulated pus-forming infection under the skin. A common result of animal bites, fights and untreated injuries.

WHAT TO DO
• **Consult your veterinarian.**

• **For home care:** Apply hot compresses to help relieve discomfort and bring the abscess to a head. When the abscess opens, keep the area clean of discharge and debris.
• To prevent abscesses, treat all skin wounds promptly.

ANAPHYLAXIS

SYMPTOMS

Tremendous sudden swelling and thickening of the skin on the face, lips and eyelids. The eyes may be swollen nearly closed and the mouth greatly distorted. The dog's head may seem too large for its body. The dog may scratch violently at itself. The female's vulva may become swollen. An allergic reaction of the skin caused by an insect bite or something that has been eaten, inhaled or touched. Sometimes develops without any notable change in diet or environment. Not usually recurrent.

WHAT TO DO

• **Consult your veterinarian.**

• **For home care:** In mild cases, the dog usually recovers without treatment. Administer antihistamine syrup or antihistamine tablet (a child's dosage for a small or medium dog; an adult's dosage for a large or giant dog). See **ADMINISTERING LIQUID MEDICINE,** page 220, or **ADMINISTERING PILLS,** page 221.

• As a precaution, always advise your veterinarian of any allergic reaction.

BACTERIAL SKIN INFECTION (PYODERMA)

SYMPTOMS

Surface infections develop small pustules, which may rupture. The dog may lick or scratch at the irritated area. The affected skin becomes reddened and angry. As the infection progresses and affects deeper layers of skin, it may ulcerate, ooze pus and spread to cover larger areas of the body. Caused by the bacteria normally on the skin becoming infective. Tends to affect parts of the body where there are folds of skin, such as the nose, lips, vulva and between the toes. Bacterial infections on the vulva often affect female puppies under 1 year old, particularly if they have already been spayed. Often results from untreated cases of flea allergy dermatitis, and inhalant allergy dermatitis. May also be a result of skin irritation due to injury, moisture or collected debris. Often seen in connection with malnutrition, distemper or parasite infestation where the dog has become run-down. Tends to be recurrent, particularly when the deeper layers of skin are affected.

WHAT TO DO

• **Consult your veterinarian. Early treatment is important.** May require lengthy treatment or surgery to remove the folds that collect debris. Must be completely cured to prevent the progress of the infection or later recurrence.
• Try to prevent an affected dog from biting or licking the infected areas.
• As a prevention: Keep the areas of folding skin clean and dry, and apply petroleum jelly to protect them from saliva and moisture. Also keep the hair in these areas clipped short.

CONTACT ALLERGY DERMATITIS

SYMPTOMS

Angry red and inflamed paws, stomach or other part of the body that has come into contact with an irritating substance. The dog may worsen the condition by biting or chewing at the affected areas. An inflammatory reaction of the skin caused by direct contact with an irritating substance. Can occur on any part of the body. May be seasonal if caused by weeds, grass, etc., or chronic if caused by carpeting or similar materials.

WHAT TO DO

• **Consult your veterinarian.**
• Try to determine the source of irritation, then eliminate it.
• Observe for **BACTERIAL SKIN INFECTION,** see above.

DEMODECTIC MANGE

SYMPTOMS

Subtle hair loss around the cheeks and the corners of the mouth and eyes, which later spreads to the legs and chest. (Often difficult to detect. Can best be seen by examining the dog's fur against the direction of growth.) No scratching, except in some advanced

cases. Caused by a common external skin parasite. For unknown reasons, the parasite may affect some dogs in a litter or household but not others. Common in puppies more than 3 months old.

WHAT TO DO
• **Consult your veterinarian.** Treatment should be started early and continued until all symptoms are completely eliminated.

• As a precaution, continue to observe an affected dog after treatment. Demodectic mange may lead to **BACTERIAL SKIN INFECTION;** see page 130.

FLEA ALLERGY DERMATITIS

SYMPTOMS
Hair loss and extremely reddened skin, usually around the back and the base of the tail. Severe scratching and chewing at the irritated areas. Possible scabs or infection. Dark specks of flea excrement on the dog's skin that turn red when moistened with water. Fleas may or may not be seen. An allergic reaction to the saliva of fleas. Occurs wherever fleas are prevalent. Affects some dogs but not others.

WHAT TO DO
• **Consult your veterinarian** for treatment of the skin condition.

• Treat the dog and all other dogs and cats in your household for **FLEAS;** see page 123.

• Observe for **BACTERIAL SKIN INFECTION;** see page 130.

HIVES

SYMPTOMS
Small areas of localized swelling that may be limited to one region or distributed all over the dog. The dog may have a "checkerboard" or spotted appearance from the hair in the affected areas pointing in a slightly different direction from the surrounding hair. Temporary thickening of the affected skin. An allergic reaction of the skin caused by something that has been eaten, inhaled, injected or touched. Sometimes develops without any notable change in diet or environment. Not usually recurrent.

WHAT TO DO
• **Consult your veterinarian.**

• **For home care:** Administer antihistamine syrup or antihistamine tablet (a child's dosage for a small or medium dog; an adult's dosage for a large or giant dog). See **ADMINISTERING LIQUID MEDICINE,** page 220, or **ADMINISTERING PILLS,** page 221.

• As a precaution, always advise your veterinarian of any allergic reaction.

INHALANT ALLERGY DERMATITIS

SYMPTOMS
Severe scratching. Hair loss and extremely reddened skin, usually on the abdomen, neck, back and base of the tail, paws and face. The dog may bite or chew at the affected areas. In the acute form, a "hotspot" resembling eczema or a burn may occur, which becomes bald and oozes serum. Caused by sensitivity to one or more airborne irritants such as grass or ragweed pollen, wool or dust. Depending upon the source of irritation, the reaction can occur seasonally or chronically. Sea-sonal episodes take place at about the same time each year, occasionally skipping a year. Dogs with multiple allergies may show symptoms throughout the year.

WHAT TO DO
• **Consult your veterinarian.**
• Try to determine the source of irritation, then eliminate it.
• Observe for **BACTERIAL SKIN INFECTION;** see page 130.

LICK GRANULOMA

SYMPTOMS
Constant licking or biting at one spot, usually on top of the front paw near the wrist. Loss of hair around the bitten area. The affected skin becomes fat and angry looking. As the condition progresses, the skin thickens and may ulcerate, become infected and ooze pus. The cause is unknown but may begin with a scrape, insect bite or other irritation.

WHAT TO DO
• **Consult your veterinarian. Early treatment is necessary to prevent serious infection.** An important part of the treatment involves preventing the dog from licking at itself while the area heals. Bandages or an Elizabethan collar are usually used to prevent this further irritation. When prevented from licking the

affected spot, the dog may begin to lick a new spot above the bandage or on the opposite paw.

- Continue to watch the dog after treatment has been completed. The condition tends to recur.

RINGWORM

SYMPTOMS

Well-defined round or oval scaly patches, usually with stubbly hair, on the head or elsewhere on the body. A skin infection caused by many types of fungi. Usually results from contact with an infected animal (most often a cat) or contaminated hair.

WHAT TO DO

- **Consult your veterinarian. Treatment should be started early** and continued until all symptoms are completely eliminated. May take a considerable time.
- Some forms of ringworm are highly contagious to dogs, cats and humans, so it may be necessary to isolate the affected dog. As a further precaution, keep the dog's area free of loose hair.

SARCOPTIC MANGE

SYMPTOMS

Crusty, scaly and reddened skin. Scaliness of the edges of the ears. Hair loss around the face, muzzle, front legs and between the toes. Scabs. Pustules. Severe continuous scratching. Caused by an external parasite. Young puppies are especially susceptible.

WHAT TO DO

- **Consult your veterinarian. Early treatment is important.** Sarcoptic mange reproduces very rapidly.
- Apply flea or tick insecticide made especially for use on dogs to the dog's bedding and the other areas it frequents. Recontamination is a frequent problem.
- The disease is contagious to dogs, cats and humans, so it may be necessary to isolate the affected dog.

SEBORRHEA

SYMPTOMS

There are 3 different types of seborrhea: dry, oily and dermatitis. SYMPTOMS OF DRY SEBORRHEA: White, gray or silver scabs scattered throughout the dog's hair in little crusts. SYMPTOMS OF OILY SEBORRHEA: Greasy, scaly patches. Foul, rancid odor. SYMPTOMS OF DERMATITIS SEBORRHEA: Scaly or oily patches all over the dog's body. Scratching. Reddened skin. A chronic skin condition caused by an increased production of skin oils. The cause is unknown.

WHAT TO DO

- **Consult your veterinarian.** Long-term treatment may be necessary. Seborrhea can be controlled but not completely cured. Some cases respond to hormone therapy.
- If your dog has oily seborrhea, shampoo it frequently to control the objectionable odor.

WALKING MANGE

SYMPTOMS

What appears to be heavy dandruff all over the dog's back. Under a magnifying glass, the "dandruff" is seen to be tiny moving insects. Scratching. Caused by external parasites. Usually affects young puppies 4 to 12 weeks old. Easily passed to other young puppies.

WHAT TO DO

- Can usually be cured at home by treating the affected dog with flea powder, bath or spray made especially for dogs. If you give the dog a flea collar, **do not** also treat it with a flea bath. Using both can cause serious poisoning.

- For 4 to 6 weeks following treatment (or as long as necessary), apply flea powder weekly to the dog's bedding and the other areas it frequents.

WARTS

SYMPTOMS

Small pea-sized gray or white, rough-surfaced fleshy masses on the skin or inside the mouth. The dog may lick or chew at them. May bleed if irritated. May occur individually or in groups. Caused by a virus. Most common in older dogs.

WHAT TO DO

- **Consult your veterinarian.** May have to be removed surgically.
- Continue to observe an affected dog after treatment has been completed. Warts can recur, even after surgical removal.

TRAUMA

HEAD INJURY

SYMPTOMS

Unconsciousness or semiconsciousness. Bleeding from the face, nose, mouth or ears. Fractures of the bones in the face. Convulsions may occur if the injury creates pressure on the brain. Caused by a sudden injury to the head. Commonly the result of a car accident, fall or severe blow. Potentially serious because it may affect the brain or the delicate structures of the eyes, ears, nose or mouth.

WHAT TO DO

• **Consult your veterinarian.**

LAMENESS

SYMPTOMS

Vary with severity. In a fairly mild case involving muscle or soft tissue injury, the dog may limp with pain or discomfort but still puts its weight on its leg when it walks. If there is a more severe injury such as a cracked bone, fracture, dislocation or serious muscle damage, the dog will not use the leg as it walks but carry it up close to its body away from the ground. A young puppy that has suffered only minor injury may also carry its leg.

WHAT TO DO

• **Consult your veterinarian** if the dog carries its leg.
• Also **consult your veterinarian** if a puppy carries its leg for more than 2 hours, even if the injury seems only minor.

RUPTURED BLADDER

SYMPTOMS

Repeated futile attempts to urinate. After 1 to 3 days, additional symptoms may include: Painfully distended belly. Vomiting. Loss of appetite. Depression. Dehydration. Symptoms may develop slowly. A sudden breaking of the bladder caused by being hit by a car or some other severe blow to the belly while the bladder is full. May also be caused by an obstruction that prevents the bladder from releasing urine.

WHAT TO DO

• **Consult your veterinarian. Early treatment is important.** Surgical repair is required.
• A ruptured bladder is to be suspected whenever a dog has had a serious accident involving a sharp blow to the belly. As a precaution, observe the dog closely for up to 48 hours to make sure it is still producing urine.

URINARY DISORDERS

BACTERIAL CYSTITIS

SYMPTOMS

Frequent efforts to urinate, producing only small amounts of urine. Straining. Pain. The dog stays in the urinating position longer than usual. It wets in the house, producing small puddles in many locations. Blood in the urine. A bacterial infection of the bladder. Usually travels up the urinary tract from the outside as a result of an injury or some other cause. More common in females than males. Dogs that do not get the chance to void their bladders frequently are predisposed to this condition, as well as to urolithiasis.

WHAT TO DO

• **Consult your veterinarian. Early treatment is important.** May become a chronic condition and lead to more serious urinary problems if left untreated.
• After treatment, watch the dog carefully for symptoms of recurrence.

END STAGE KIDNEY DISEASE

SYMPTOMS

Dogs whose kidneys function only marginally are usually excessively thirsty and urinate frequently. The gums, tongue and inner linings of the eyelids may also become progressively more pale. As a result of stress or further loss of kidney function, additional symptoms may include: Vomiting. Diarrhea. Loss of appetite. Depression. Weakness. Dehydration. The result of damage to the kidneys from any number of other kidney diseases. May develop slowly as kidney function is lost because of aging or chronic or repeated kidney illness, or more quickly as a result of serious acute kidney damage. Symptoms usually appear when the dog is placed under stress from such things as fighting, being in the hot sun, going to a veterinarian or kennel, or undergoing any sort of illness.

WHAT TO DO

• **Consult your veterinarian.** Treatment is aimed at reducing stress and maintaining the dog's balance with its environment so that the remaining minimal kidney function suffices to serve its needs. The vet may prescribe a special diet containing a small amount of high quality protein.

INCONTINENCE

SYMPTOMS

Loss of bladder control, often while the dog is sleeping. A very common problem in dogs with no diagnosable illness. Most common in spayed females, but occasionally also affects males.

WHAT TO DO

• **Consult your veterinarian.** The problem can often be controlled by low doses of supplemental female hormones.

PROSTATITIS

SYMPTOMS

Vary according to severity. May include: Isolated drops of blood on the floor or in the urine. (Occasionally, the blood may be profuse.) Difficulty, straining and pain while urinating or defecating. The dog may remain in the defecating position longer than usual. An inflammation of the prostate gland, causing it to become enlarged or infected. Occurs only in male dogs.

WHAT TO DO

• **Consult your veterinarian. Early treatment is impor-** tant. Continued straining can result in a breakdown in the attachments holding the prostate gland in place and cause it to press against the rectum, making defecation even more difficult; see **PERINEAL HERNIA,** page 116. If the prostatitis is severe or recurrent, or the affected dog is young, your vet may recommend castration.

• Prostatitis tends to be recurrent, so continue to watch your dog for the return of symptoms.

PYOMETRA (UTERINE INFECTION)

SYMPTOMS

Excessive thirst and urination. The dog has difficulty holding its urine and wets in the house. May also include foul-smelling vulvar discharge containing blood or pus. In severe cases, there may also be vomiting and dehydration. A bacterial infection of the uterus caused by an underlying hormonal imbalance. Occurs only in female dogs, usually within a month after being in heat. Most common in females over 5 years old.

WHAT TO DO

• **Consult your veterinarian. Early treatment is essential.** Surgery is usually required. An affected animal may also develop other hormone-related conditions such as **MAMMARY TUMORS,** page 105.

• Can be prevented by spaying the dog when it is young.

UROLITHIASIS (URINARY CALCULI)

SYMPTOMS

Frequent efforts to urinate, producing only small amounts of urine. Straining. Pain. The dog stays in the urinating position longer than usual. It wets in the house, producing small puddles in many locations. Inability to hold urine. Clots of blood in the urine. When the bladder is totally obstructed, further symptoms include: No urinating. Intense pain. Tender abdomen. Acute distress. Caused by pea-sized or larger stones accumulating in the bladder. Often the result of an untreated bladder infection. Most common in females but also affects males. Frequently affects Schnauzers.

WHAT TO DO

• **Consult your veterinarian. Prompt treatment is essential.** Total obstruction can be fatal. Before the underlying infection can be cured, surgery is usually required to remove the stones from the bladder.

• An affected dog should be watched closely for reduced production of urine.

• To help prevent recurrence: Add salt to the dog's diet to encourage drinking and make sure that plenty of water is available.

VAGINAL HYPERPLASIA (PROLAPSE OF THE VAGINAL MUCOSA)

SYMPTOMS

A sizeable red fleshy mass resembling a tumor protrudes from the female's vulva. May be visible only intermittently. The dog may scratch or chew at the tissue. If irritated or injured, the surface may be dry or ulcerated and bloody. An abnormal swelling of the lining of the vagina. Occurs during the fertile phase of the heat cycle. May shrink in size and disappear after the heat cycle, then reappear during the next heat period.

WHAT TO DO

• **Consult your veterinarian.** Surgery is usually recommended to remove the tissue. The dog may have to be spayed to prevent further heat cycles.

• Exposed tissues are subject to injury and irritation, so try to prevent your dog from licking or chewing at the affected area.

ALPHABETICAL INDEX OF ILLNESSES AND DISORDERS

EMERGENCIES: FIRST-AID PROCEDURES

First aid is not a substitute for professional veterinary care. If your dog becomes seriously injured or ill, you should always try to get the immediate assistance of a veterinarian. Unfortunately, this isn't always possible. Emergencies have a way of happening when help isn't available right away, and if they aren't dealt with promptly, the dog's life may be jeopardized. Under such circumstances, your ability to provide quick, effective first aid may make the difference between your dog's life and death.

This section provides the most up-to-date first-aid procedures for all the common emergencies that are most likely to afflict your pet. To help you act quickly and correctly, each procedure combines clear, simple instructions printed in large type with easy to follow step-by-step illustrations. As a further help, the back cover of this book is thumb indexed to give you immediate access to the relevant procedures. Each procedure is also listed in the **CONTENTS** in the front of the book, and the symptoms for all emergencies are included in the **SYMPTOM RECOGNITION INDEX** that begins on page 83.

There are several crucial points to keep in mind whenever you have to come to your dog's aid:

• It is, of course, terribly distressing to see a cherished pet suffering from an illness or injury, but if you are to alleviate the emergency you must do your best to remain calm and clearheaded so you can follow the appropriate procedures correctly.

• If you are unsure about the nature or extent of an emergency, see **ASSESSING THE EMERGENCY,** page 141, before attempting any first aid. There are times when doing the incorrect thing can be more injurious than not doing anything at all. The **SYMPTOM RECOGNITION INDEX** will also help you determine what is wrong.

• An injured dog that is still conscious should always be restrained before it is examined or treated. Restraint places the animal under your control, prevents it from injuring you or worsening its own condition and makes it easier for you to administer first aid. Pain, fright and confusion can cause a normally gentle pet to become vicious and strike out at a helping hand offered too quickly. We suggest that you study the section on **RESTRAINTS,** page 209, to acquaint yourself with this single most important aspect of emergency care.

ASSESSING THE EMERGENCY

IMPORTANT

- Always approach an injured dog with caution. Speak in a gentle, reassuring voice. If possible, protect your hands with gloves.

- **Consult your veterinarian as soon as possible for any injury that seems serious.** See **TRANSPORTING AN INJURED DOG,** pages 204-205.

1 Restrain the dog if it is conscious. See **RESTRAINTS, pages 209-217.**

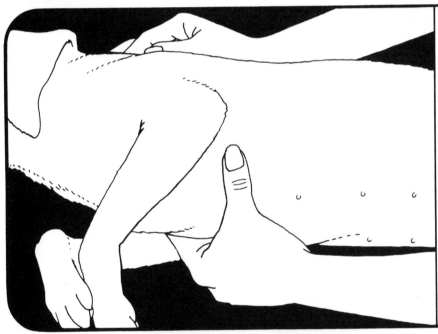

2 **Check the heartbeat** by gently squeezing the lower third of the dog's chest between your thumb and fingers. If no heartbeat is felt, see **HEART FAILURE,** pages 189-190.

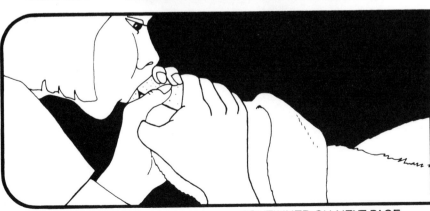

3 **Check the dog's breathing.** If necessary, see **BREATHING: ARTIFICIAL RESPIRATION,** pages 163-165.

CONTINUED ON NEXT PAGE

141

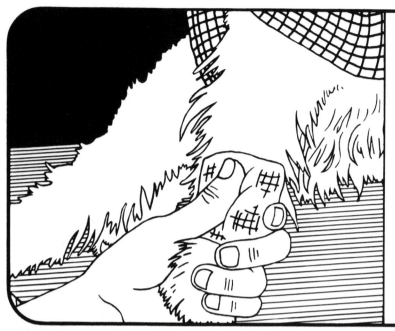

4 **Check for bleeding.** Quickly and gently examine the dog's head and body for injuries. Make sure not to overlook any concealed wounds. Control the most serious bleeding first. See **BLEEDING: CUTS & WOUNDS,** pages 153-159.

5 If there are burns or stains on the dog's mouth or other signs of poisoning (pills, chemicals, etc.), see **POISONING,** pages 196-201.

6 If the dog is unconscious or unresponsive, treat for **SHOCK,** pages 202-203.

7 For broken bones, see **BREAKS: FRACTURES & DIS-LOCATIONS,** pages 161-162.

ANAL SAC IMPACTION

IMPORTANT

- **Consult your veterinarian. Do not** clear the dog's anal sacs yourself unless your veterinarian recommends it.

- Speak in a gentle, reassuring voice.

- The anal sacs are teardrop shaped and have their openings at the edge of the anus.

SYMPTOMS

The dog "scoots" on its rear end and rubs or licks its anus.

1 **Restrain the dog. See RESTRAINTS, pages 209-217.** Lift its tail firmly.

CONTINUED ON NEXT PAGE

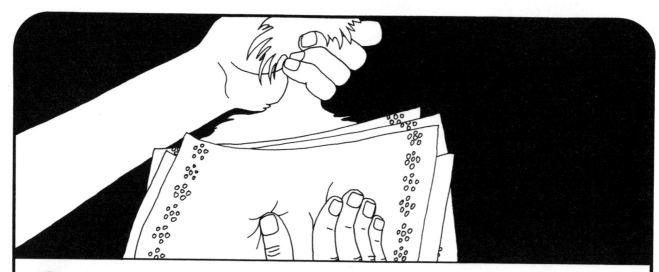

2 Place your thumb at an 8 o'clock position slightly below the dog's anus and your other fingers at a 4 o'clock position. Cover the anal opening with a large wad of paper towels.

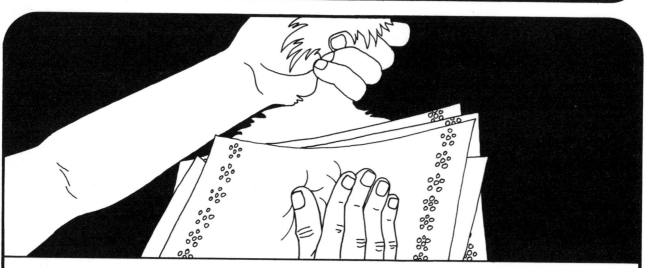

3 In one continuous motion, bring your thumb and fingers together and push inward and upward against the edge of the dog's anus. Collect the material emitted by the anal sacs in the paper towel.

4 Repeat the process 2 or 3 times until the sacs are completely cleared.

BITES & STINGS

ANIMAL BITES

IMPORTANT

• **If the skin is penetrated, consult your veterinarian.**

• Try to capture or confine the other animal for examination. Take care not to be bitten yourself. If you kill the other animal, keep its head intact. The head can provide the public health authorities with information that may save your dog a long quarantine.

• Observe for **SHOCK,** pages 202-203.

1 **Restrain the dog. See RESTRAINTS, pages 209-217.** Control the bleeding. See **BLEEDING: CUTS & WOUNDS,** pages 153-156.

CONTINUED ON NEXT PAGE

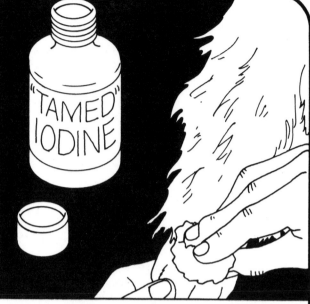

2 Wash the wound with soap and water. Apply "tamed" iodine or other antiseptic. **Do not** use ointments or other medications.

3 Apply a sterile dressing or clean cloth, and hold it firmly in place with a bandage. **Do not** bind too tightly.

BITES & STINGS

INSECTS

IMPORTANT

- **Consult your veterinarian as soon as possible** for bites and stings from **Black Widow** and **Brown Recluse Spiders, Scorpions** and **Tarantulas,** particularly if the dog is subject to an allergic reaction or is bitten on the mouth or eye.

- Observe for **SHOCK,** pages 202-203.

BEE (WASP, HORNET & YELLOW JACKET)

NOTE: Consult your veterinarian as soon as possible if the dog is subject to an allergic reaction or if there is severe swelling anywhere on its body. Also observe for **SHOCK,** pages 202-203, and watch breathing closely. If necessary, see **BREATHING: ARTIFICIAL RESPIRATION,** pages 163-165.

SYMPTOMS: Pain. Local swelling. Itching. Allergic reaction will also cause shock, unconsciousness and severe swelling.

FIRST AID: Restrain the dog. See RESTRAINTS, pages 209-217. For a bee sting, remove the venom sac by scraping gently, not by squeezing. (Wasps, hornets and yellow jackets do not leave venom sacs.) Wash the wound with soap and water and administer antihistamine syrup or antihistamine tablet (1/2 teaspoon syrup or 1/2 tablet for a small dog; 1 teaspoon or 1 tablet for a medium or large dog; 2 teaspoons or 2 tablets for a giant dog). See **ADMINISTERING LIQUID MEDICINE,** page 220, or **ADMINISTERING PILLS,** pages 221-222. For severe reactions, follow first aid for **BLACK WIDOW SPIDER.**

BLACK WIDOW SPIDER

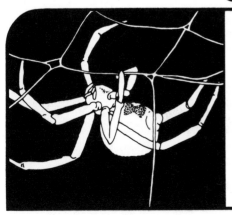

SYMPTOMS: Severe pain. Difficulty breathing. Swelling.

FIRST AID: Restrain the dog. See RESTRAINTS, pages 209-217. Watch breathing closely. If it stops, see **BREATHING: ARTIFICIAL RESPIRATION,** pages 163-165. Keep the dog quiet and avoid unnecessary movement. Keep the affected part below heart level. Place a constricting band about 1 inch wide 2 to 4

CONTINUED ON NEXT PAGE

147

BITES & STINGS

INSECTS
CONTINUED

BLACK WIDOW SPIDER, CONTINUED

inches above the wound. **Do not** bind too tightly. You should be able to slide your finger under it. Apply ice wrapped in a cloth. Remove the band after 30 minutes. Administer antihistamine syrup or antihistamine tablet (1/2 teaspoon syrup or 1/2 tablet for a small dog; 1 teaspoon or 1 tablet for a medium or large dog; 2 teaspoons or 2 tablets for a giant dog). See **ADMINISTERING LIQUID MEDICINE,** page 220, or **ADMINISTERING PILLS,** pages 221-222.

BROWN RECLUSE SPIDER

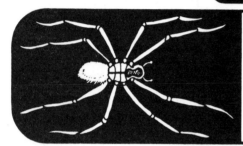

SYMPTOMS: The bite may be hardly noticed, but hours later severe pain, swelling and blisters occur.

FIRST AID: Follow first aid for **BLACK WIDOW SPIDER.**

SCORPION

SYMPTOMS: Excruciating pain at the sting. Swelling. Fever. Convulsions. Coma.

FIRST AID: Restrain the dog. See RESTRAINTS, pages 209-217. Wash the wound with soap and water. Cover lightly with a sterile dressing or clean cloth. For severe reactions, follow first aid for **BLACK WIDOW SPIDER.**

TARANTULA

SYMPTOMS: May vary from pin prick to severe wound.

FIRST AID: Restrain the dog. See RESTRAINTS, pages 209-217. Wash the wound with soap and water. Cover lightly with a sterile dressing or clean cloth. For severe reactions, follow first aid for **BLACK WIDOW SPIDER.**

BITES & STINGS

PORCUPINE QUILLS

- Carefully check the dog's paws, face and mouth for quills. If there are many quills or quills in the eyes or mouth, have your veterinarian remove them.

- Over the next week continue to check for quills and abscesses or infections. Broken quills often take that long to rise to the surface.

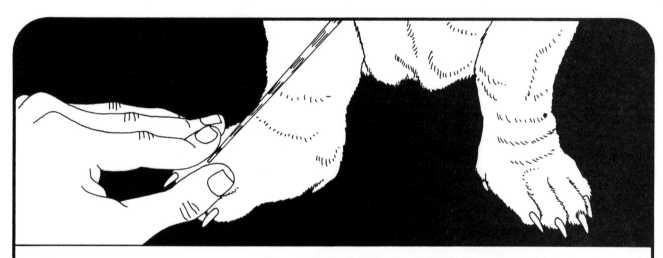

1 **Restrain the dog. See RESTRAINTS, pages 209-217.** Position the dog so the quills are exposed. Place one finger on each side and close to the quill.

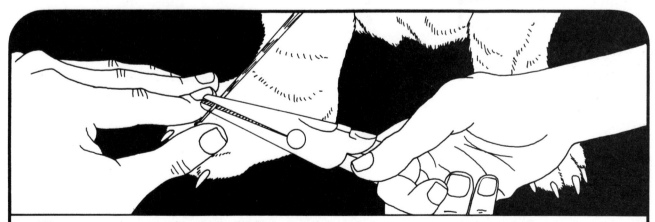

2 Grasp the quill near the skin with a needlenose pliers or your thumb and index finger. Avoid grasping the dog's fur.

CONTINUED ON NEXT PAGE

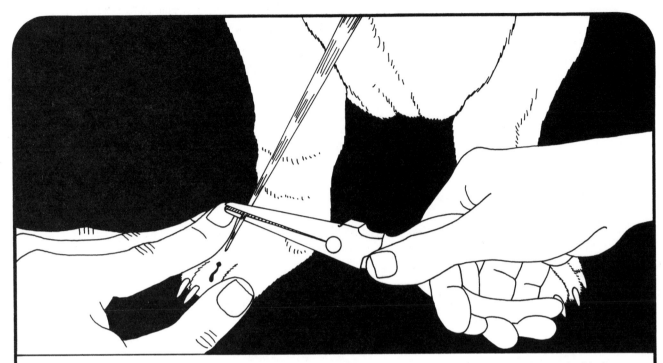

3 Using a quick, jerking motion, pull the quill straight out. **Do not** pull at an angle.

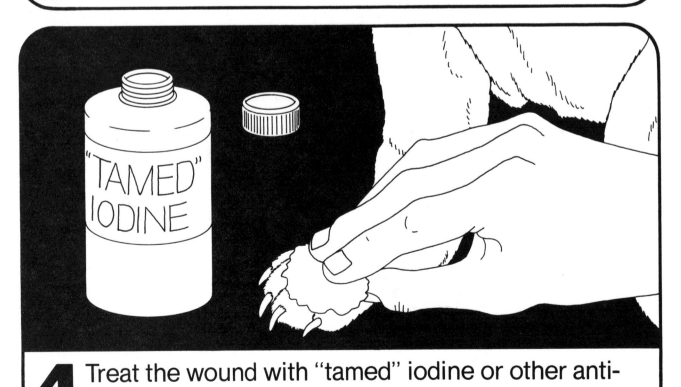

4 Treat the wound with "tamed" iodine or other anti-septic.

BITES & STINGS

SNAKEBITE

IMPORTANT

POISONOUS   NONPOISONOUS

- To determine if the bite is from a poisonous snake, look for fang marks at the wound. **If nonpoisonous, follow Step 4 only.**

- **Consult your veterinarian as soon as possible.**

- **Do not** let the dog walk or move the affected part.

- Watch breathing closely. If necessary, see **BREATHING: ARTIFICIAL RESPIRATION**, pages 163-165.

- Observe for **SHOCK**, pages 202-203.

SYMPTOMS

Pain. Swelling. May also include vomiting, difficulty breathing, weakness, paralysis, convulsions.

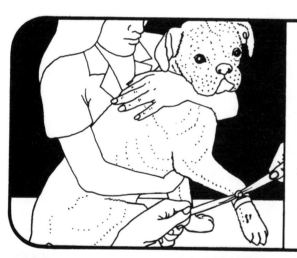

1 **Restrain the dog. See RESTRAINTS, pages 209-217.** Apply a constricting band about 1 inch wide between the bite and the heart 2 to 4 inches above the puncture. **Do not** bind too tightly. The wound should ooze. Keep the affected part below heart level.

2 Sterilize a knife or razor blade over an open flame, and make a **shallow vertical incision 1/2 inch long over each fang mark. Do not** cut deeply or crisscross.

CONTINUED ON NEXT PAGE

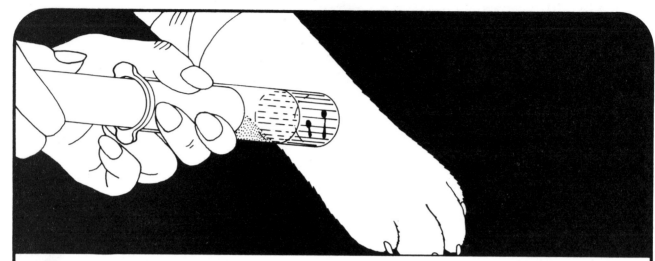

3 Draw the venom from the wound with a suction cup or your mouth, if it is free of open sores. Maintain suction for 30 minutes. If swelling reaches the band, leave it in place and apply a second band 2 to 4 inches above the first.

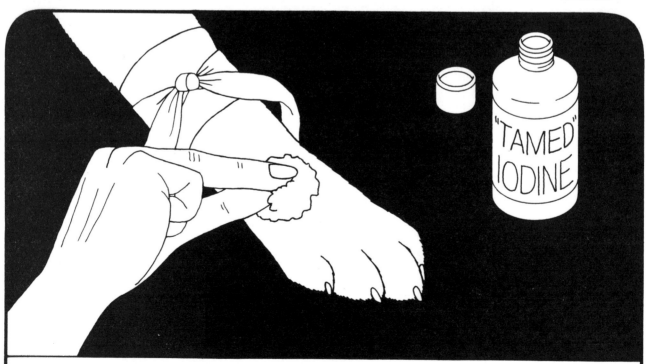

4 Wash thoroughly with soap and water and apply "tamed" iodine or other antiseptic.

DIRECT PRESSURE

IMPORTANT

- Consult your veterinarian for any serious bleeding.

- Observe for **SHOCK,** pages 202-203.

- First try to control the bleeding by **DIRECT PRESSURE**; see below.

- If serious blood loss continues and becomes critical, apply a **TOURNIQUET** as a last resort; see pages 154-156.

1 **Restrain the dog. See RESTRAINTS, pages 209-217.** Press a heavy gauze compress or clean cloth directly over the wound to control the bleeding.

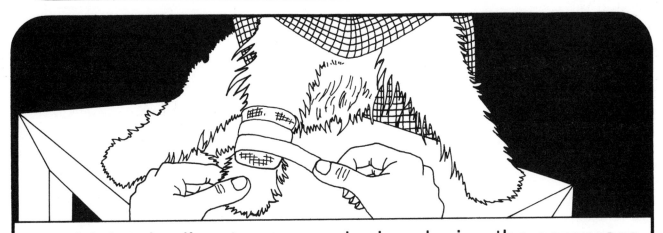

2 Maintain direct pressure by bandaging the compress firmly in place with adhesive tape. If bleeding does not stop, increase pressure by taping more tightly.

BLEEDING: CUTS & WOUNDS

TOURNIQUET

IMPORTANT

- Consult your veterinarian as soon as possible.

- **Do not use except in a critical emergency where it is a matter of life over limb.** Always try **DIRECT PRESSURE** first; see page 153.

- The tourniquet band should be about 1 inch wide.

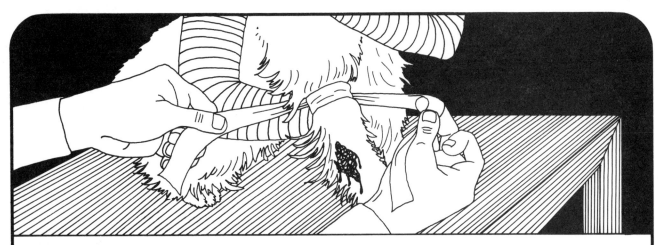

1 **Restrain the dog. See RESTRAINTS, pages 209-217.** Place the tourniquet band over the artery to be compressed, **slightly above** the wound. If a joint intervenes, position the band above the joint.

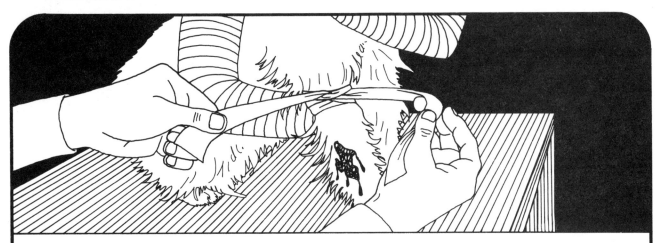

2 Wrap the band tightly around the limb twice, and tie a half knot.

TOURNIQUET

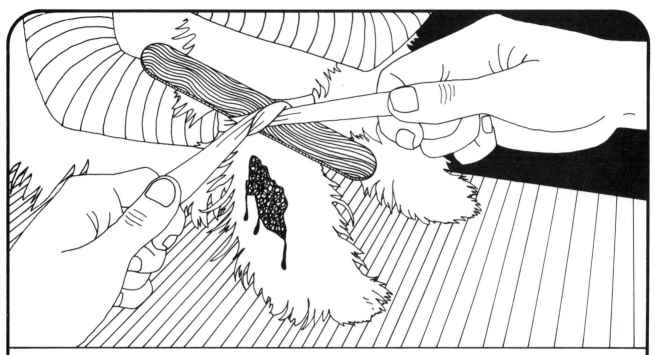

3 Place a short, strong stick on the band, and complete the knot on the top of the stick.

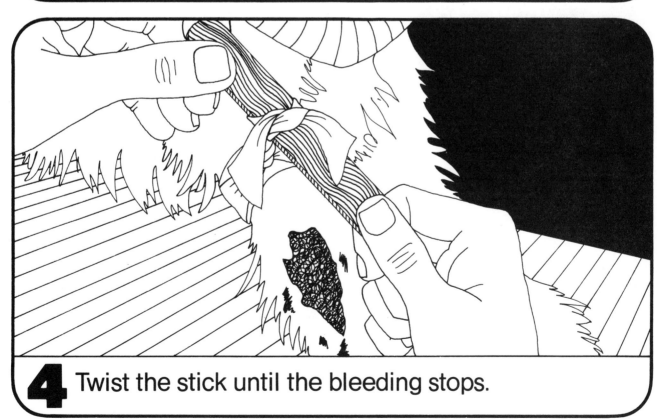

4 Twist the stick until the bleeding stops.

CONTINUED ON NEXT PAGE

TOURNIQUET
CONTINUED

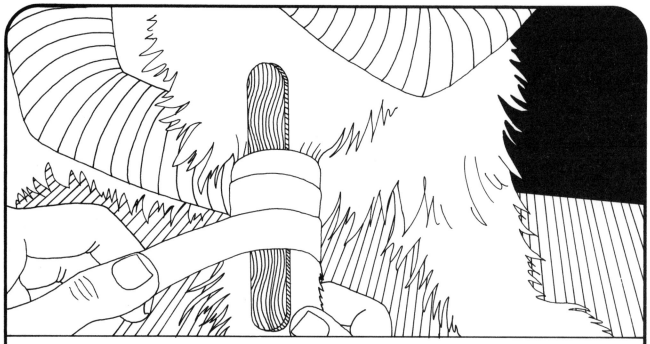

5 Secure the stick in place with adhesive tape. **Do not** loosen unless a veterinarian so advises.

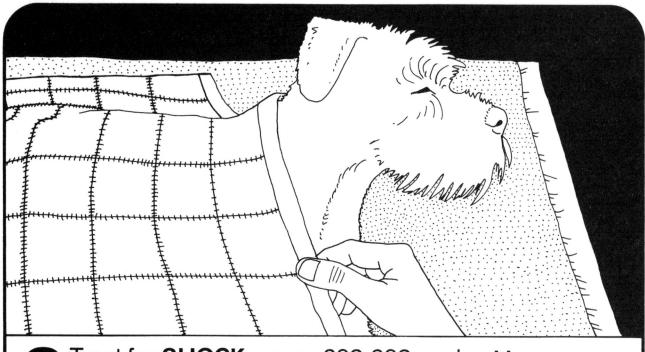

6 Treat for **SHOCK,** pages 202-203, and **get to a veterinarian immediately.**

BLEEDING: CUTS & WOUNDS

AMPUTATIONS

IMPORTANT

- Stay calm and act quickly. Bleeding must be stopped.
- Consult your veterinarian as soon as possible.

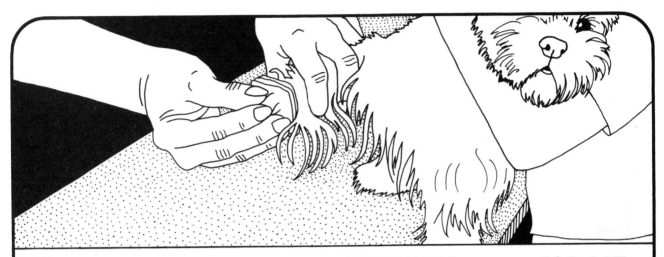

1 **Restrain the dog. See RESTRAINTS, pages 209-217.** Control the bleeding by pressing a heavy gauze compress or clean cloth directly over the wound.

2 Maintain direct pressure by bandaging the compress firmly in place with adhesive tape. If bleeding does not stop, increase pressure by taping more tightly. If serious blood loss continues and becomes critical, a **TOURNIQUET** may be necessary as a last resort; see pages 154-156.

BLEEDING: CUTS & WOUNDS

IMPALED OBJECTS

IMPORTANT

- **Get to a veterinarian as soon as possible.**

- **Do not** move the dog off an impaling object unless its life is in imminent danger. If you must, remove it as gently as possible, tend to the wounds immediately and treat for shock. See **BLEEDING: DIRECT PRESSURE,** page 153, and **SHOCK,** pages 202-203.

1 **Restrain the dog. See RESTRAINTS, pages 209-217.** If possible, cut off the impaled object several inches from the wound without moving or removing it.

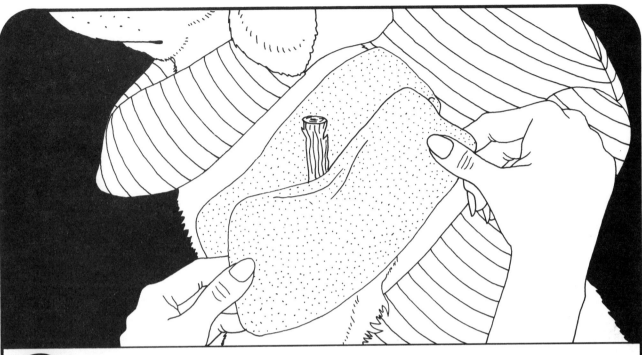

2 Place bulky dressings around the object.

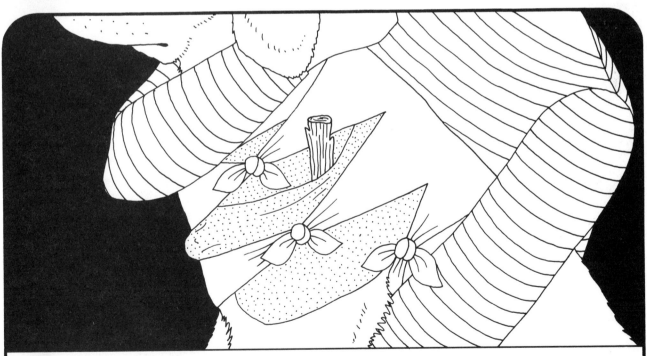

3 Secure the dressings in place with bandages. Observe for **SHOCK,** pages 202-203.

BLEEDING: CUTS & WOUNDS

INTERNAL BLEEDING

IMPORTANT

- To be suspected if the dog has had a sharp blow or crushing injury to the body.

- **Do not** give the dog anything to drink.

- **Consult your veterinarian.**

- Observe for **SHOCK,** pages 202-203.

SYMPTOMS

There is usually no visible bleeding, although the dog may bleed from its ears, nose, mouth or anus. Progressive weakness. Pale or blue gums. Progressive difficulty breathing. May also include bloody vomit, excrement or urine.

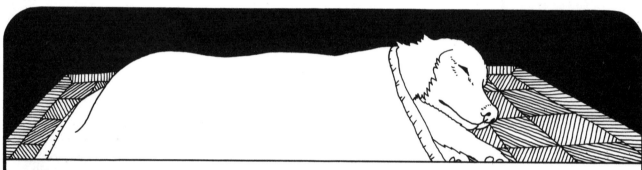

1 **Restrain the dog if necessary. See RESTRAINTS, pages 209-217.** Keep the dog lying down and covered lightly.

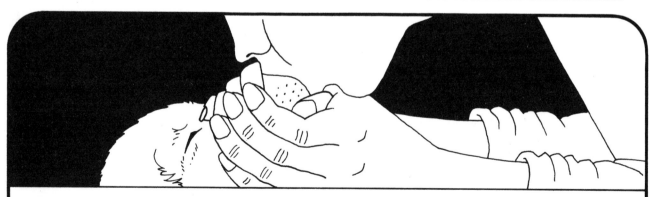

2 Watch breathing closely. If necessary, see **BREATH-ING: ARTIFICIAL RESPIRATION,** pages 163-165.

BREAKS: FRACTURES & DISLOCATIONS

LOWER LEG, PAW, TOES & TAIL

IMPORTANT

- **Consult your veterinarian.**
- **Do not** treat fractures or dislocations other than of the lower leg, paw, toes or tail. **See your veterinarian immediately.**
- **Do not** try to reset dislocations yourself. Treat the same as fractures.
- Observe for **SHOCK,** pages 202-203.

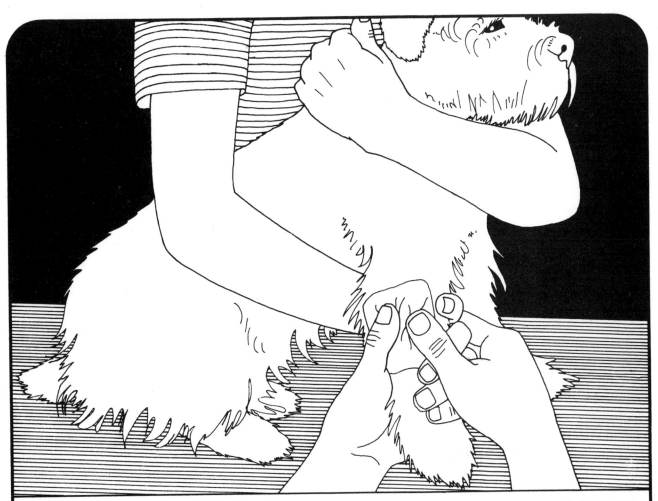

1 **Restrain the dog. See RESTRAINTS, pages 209-217.** If any bones protrude, control the bleeding with **DIRECT PRESSURE,** page 153, and cover the wound with a large clean dressing or cloth. **Do not** clean the wound.

CONTINUED ON NEXT PAGE

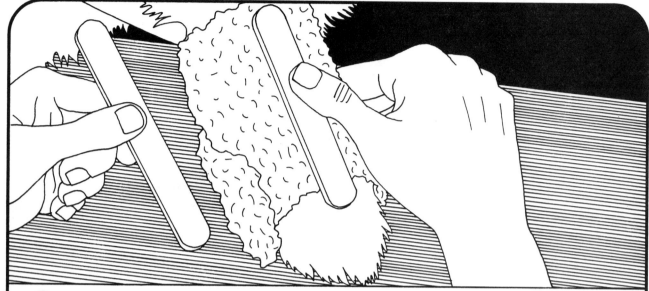

2 Wrap cotton batting or cloth around the entire bone for padding, then place tongue depressors or other splints on opposite sides of the break for rigidity. The splints should extend past the joints at both ends of the break.

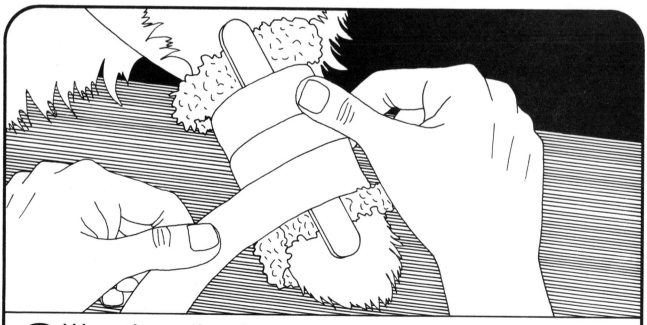

3 Wrap the splints in place with adhesive tape. **Do not** bind too tightly.

BREATHING: ARTIFICIAL RESPIRATION

IMPORTANT

- **Consult your veterinarian as soon as possible.**

- If the dog has drowned or inhaled vomit, liquid medication or other fluids, quickly suspend it by its rear feet for 15 seconds, giving 3 or 4 downward shakes to help drain the air passages. If the dog is too large to suspend, lift its pelvis and hind-quarters as high as possible and give 3 or 4 downward shakes.

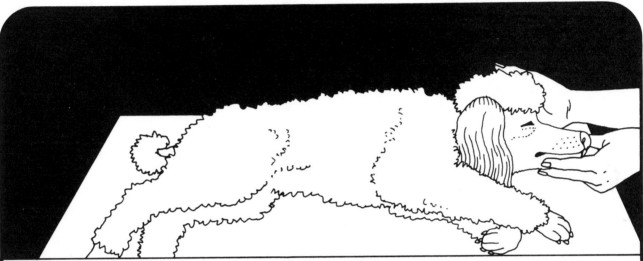

1 Place the dog on its side with its head extended. Remove its collar or harness.

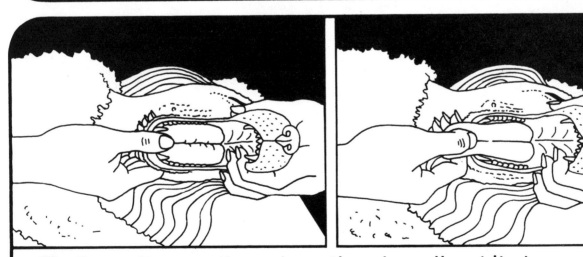

2 Open its mouth and cautiously pull out its tongue with your fingers or a cloth. Hold the tongue to keep the airway open. If necessary, clear out its mouth with your fingers or a cloth.

CONTINUED ON NEXT PAGE

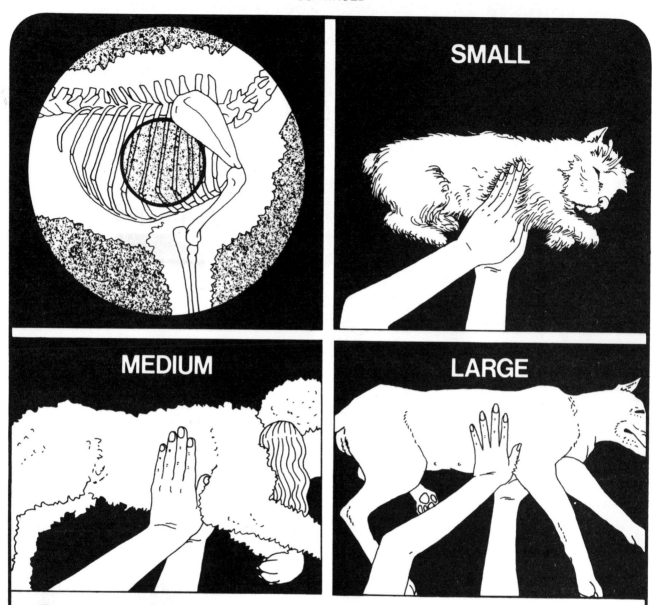

SMALL

MEDIUM

LARGE

3 **If breathing does not resume:** Compress the rib cage sharply between the palms of your hands at the exact spot shown, then release immediately. Adjust the force to the dog's size (fingertips only for a small dog; fingers extended and closed for a medium dog; fingers extended and open for a large dog). Look and listen for the air leaving its lungs. If the entry or return of air seems blocked, see **CHOKING,** pages 171-172, then resume artificial respiration. Repeat compressions every 5 seconds for 1 minute, then recheck breathing.

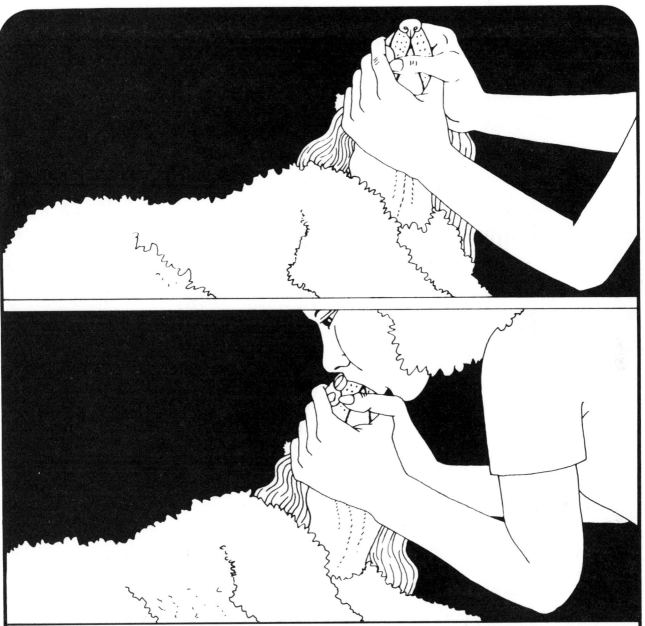

4 **If breathing has not resumed:** Grasp the dog's muzzle firmly and compress the lips and mouth shut. Place your mouth against the dog's nose and blow gently, watching for the chest to rise. If necessary, re-adjust your hand to seal air leaking from the mouth. Remove your mouth and look and listen for air leaving the dog's lungs. Repeat every 5 seconds for 1 minute, then recheck breathing. Repeat the process until the dog begins to breathe.

BURNS: CHEMICAL

- **Consult your veterinarian as soon as possible.**
- Protect your hands with rubber gloves.

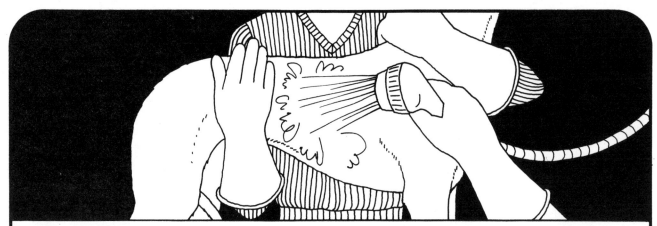

1 **Restrain the dog. See RESTRAINTS, pages 209-217.**
Place it immediately under a faucet, hose or other heavy stream of cool water. Remove its collar or harness. Make sure the water reaches the lower layers of fur and the skin. Check the dog's mouth and wash it out if it appears to be red or burned.

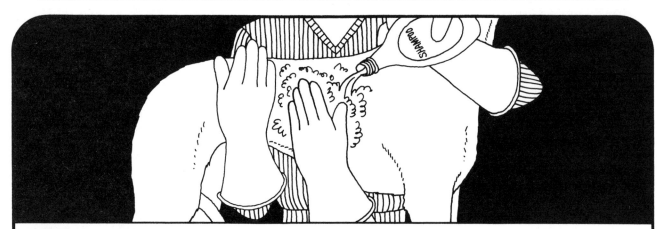

2 Soak the fur for 2 minutes, then apply hand soap or gentle shampoo. Lather and rinse well, then repeat the process. Keep the dog under the stream of water for at least 10 minutes, until all traces of the chemical have washed away.

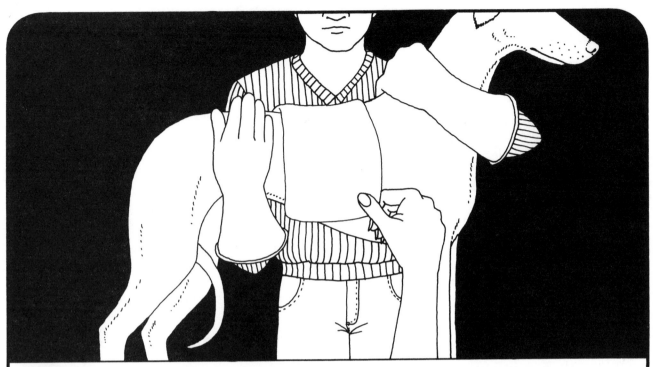

3 Cover the burned skin loosely with a clean, non-adhering dressing or cloth.

4 Hold the dressing lightly in place with a bandage. Treat for **SHOCK,** pages 202-203.

167

1st & 2nd DEGREE

- **Do not** remove shreds of tissue or break blisters.

- **Do not** use antiseptic sprays, ointments or home remedies.

- **Do not** put pressure on burned areas.

- Observe for **SHOCK,** pages 202-203.

- **Consult your veterinarian as soon as possible.**

Determine the degree of the burn and treat accordingly.

First Degree: Fur singed or burned off. Red or discolored skin. **See below.**

Second Degree: Fur burned off. Blisters and red or mottled skin. **See below.**

Third Degree: White or charred skin. **See page 170.**

1A Restrain the dog. See RESTRAINTS, pages 209-217. Immerse it in cold (not ice) water for 5 minutes.

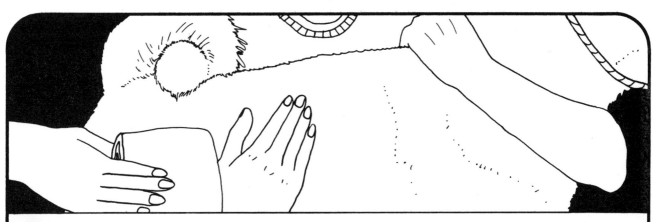

1B Or lightly apply cold clean compresses that have been wrung out after being immersed in ice water.

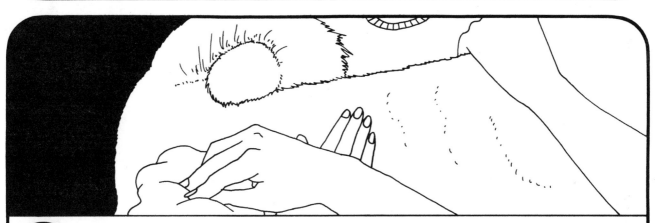

2 Gently blot dry with sterile gauze or a clean cloth.

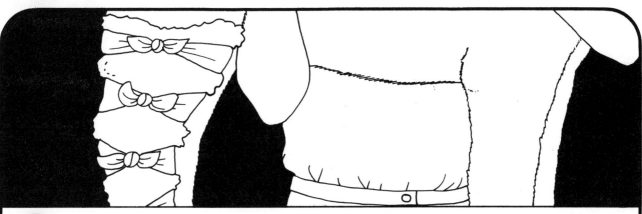

3 Cover loosely with a dry, clean dressing.

BURNS: HEAT

3rd DEGREE

IMPORTANT

- **Consult your veterinarian as soon as possible.**

- **Do not** apply water, antiseptic sprays, ointments or home remedies.

- **Do not** remove adhered particles of fur.

- **Do not** remove shreds of tissue or break blisters.

- **Do not** use absorbent cotton.

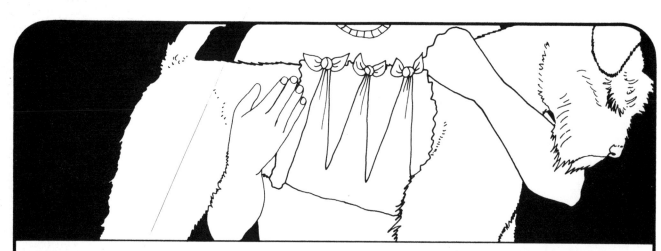

1 **Restrain the dog. See RESTRAINTS, pages 209-217.** Lightly cover the burned area with a nonadhering dressing or a dry, clean cloth.

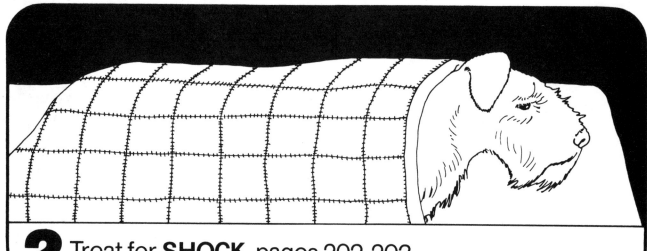

2 Treat for **SHOCK,** pages 202-203.

CHOKING

IMPORTANT

- **Do not** pull thread or string from the dog's throat. A needle or hook may be attached. Get to a veterinarian as soon as possible.

SYMPTOMS

Violent pawing at the face. Gasping and gulping. Great agitation and anxiety.

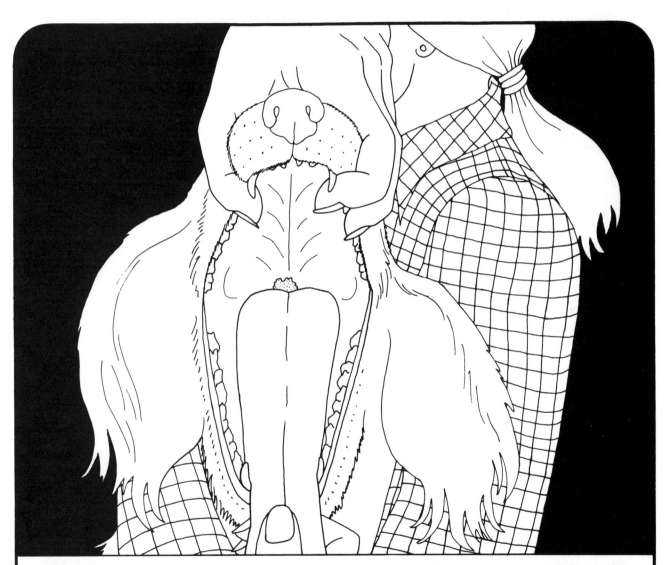

1 **Restrain the dog. See RESTRAINTS, pages 209-217.** Open its mouth wide, and pull out its tongue with your fingers or a cloth. Holding the tongue, look deeply into the dog's throat with a bright light.

CONTINUED ON NEXT PAGE

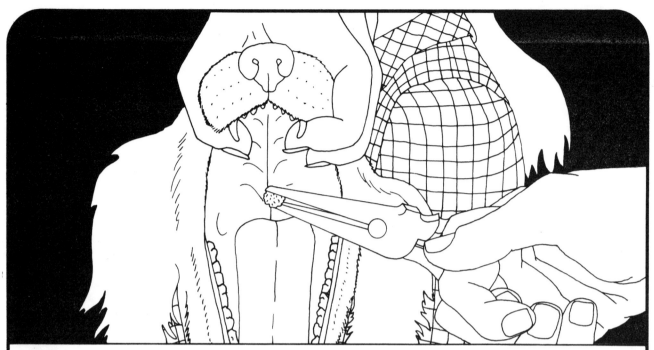

2A If you can see the obstruction, grasp it firmly and gently remove it.

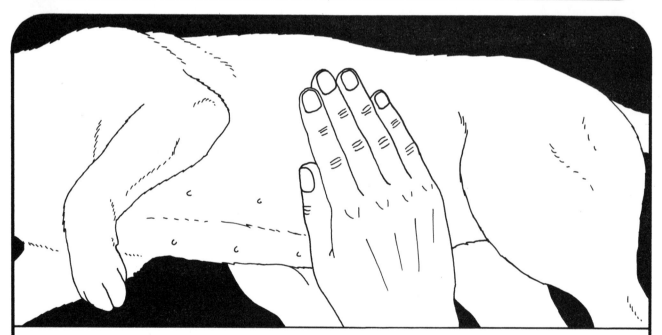

2B If you cannot see the obstruction, lay the dog on its side, place your palms just behind the last rib and give 4 quick thrusts. Recheck the throat. Repeat thrusts if necessary.

CONVULSIONS & SEIZURES

IMPORTANT

- **Do not** handle the dog during a convulsion or for 15 minutes afterward.

- **Do not** try to pull out its tongue.

- **Do not** give the dog anything to drink during the convulsion.

- Although convulsions are rarely fatal unless repetitive, tell your veterinarian about all of them, no matter how brief or infrequent. If a seizure recurs within 2 hours, see your veterinarian immediately.

SYMPTOMS

Falling. Chomping jaws. Stiffening of the body. May void bladder and bowels. Paddling motion of the legs. Jerky, uncontrollable movements, usually lasting 2 to 3 minutes. The dog is conscious but unresponsive. A mild seizure may involve just a short period of body stiffening and confusion.

1 Clear the area of hard or sharp objects that might cause harm. Try to remove its collar or harness, but **do not** restrain the dog.

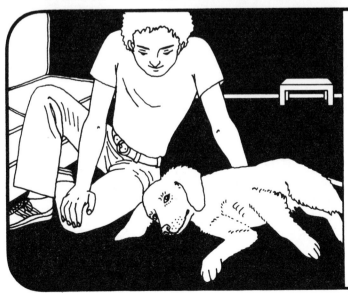

2 When the convulsion subsides, watch breathing closely. If necessary, see **BREATHING: ARTIFICIAL RESPIRATION,** pages 163-165. The dog may show fright and disorientation for 10 to 15 minutes following a seizure.

DIARRHEA

- Consult your veterinarian if the diarrhea contains blood or lasts longer than 24 hours.

- Treat promptly. Diarrhea can seriously dehydrate and weaken the dog.

- Diarrhea can be caused by illness, internal parasites, emotional or environmental factors, or by eating spoiled food or indigestible substances such as grass. It often follows bouts of vomiting within 24 hours.

- To help the veterinarian determine the cause, note if there are worms, grass, mucus or bones in the dog's droppings.

- When the diarrhea has ceased, bring a stool specimen to your veterinarian for analysis.

1 Take the dog's temperature; see **TAKING THE DOG'S TEMPERATURE,** pages 230-231. Consult your veterinarian if it has a fever or shows other symptoms of illness.

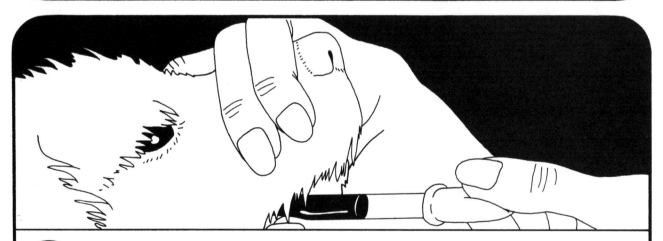

2 If the dog's temperature is normal, withhold food and water and give it Pepto-Bismol or Kaopectate every 2 hours for 12 hours (1/2 teaspoon for a small dog; 1 teaspoon for a medium or large dog; 2 teaspoons for a giant dog); see **ADMINISTERING LIQUID MEDICINE,** page 220. Consult your veterinarian if the dog vomits the medicine.

DIARRHEA

3 After 12 hours, give the dog a small drink of water. If diarrhea does not resume, give it small quantities of water every 3 hours. Consult your veterinarian if diarrhea resumes.

4 After 24 hours, give the dog a small amount of bland food such as cooked hamburger mixed with an equal amount of boiled rice or cooked eggs. Consult your veterinarian if diarrhea resumes. If diarrhea does not resume, repeat small portions of bland food every 3 hours for 24 hours and give normal quantities of water. Continue bland foods in normal portions for 5 days, then return to the dog's regular diet.

DROWNING

- **Send for help immediately.**

- **Do not** swim to the dog without a reaching assist. Try to stay at a safe distance. A panicky dog may claw at you.

1A Try to reach the dog from land with a buoy, board or anything that floats.

1B If the dog is too far away to reach, wade in closer with a reaching assist.

DROWNING

1c If you must swim to it, keep watching it or the spot you saw it last. Bring something for the dog to cling to or climb on, and pull it to shore.

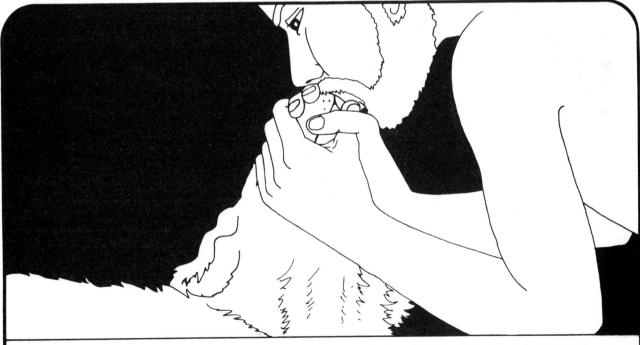

2 If necessary, see **BREATHING: ARTIFICIAL RESPIRATION,** pages 163-165.

EAR INJURIES

IMPORTANT
- **Consult your veterinarian for serious bleeding.**

1 **Restrain the dog. See RESTRAINTS, pages 209-217.** Place gauze or a clean cloth behind the dog's ear.

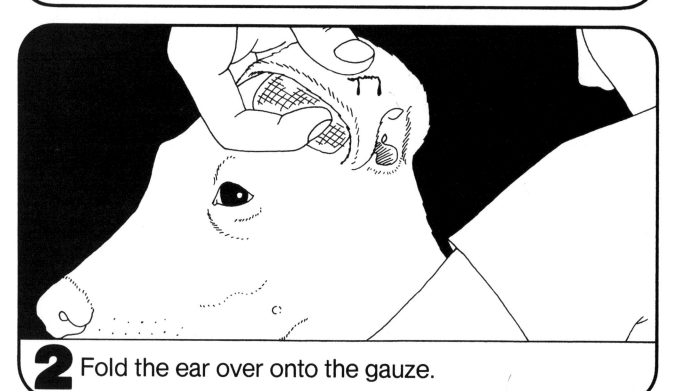

2 Fold the ear over onto the gauze.

178

EAR INJURIES

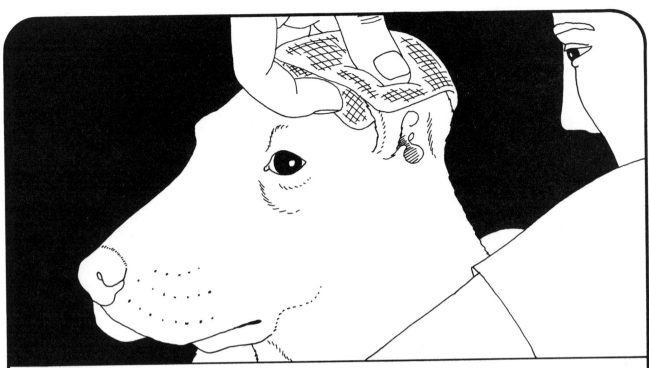

3 Control the bleeding by pressing the wound against the skull with gauze or a clean cloth.

4 Maintain direct pressure by bandaging the gauze firmly in place.

ELECTRIC SHOCK

IMPORTANT

- **Do not** touch the dog while it remains in contact with the current.

- Suspect electric shock from biting an electrical cord if the dog has red sores in the corners of its mouth; charred lips, gums and teeth; profuse thick salivation; dazed expression. See Step 2 below.

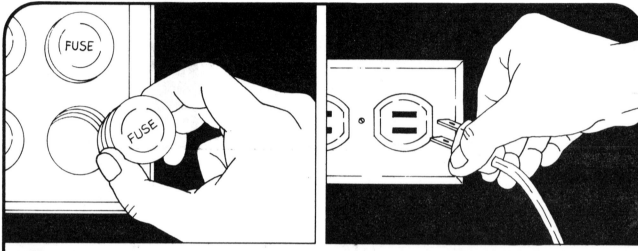

1A Try to turn off the current by removing the fuse or unplugging the electrical cord from the outlet.

1B If that isn't possible, stand on something dry— a blanket, rubber mat, newspapers, etc.—and push the dog away with a dry board or pole.

ELECTRIC SHOCK

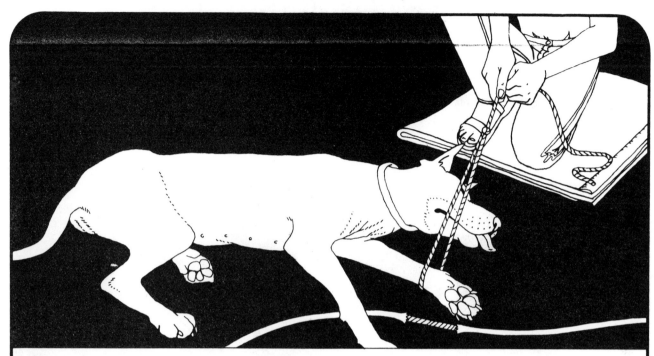

1c Or pull the dog away with a dry rope looped around one of its legs.

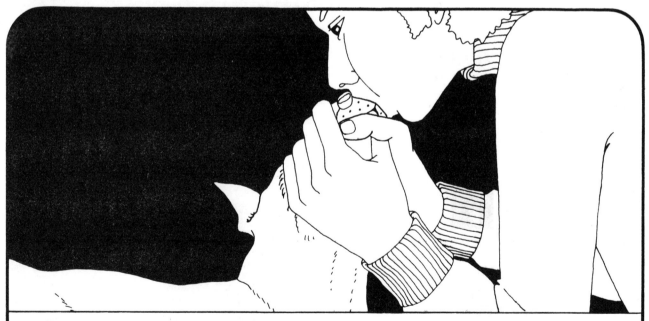

2 If necessary, begin rescue breathing immediately; see **BREATHING: ARTIFICIAL RESPIRATION,** pages 163-165. Treat for **SHOCK,** pages 202-203, and **BURNS,** pages 168-170. **Consult your veterinarian.**

EYE INJURIES

CHEMICALS IN THE EYE

- Be aware that the dog has an opaque third eyelid which is not normally seen but may come up to protect an injured eye. Should this happen, **do not** try to remove it or otherwise interfere with it.

1 **Restrain the dog. See RESTRAINTS, pages 209-217.** Holding the eyelid open, flush the eye immediately with gently running water for up to 2 minutes. **Do not** let the water run into the other eye.

2 Apply gauze or a clean cloth. Hold it in place with a loosely fastened bandage. **Consult your veterinarian as soon as possible.**

EYE INJURIES

FOREIGN OBJECTS

IMPORTANT

- Be aware that the dog has an opaque third eyelid which is not normally seen but may come up to protect an injured eye. Should this happen, **do not** try to remove it or otherwise interfere with it.

1 **Restrain the dog. See RESTRAINTS, pages 209-217.** Facing the dog, grasp the lower lid between your thumb and index finger and gently pull it away from the eyeball. If you cannot see the object, grasp the upper lid and elevate the head to expose the upper surface of the eye.

CONTINUED ON NEXT PAGE

EYE INJURIES
FOREIGN OBJECTS
CONTINUED

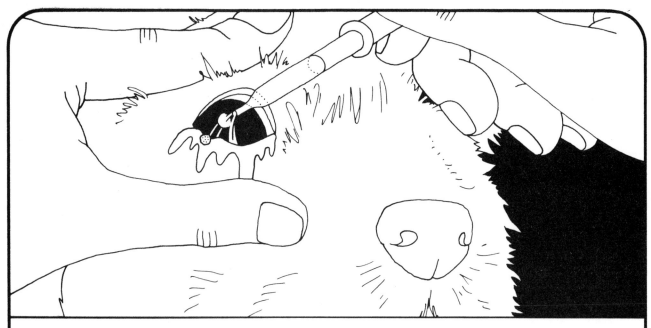

2A For a small foreign object, wash out the eye with water, letting the water drain down and away from the eye.

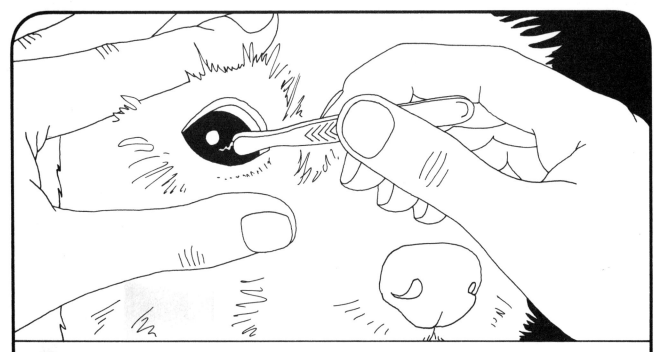

2B Carefully use blunt tweezers to remove thorns, etc. that cling to the surface of the eye or the lid.

EYE INJURIES

EYELID, EYEBALL & IMPALED OBJECTS

IMPORTANT

- **Consult your veterinarian as soon as possible.**

- **Restrain the dog before administering first aid. See RESTRAINTS, pages 209-217.**

- **Do not** wash out the eye.

- Be aware that the dog has an opaque third eyelid which is not normally seen but may come up to protect an injured eye. Should this happen, **do not** try to remove it or otherwise interfere with it.

LACERATED EYELID

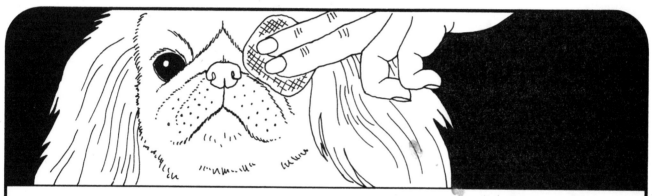

Control the bleeding by applying direct pressure against the lid and bone with gauze or a clean cloth.

LACERATED EYEBALL

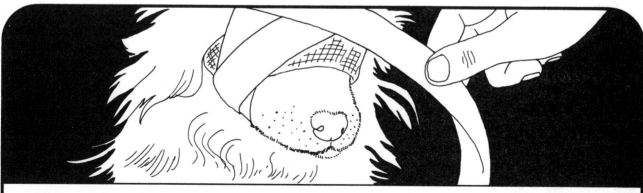

Cover **both** eyes loosely with gauze or a clean cloth. **Do not** apply pressure.

CONTINUED ON NEXT PAGE

EYE INJURIES

EYELID, EYEBALL & IMPALED OBJECTS
CONTINUED

IMPALED OBJECTS

NOTE: Try to remove the object if it is sharp, smooth and straight. It is better not to transport the dog with an impaled object still in its eye, but if the object cannot be removed, follow Step 3 only.

1 Using great gentleness and care, remove the object with your fingers, tweezers, needlenose pliers, etc.

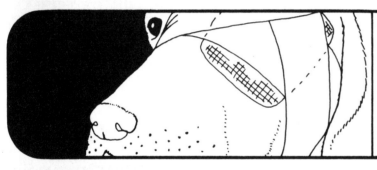

2 Apply gauze or a clean cloth and hold it in place with a loosely fastened bandage.

3 Bind the front paws together by wrapping adhesive tape around them twice. Immobilize the hind paws the same way, then bind the front and hind paws together. **Take the dog to the veterinarian immediately.** See **TRANSPORTING AN INJURED DOG,** pages 204-205.

FISHHOOKS

- **Do not** attempt to remove a fishhook in or near the dog's eye. **Consult your veterinarian immediately.**

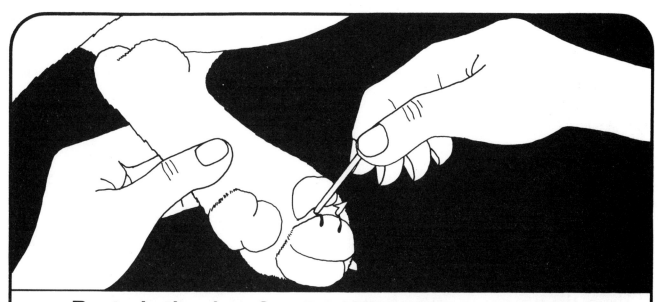

1 **Restrain the dog. See RESTRAINTS, pages 209-217.** Push the shank through the skin until the point appears.

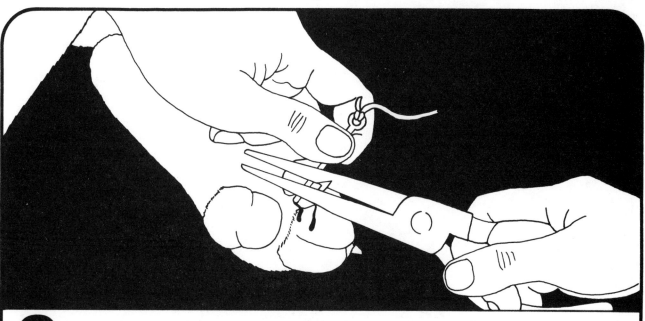

2 Cut off the barbed end with clippers or pliers.

CONTINUED ON NEXT PAGE

187

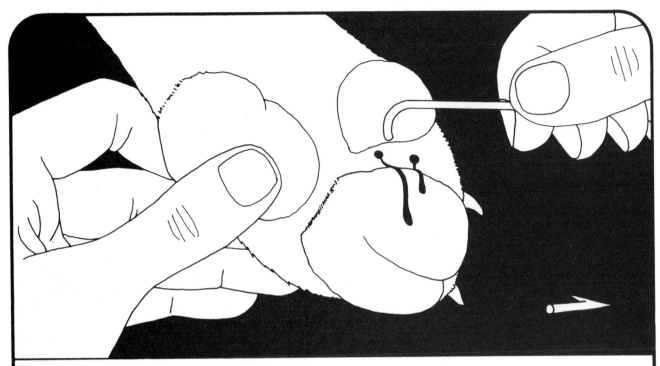

3 Remove the shank from the wound.

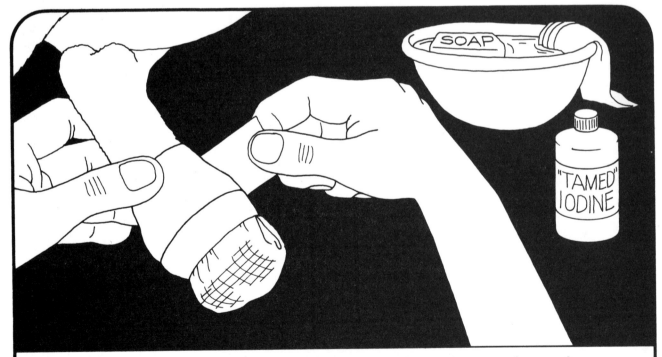

4 Wash the wound with soap and water and apply "tamed" iodine or other antiseptic. Cover with gauze or a clean cloth. **Consult your veterinarian.**

HEART FAILURE

IMPORTANT

- **Consult your veterinarian as soon as possible.**

- Waste no time, but be certain all symptoms are present before beginning first aid.

SYMPTOMS

Unconsciousness. No breathing. No heartbeat can be felt when you gently squeeze the lower third of the dog's chest between your thumb and fingers.

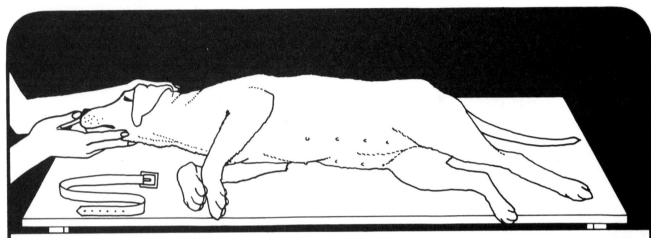

1 Place the dog on its side with its head extended. Remove its collar or harness.

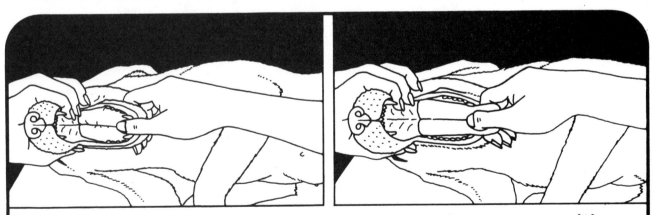

2 Open the dog's mouth and pull out its tongue with your fingers or a cloth. Hold the tongue to keep the airway open. If necessary, clear out its mouth with your fingers or a cloth.

CONTINUED ON NEXT PAGE

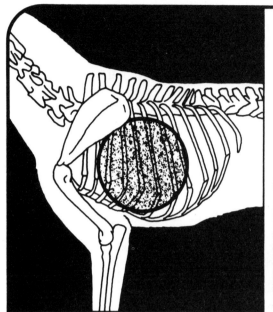
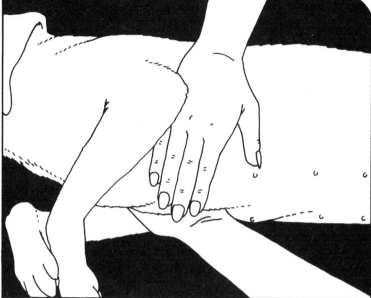

3 Recheck all symptoms. If the heartbeat has not resumed, quickly and firmly compress the lower third of the dog's chest between the palms of your hands at the exact spot shown. Release immediately. Adjust your force according to the dog's size. Repeat once a second for 1 minute.

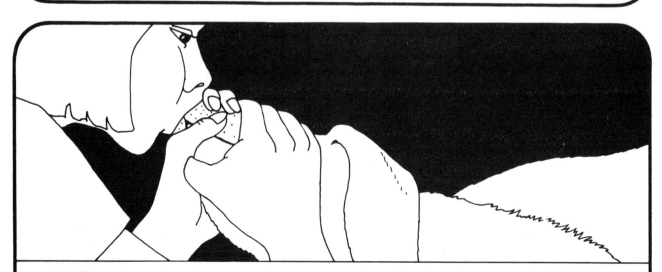

4 Recheck all symptoms again. If the heartbeat still has not resumed, repeat Step 3. When heartbeat resumes, begin rescue breathing; see **BREATHING: ARTIFICIAL RESPIRATION,** pages 163-165.

HEATSTROKE

IMPORTANT

- **Consult your veterinarian as soon as possible.**

- Act quickly. Body temperature must be immediately lowered to 103°F. (39.4°C.). See **TAKING THE DOG'S TEMPERATURE,** pages 230-231.

- Watch temperature closely; repeat first aid if it rises again.

- Watch breathing closely. If necessary, see **BREATHING: ARTIFICIAL RESPIRATION,** pages 163-165.

- Heatstroke is most likely to occur in St. Bernards, Bulldogs, Pekinese and other breeds with "pug" faces. They are susceptible even in moderate temperatures.

SYMPTOMS

Extremely high body temperature (105°F. — 110°F.; 40.6°C. — 43.3°C.). Uncontrollable panting. Foaming at the mouth. Depression. Agitation. Loss of consciousness. Tongue and gums become progressively blue or gray.

1A **Restrain the dog if necessary. See RESTRAINTS, pages 209-217.** Bathe or hose the dog with cold water until temperature subsides.

CONTINUED ON NEXT PAGE

1B Or take the dog to a cool, well-ventilated place and wrap it in a wet, cold sheet or towel until temperature subsides.

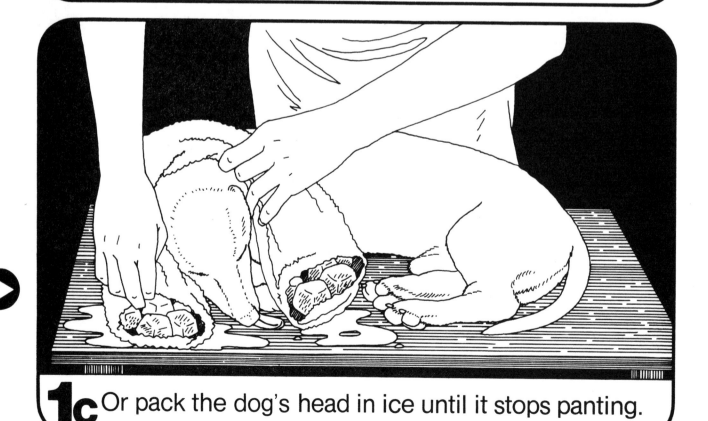

1C Or pack the dog's head in ice until it stops panting.

MOUTH INJURIES

GUMS, PALATE, TEETH, LIPS & TONGUE

IMPORTANT

- **Restrain the dog before administering first aid.** See **RESTRAINTS,** pages 209-217.

- Cautiously clear the mouth of broken teeth.

- Keep the dog sitting up with its head lowered slightly so it does not inhale blood.

- **Do not** treat mouth injuries if the dog is vicious. Consult your veterinarian immediately.

GUMS & PALATE

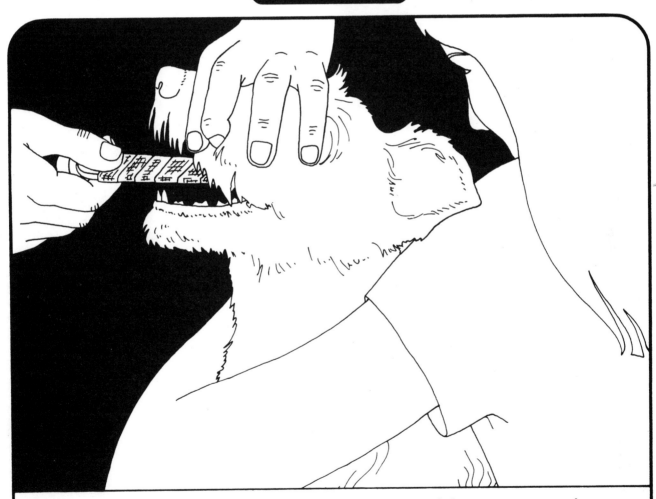

Control bleeding by direct pressure with gauze pads or a clean cloth wrapped around a tongue depressor, spoon, tweezers, etc.

CONTINUED ON NEXT PAGE

MOUTH INJURIES

GUMS, PALATE, TEETH, LIPS & TONGUE
CONTINUED

TEETH

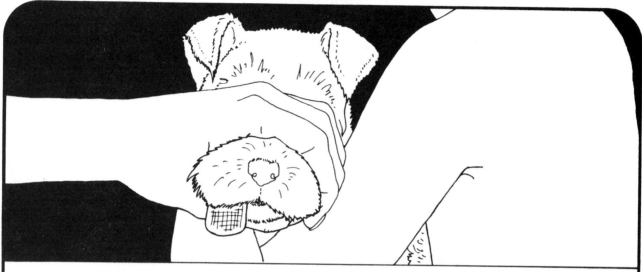

Control bleeding by direct pressure on the tooth socket with gauze pads or a clean cloth. Hold the mouth shut so the dog bites down firmly on the gauze to keep it in place.

LIPS

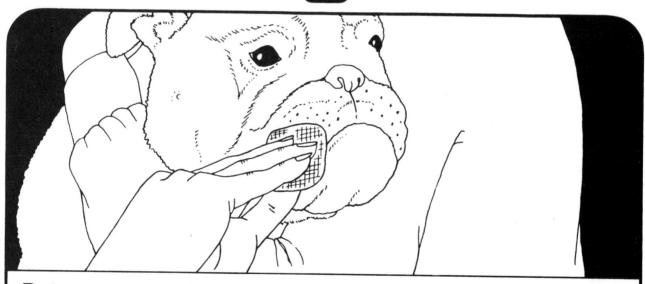

Put a gauze pad or clean cloth directly over the wound. Place your thumb on the lip behind the wound and your other fingers over the pad, then apply direct pressure by squeezing your fingers together.

MOUTH INJURIES

GUMS, PALATE, TEETH, LIPS & TONGUE

TONGUE

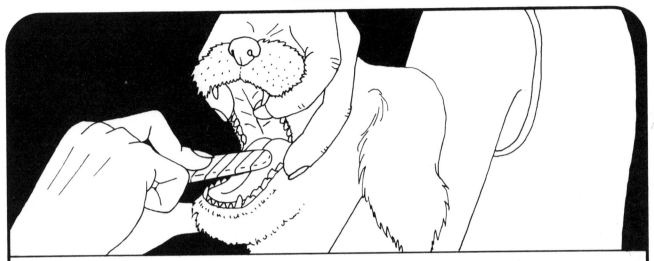

If the dog is conscious: Apply direct pressure with several gauze pads wrapped around a tongue depressor, spoon, etc. held in place with your index and middle fingers. Apply counterpressure by placing your thumb behind the chin and pressing up firmly.

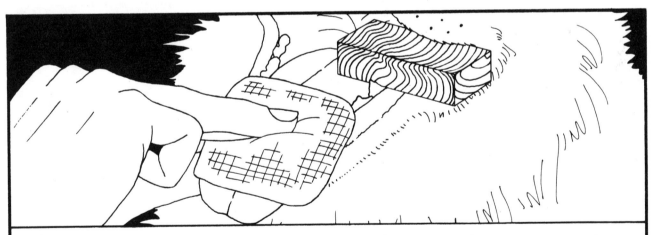

If the dog is unconscious: Prop the jaws apart by placing a small block of wood or the like between the teeth at the back of the mouth. Control bleeding by pressing both sides of the tongue with gauze or a clean cloth. For more severe bleeding, gently pull the tongue and hold it for about 5 minutes.

POISONING

CONTACT

IMPORTANT

- **Consult your veterinarian if there is a severe reaction or if the dog is highly allergic.**

- Burns on the mouth could indicate **ELECTRIC SHOCK,** pages 180-181, or **SWALLOWED POISONS,** pages 200-201.

- Watch breathing closely. If necessary, see **BREATHING: ARTIFICIAL RESPIRATION,** pages 163-165.

- **Do not** use chemical solvents unless your veterinarian so advises.

- Contact poisoning is frequently caused by treating the dog with a parasite bath in combination with a flea collar.

SYMPTOMS

Burns. Vomiting. Profuse salivation. Swelling. Fever. Convulsive seizures (usually occur within 24 hours after contact with such toxic substances as poisons, oil, gasoline, turpentine, benzine and chemical dips).

1 **Restrain the dog. See RESTRAINTS, pages 209-217.** Remove its collar or harness. Bathe or hose the dog with lukewarm water.

2 Apply mild hand soap or shampoo. Lather and rinse well. Repeat the process until all traces of the toxic substance have washed away.

197

POISONING

INGESTED PLANTS

IMPORTANT

- **Call your veterinarian or Poison Control Center immediately.**

- Dogs rarely ingest poisonous plants. **Do not** treat for poisoning unless you have witnessed the poisoning or are certain that poison is involved.

- Watch breathing closely. If necessary, see **BREATHING: ARTIFICIAL RESPIRATION,** pages 163-165.

- **Do not** give the dog anything to drink if it is unconscious.

- **If you cannot reach your veterinarian or Poison Control Center, see POISONING: SWALLOWED POISONS, page 201, and follow treatment Ⓑ.**

COMMON POISONOUS PLANTS

BANEBERRY

BITTERSWEET

CASTOR-OIL PLANT

DAPHNE

FOXGLOVE

198

POISONING

INGESTED PLANTS

JIMSON WEED
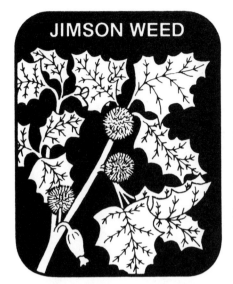

LARKSPUR

LILY-OF-THE-VALLEY

MONKSHOOD

NIGHTSHADE

POISON HEMLOCK

POKEWEED

WATER HEMLOCK

YEW

CONTINUED ON NEXT PAGE

SWALLOWED POISONS

IMPORTANT

- **Call your veterinarian or Poison Control Center immediately.**

- Poisoning is relatively rare in dogs. **Do not** treat for poisoning unless you have witnessed the poisoning or are certain that poison is involved.

- Burns on the mouth could also indicate **ELECTRIC SHOCK;** see pages 180-181.

- Save the poison container and a sample of the vomit.

- Watch breathing closely. If necessary, see **BREATHING: ARTIFICIAL RESPIRATION,** pages 163-165.

- **Do not** give the dog anything to drink if it is unconscious.

If you cannot reach your veterinarian or Poison Control Center:

- Find the poison swallowed on the list below.

- Follow the corresponding treatment on the opposite page.

- If you don't know what was swallowed, follow Treatment **Ⓐ**. If there are no burns around the mouth, also have the dog drink a mixture of activated charcoal and water (1 teaspoon of activated charcoal in 1 ounce of water for a small dog; 2 teaspoons in 2 ounces of water for a medium or large dog; 3 teaspoons in 3 ounces of water for a giant dog). See **ADMINISTERING LIQUID MEDICINE,** page 220.

Acetone Ⓑ
After Shave Lotion Ⓑ
Alcohol Ⓑ
Antifreeze Ⓑ
Arsenic Ⓑ
Battery Acid Ⓐ
Benzine Ⓑ
Bichloride of Mercury Ⓑ
Bleach Ⓑ
Body Conditioner Ⓑ
Boric Acid Ⓑ
Brush Cleaner Ⓐ
Camphor Ⓑ
Carbon Tetrachloride Ⓑ
Charcoal Lighter Ⓐ
Chlordane Ⓑ
Cologne Ⓑ
Corn Remover Ⓐ
Cosmetics Ⓑ
DDT Ⓑ
Deodorant Ⓑ
Detergent Ⓑ
Dishwasher Granules Ⓐ
Drain Cleaner Ⓐ
Fabric Softeners Ⓑ

Fingernail Polish & Remover Ⓑ
Fireworks Ⓑ
Floor Polish Ⓐ
Fluoride Ⓑ
Furniture Polish Ⓐ
Gasoline Ⓐ
Grease Remover Ⓐ
Gun Cleaner Ⓐ
Hair Dye Ⓑ
Hair Permanent Neutralizer Ⓑ
Hair Preparations Ⓑ
Hydrogen Peroxide Ⓑ
Indelible Markers Ⓑ
Ink (Green & Purple) Ⓑ
Insecticides Ⓑ
Iodine Ⓑ
Kerosene Ⓐ
Lacquer Thinner Ⓐ
Liniment Ⓑ
Lye Ⓐ
Matches (more than 20 wooden matches or 2 match books) Ⓑ
Mercury Salts Ⓑ
Metal Cleaner Ⓐ
Mothballs, Flakes or Cakes Ⓑ

Naphtha Ⓐ
Oil of Wintergreen Ⓑ
Oven Cleaner Ⓐ
Paint (Lead) Ⓑ
Paint Thinner Ⓐ
Perfume Ⓑ
Pesticides Ⓑ
Pine Oil Ⓑ
Quicklime Ⓐ
Rat or Mouse Poison Ⓑ
Roach Poison Ⓑ
Shoe Polish Ⓐ
Strychnine Ⓑ
Suntan Preparations Ⓑ
Toilet Bowl Cleaner Ⓐ
Turpentine Ⓑ
Typewriter Cleaner Ⓐ
Wart Remover Ⓐ
Washing Soda Ⓐ
Wax (Floor or Furniture) Ⓐ
Weed Killer Ⓑ
Wick Deodorizer Ⓑ
Wood Preservative Ⓐ
Zinc Compounds Ⓐ

POISONING

SWALLOWED POISONS

Ⓐ FOR ACID, ALKALI & PETROLEUM POISONING

IMPORTANT

• **Do not induce vomiting.**

SYMPTOMS OF ACID & ALKALI POISONING Burns around the mouth, lips and tongue.

SYMPTOMS OF PETROLEUM POISONING Coughing. Petroleum odor on the breath. Bloody vomit. Coma.

1 **Restrain the dog. See RESTRAINTS, pages 209-217.**
If the dog is conscious, give it 1 cup of milk (or as much as it will accept) to dilute the poison. (If milk isn't available, use water.) See **ADMINIS-TERING LIQUID MEDICINE,** page 220.

2 Observe for **SHOCK,** pages 202-203.

Ⓑ FOR OTHER POISONING

SYMPTOMS May include vomiting, pain, lack of coordination, panting, slimy mouth, convulsions, coma.

1 **Restrain the dog. See RESTRAINTS, pages 209-217.**
If the dog is conscious, give it 1 cup of milk (or as much as it will accept) to dilute the poison. (If milk isn't available, use water.) See **ADMINIS-TERING LIQUID MEDICINE,** page 220.

2 Induce vomiting by giving the dog 3% medicinal hydrogen peroxide U.S.P. (1 teaspoon for a small dog; 2 teaspoons for a medium or large dog; 3 teaspoons for a giant dog).
If hydrogen peroxide isn't available, give the dog table salt mixed with water (1/2 teaspoon of salt in 1 tablespoon of water for a small dog; 1 teaspoon in 2 tablespoons of water for a medium or large dog; 1-1/2 teaspoons in 3 tablespoons of water for a giant dog). If the dog doesn't vomit within 30 minutes, give it a second dose.

3 When the dog has finished vomiting, give it activated charcoal mixed with water (1 teaspoon in 1 ounce of water for a small dog; 2 teaspoons in 2 ounces of water for a medium or large dog; 3 teaspoons in 3 ounces of water for a giant dog).

4 Observe for **SHOCK,** pages 202-203.

201

SHOCK

IMPORTANT

- **Always check a seriously injured dog for shock.**
- **Consult your veterinarian as soon as possible.**
- **Do not** give the dog anything to drink.

SYMPTOMS

Weak or rapid but shallow breathing. Confusion. Pale gums. Weakness. Semiconsciousness or unconsciousness.

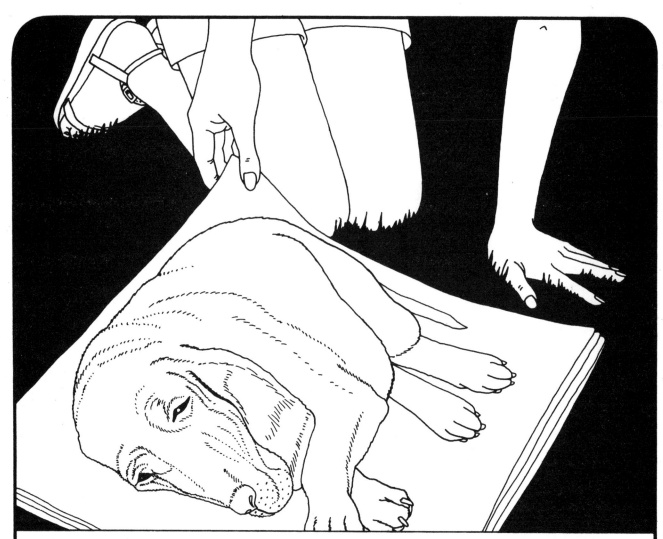

1 Restrain the dog if necessary. See RESTRAINTS, pages 209-217. Place the dog on its side with its head extended. Put a blanket or jacket under it if it is cold or damp.

SHOCK

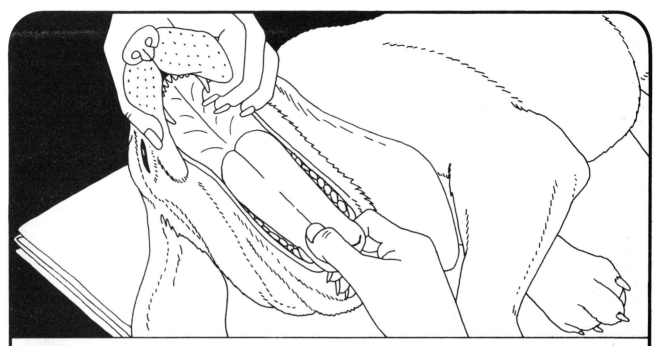

2 Open the dog's mouth and cautiously pull out its tongue with your fingers or a cloth. Hold the tongue to keep the airway open. If the dog is unconscious, elevate its hindquarters slightly.

3 Cover the dog lightly with a blanket. **Do not** overheat.

TRANSPORTING A DOG

- **Always use a stretcher to move a dog that cannot walk.**

- **Always approach an injured dog with caution.** Speak in a gentle, reassuring voice.

- **Do not** handle the dog more than necessary. If possible, call ahead to the veterinarian.

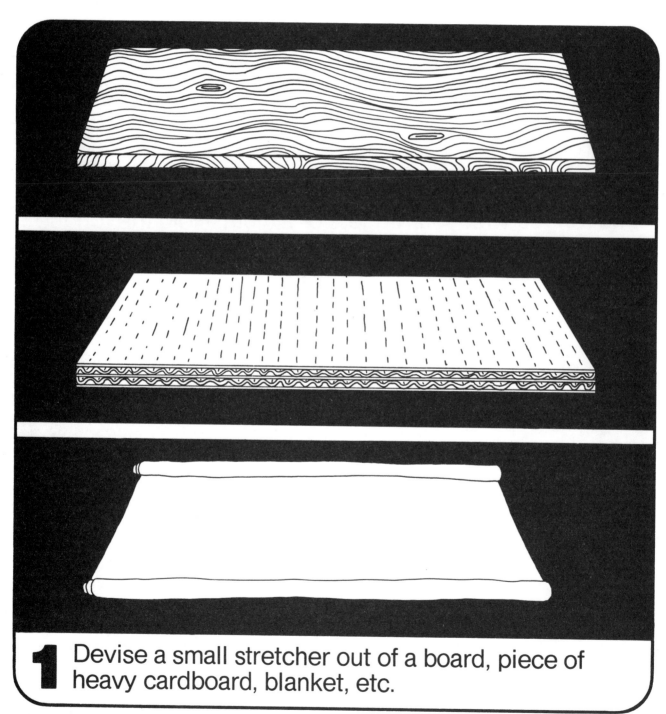

1 Devise a small stretcher out of a board, piece of heavy cardboard, blanket, etc.

2 **Muzzle the dog if necessary. See IMPROVISING A MUZZLE, page 217.** Slide the dog gently onto the stretcher. Move it carefully as a single unit without bending or twisting any part of its body.

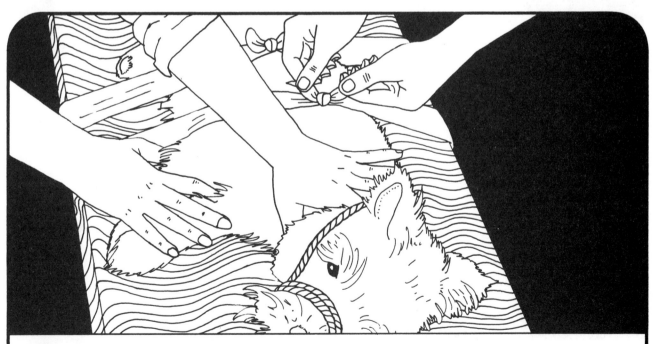

3 Bind the dog in place with belts, adhesive tape, a pinned towel, etc.

VOMITING

IMPORTANT

- Vomiting can be caused by illness, emotional or environmental factors, or by eating spoiled food or indigestible substances such as grass.

- Consult your veterinarian if the vomit contains blood or if vomiting occurs frequently, lasts longer than several hours or the dog seems otherwise ill or in pain.

1 Take the dog's temperature; see **TAKING THE DOG'S TEMPERATURE**, pages 230-231. Consult your veterinarian if it has a fever or shows other symptoms of illness.

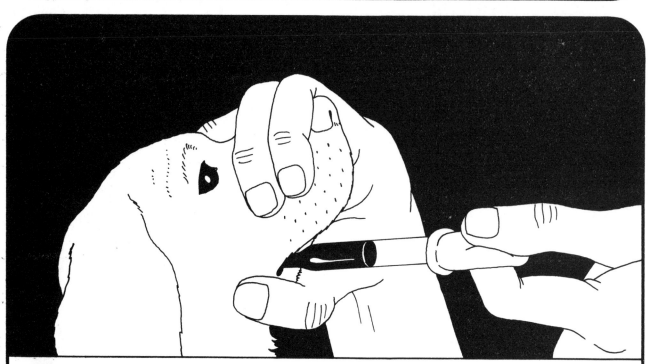

2 If the dog's temperature is normal, withhold food and water and administer Pepto-Bismol or Kaopectate every 2 hours for 12 hours (1/2 teaspoon for a small dog; 1 teaspoon for a medium or large dog; 2 teaspoons for a giant dog); see **ADMINISTERING LIQUID MEDICINE**, page 220. Consult your veterinarian if the dog vomits the medicine.

VOMITING

3 After 12 hours, give the dog a small drink of water. If it does not vomit, give it small quantities of water every 3 hours. Consult your veterinarian if the dog does not drink any water or vomits after drinking.

4 After 24 hours, give the dog a small amount of bland food such as cooked hamburger mixed with an equal amount of boiled rice or cooked eggs. If the dog still does not vomit, repeat small portions of water and food every 3 hours for 24 hours. Continue bland foods in normal portions for 3 days, then return to the dog's regular diet.

RESTRAINTS

RESTRAINTS

IF YOU HAVE ASSISTANCE & THE DOG IS COOPERATIVE

IMPORTANT

- **Always approach an injured dog with caution.** Speak in a gentle, reassuring voice.

- If possible, perform all restraints on a smooth tabletop or other elevated surface.

- An injured dog that is still conscious should always be restrained before it receives first aid.

- Whenever possible, have someone restrain the dog for you while you administer the emergency treatment. See **AIDED RESTRAINTS** below.

- If you cannot obtain assistance or if the dog is uncooperative or vicious, use the **EMERGENCY RESTRAINT** on pages 214-216.

AIDED RESTRAINT A
FOR ADMINISTERING MEDICINE
& TREATING THE HEAD, FRONT LEGS & SIDES

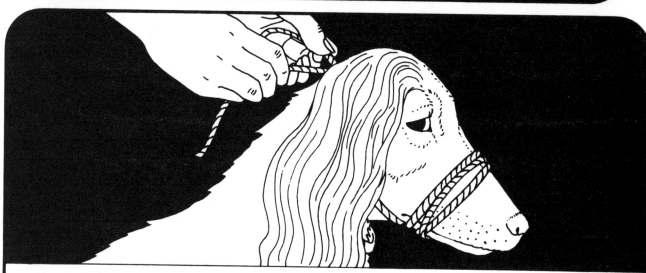

1 Muzzle the dog unless it is unconscious, having difficulty breathing, has an injury inside its mouth or requires medication. Have your assistant hold the dog while you apply the muzzle. If a muzzle isn't available, see **IMPROVING A MUZZLE,** page 217.

RESTRAINTS

2 Tell your assistant to place one arm under and around the dog's neck so that his fist points toward his shoulder. Make sure he keeps his elbow **under** the dog's neck so its breathing won't be obstructed.

3 Have him place his other arm over the dog's back and around its chest, then force the dog into a sitting position by pressing his weight down on its hindquarters.

4 Tell him to hold the dog firmly against his body to keep it still and to hold on tightly if it struggles to break loose. Proceed to administer the appropriate first aid.

RESTRAINTS

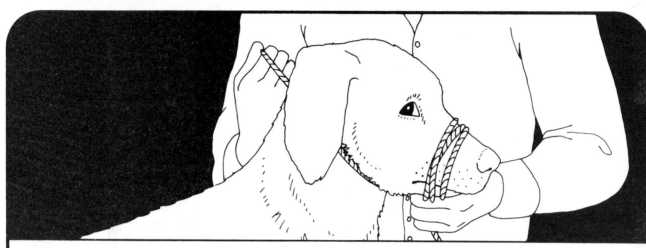

1 Muzzle the dog unless it is unconscious or having difficulty breathing. Have your assistant hold the dog while you apply the muzzle. If a muzzle isn't available or if the dog will not accept it, see **IMPROVISING A MUZZLE,** page 217.

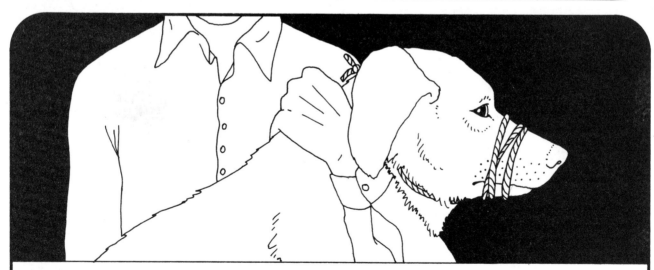

2 Tell your assistant to place one arm under and around the dog's neck so that his fist points toward his shoulder. Make sure he keeps his elbow **under** the dog's neck so its breathing won't be obstructed.

RESTRAINTS

3 Have him place his other arm under the dog's stomach and lift it to a standing position.

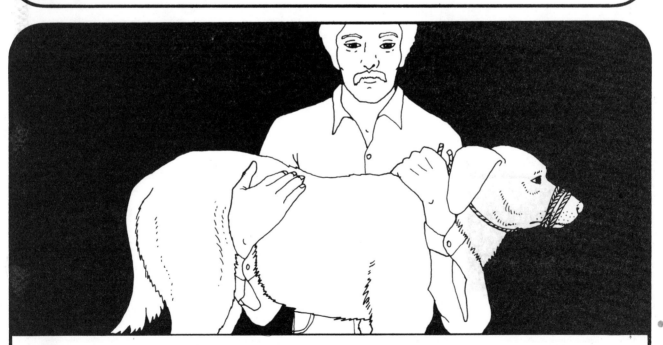

4 Tell him to hold the dog firmly against his body to keep it still and to hold on tightly if it struggles to break loose. Proceed to administer the appropriate first aid.

RESTRAINTS

IF YOU ARE ALONE OR THE DOG IS UNCOOPERATIVE OR VICIOUS

IMPORTANT

- **Always approach an injured dog with caution.** Speak in a gentle, reassuring voice.

- An injured dog that is still conscious should always be restrained before it receives first aid.

- Whenever possible, have someone restrain the dog for you while you administer the emergency treatment. See **AIDED RESTRAINTS,** pages 210-213.

- If you cannot obtain assistance or if the dog is uncooperative or vicious, use the **EMERGENCY RESTRAINT** below.

EMERGENCY RESTRAINT
IF YOU ARE ALONE OR IF THE DOG IS UNCOOPERATIVE OR VICIOUS

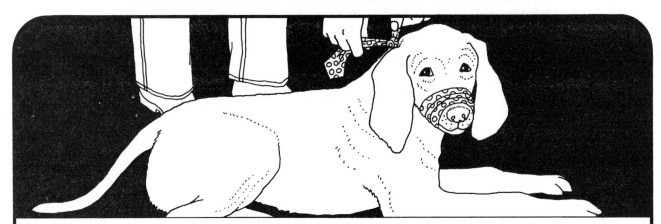

1A If the dog cannot stand, approach it from the rear and try to muzzle it unless it is unconscious, having difficulty breathing, has an injury inside its mouth or requires medication. If a muzzle isn't available, see **IMPROVISING A MUZZLE,** page 217.

1B If the dog can stand or if it refuses to accept the muzzle, wait until you have completed Step 4 below and then muzzle it.

RESTRAINTS

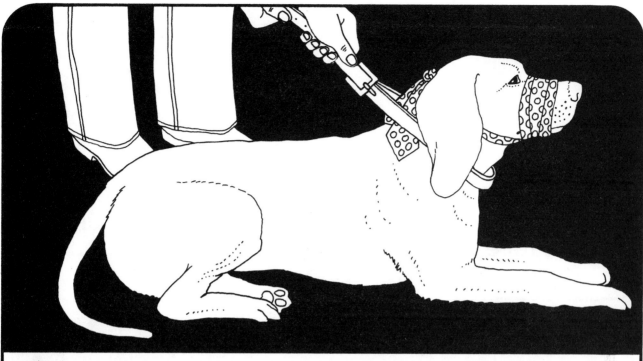

2 Improvise a noose from a length of rope, a belt, etc. and slip it cautiously over the dog's head.

3 Tighten the noose gently and pass the free end through a fence or other fixed object.

CONTINUED ON NEXT PAGE

4 Pull the dog against the fixed object and secure the rope so the dog cannot effectively move its head. Take care not to choke the dog.

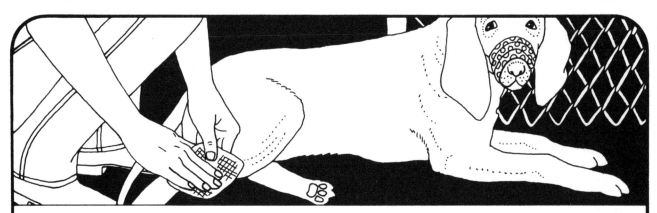

5A If you are alone, proceed to administer first aid from this position.

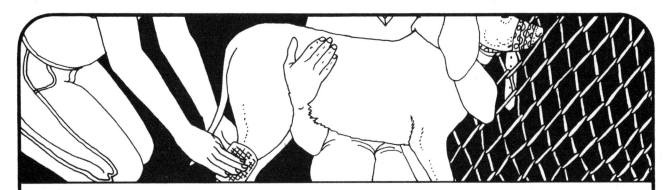

5B If you have assistance, apply the appropriate **AIDED RESTRAINT,** pages 210-213, then administer first aid.

RESTRAINTS

IMPROVISING A MUZZLE

IMPORTANT

- **Always approach an injured dog with caution.** Speak in a gentle, reassuring voice.

- **Do not** muzzle the dog if it is unconscious, having difficulty breathing, has an injury inside its mouth or requires medication.

1 Take a rope, heavy cord or the like, and holding one end behind the dog's ear, lead it down the side of its neck and under its chin.

2 Wrap the rope firmly around the dog's muzzle 2 or 3 times, then bring it back up along the other side of its neck and behind its ear.

3 Bring the ends together behind the dog's head and knot them securely.

ADMINISTERING MEDICINE AND TAKING THE DOG'S TEMPERATURE

ADMINISTERING LIQUID MEDICINE

- Be gentle but firm and decisive. Speak in a quiet, reassuring voice.

- Administer liquid slowly to keep it from being coughed out or inhaled.

1 **Restrain the dog. See RESTRAINTS, pages 209-217.** Holding the dog's mouth shut, gently tip back its head very slightly.

2 Using a plastic eyedropper or dosing syringe, slowly feed the medicine between the molar and canine teeth at the side of the mouth. **Do not** clamp the jaws shut; the dog must move its tongue to swallow.

ADMINISTERING PILLS

IMPORTANT

- Be gentle but firm and decisive. Speak in a quiet, reassuring voice.

- Lubricate capsules or large pills with butter before administering.

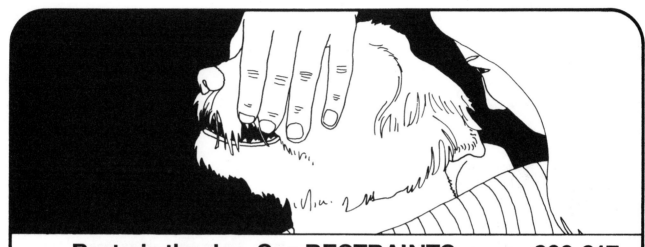

1 **Restrain the dog. See RESTRAINTS, pages 209-217.** Place one hand over the dog's muzzle, with your thumb and index finger just behind the long fang teeth.

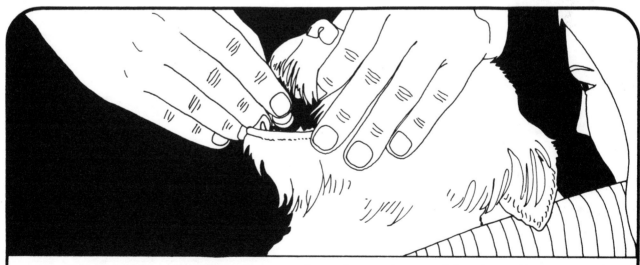

2 Hold the pill between the thumb and index finger of your other hand. Use your other three fingers to hold the dog's mouth wide open.

CONTINUED ON NEXT PAGE

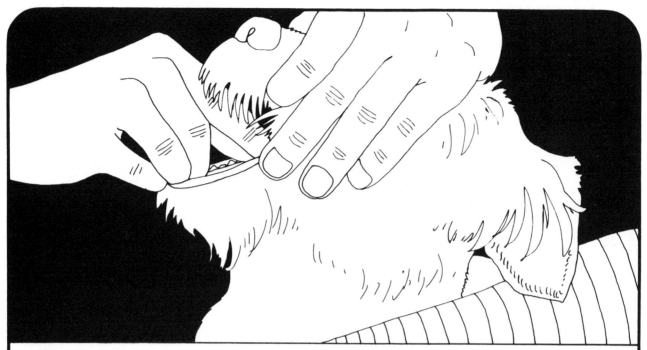

3 Tip the dog's head back slightly. Place the pill as far back on the tongue as possible, then push it into the throat with your index finger.

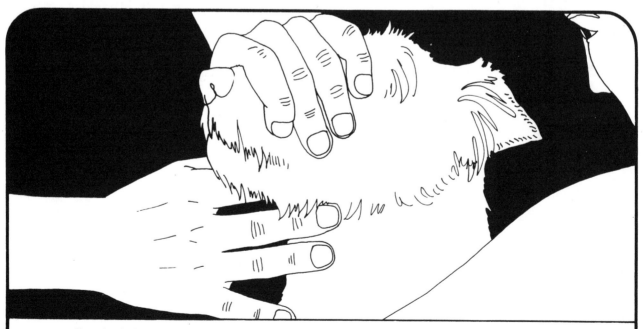

4 Quickly close the dog's mouth and lower its head to a level position. Stroke its throat to stimulate swallowing.

APPLYING MEDICINE TO THE EARS

- **Do not** put medicine in the dog's ears unless your veterinarian recommends it.

1 **Restrain the dog. See RESTRAINTS, pages 209-217.** Grasp the dog's muzzle and steady its head.

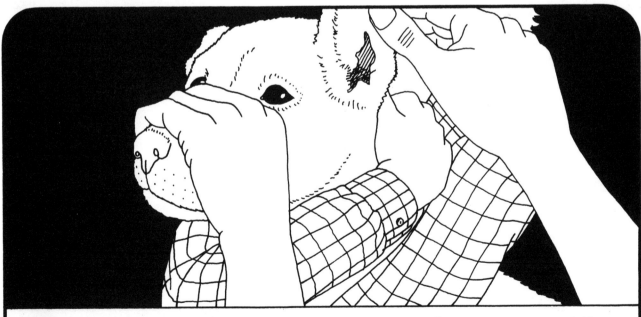

2 Using your other hand, fold the ear flap up toward the head.

CONTINUED ON NEXT PAGE

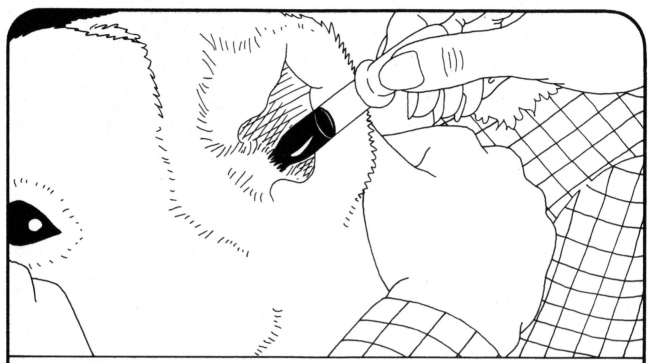

3 Put the recommended dosage of medication as far into the ear canal as you can see.

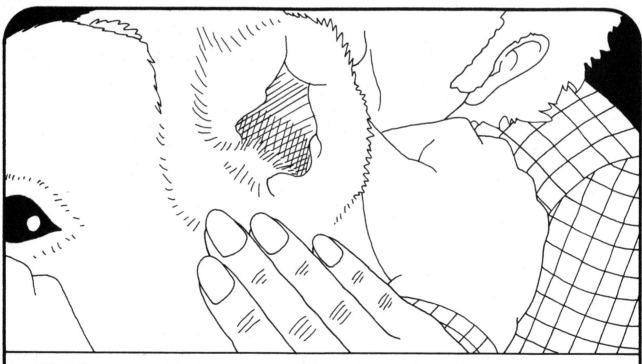

4 Massage the area outside and under the ear opening to distribute the medication.

IMPORTANT

- **Do not** put medicine in the dog's eyes unless your veterinarian recommends it.

- **Do not** touch the eyeball with the applicator when applying the drops.

- Be aware that dogs have an opaque third eyelid which normally is not seen but may come up to protect an irritated or injured eye. Should this happen, **do not** try to remove it or otherwise interfere with it.

1 **Restrain the dog. See RESTRAINTS, pages 209-217.** Place one hand under the dog's jaw, then lift it to elevate the head.

CONTINUED ON NEXT PAGE

225

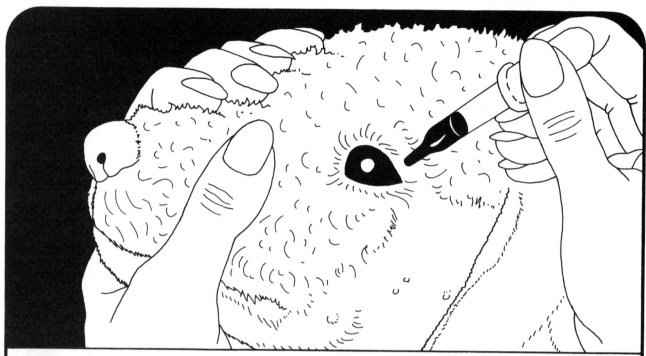

2 Steady the heel of your other hand against the dog's head, then carefully approach the inside corner of the eye with the eyedropper.

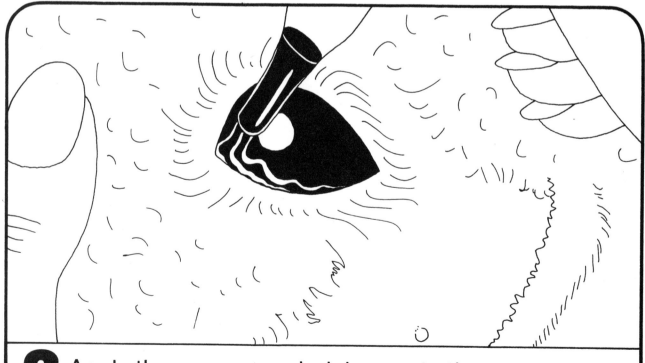

3 Apply the recommended dosage to the eye.

APPLYING OINTMENT TO THE EYES

IMPORTANT

- **Do not** put medicine in the dog's eyes unless your veterinarian recommends it.

- **Do not** touch the eyeball with the applicator when applying the ointment.

- Be aware that dogs have an opaque third eyelid which normally is not seen but may come up to protect an irritated or injured eye. Should this happen, **do not** try to remove it or otherwise interfere with it.

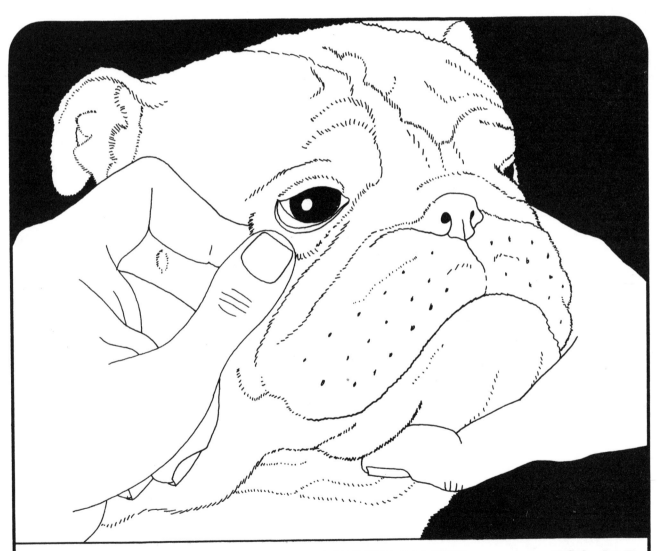

1 **Restrain the dog. See RESTRAINTS, pages 209-217.** Facing the dog, gently pull the lower lid away from the eye with your thumb and index finger. Hold the eyelid open.

CONTINUED ON NEXT PAGE

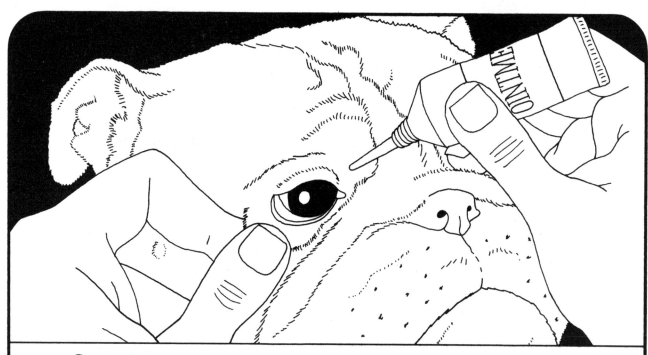

1 Steady the heel of your other hand against the dog's head, then carefully approach the inside corner of the eye with the ointment tube.

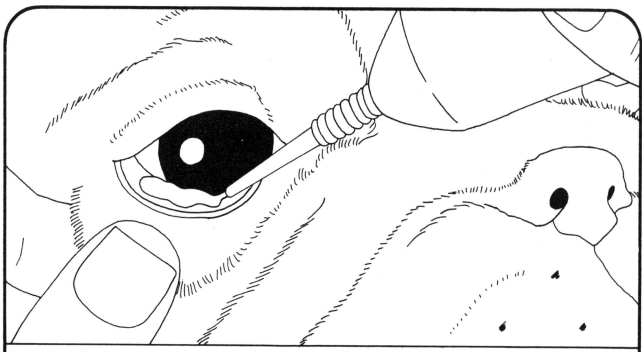

2 Apply the recommended dosage on the lower lid as close to the eye as possible.

APPLYING MEDICINE TO THE NOSE

IMPORTANT

- **Do not** put medicine in the dog's nose unless your veterinarian recommends it.

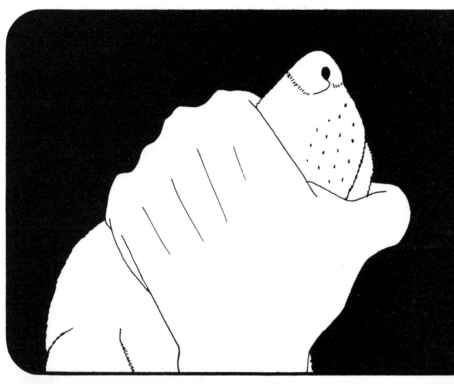

1 **Restrain the dog. See RESTRAINTS, pages 209-217.** Grasp the dog's muzzle and block its vision with your hand. Elevate the head so the nose points upward.

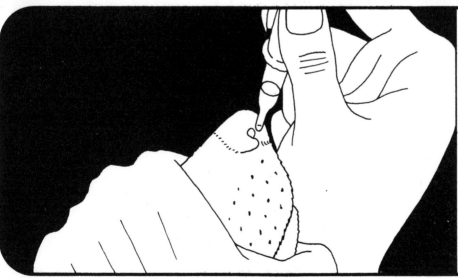

2 Holding the medicine dropper with your fingers, steady the heel of your other hand against the dog's muzzle.

3 Apply the recommended dosage directly into the nostrils. Avoid touching the nose with the medicine dropper.

TAKING THE DOG'S TEMPERATURE

IMPORTANT

- Only use a rectal thermometer.

- Shake the thermometer until it registers below 98°F. (36.7°C.).

- Lubricate it well with petroleum jelly.

- Speak in a gentle, reassuring voice.

- A dog's normal temperature ranges between 99.5°F. (38.5°C.) and 102.5°F. (39.2°C.), slightly higher if it is excited.

1 **Restrain the dog. See RESTRAINTS, pages 209-217.** Lift its tail firmly.

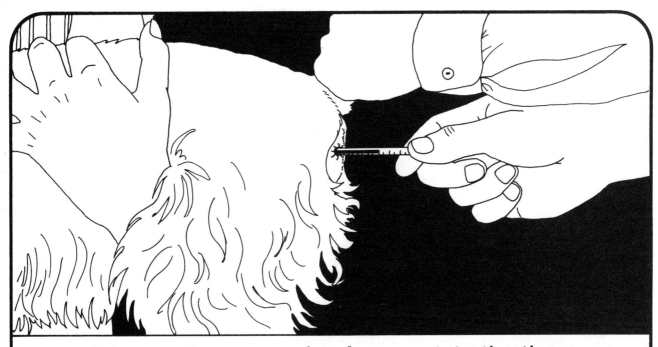

2 Without using excessive force, rotate the thermometer back and forth while inserting it about 1 inch. Hold it in place for 1 minute.

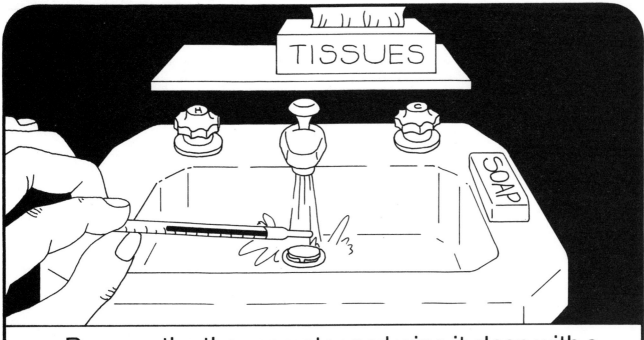

3 Remove the thermometer and wipe it clean with a tissue. Carefully read the temperature, then wash the thermometer with soap and cool water.

For our free brochure of health care and first-aid products
for your pet, send your name and address to:

**THE
HOME
PET VET
GUIDE
DOGS**

West Stockbridge, Massachusetts 01266